THE DIMENSIONS OF ROBERT FROST

THE DIMENSIONS OF
ROBERT FROST

REGINALD L. COOK

Rinehart & Company, Inc. NEW YORK TORONTO

Grateful acknowledgment is made to Henry Holt and Company, Incorporated, New York, N. Y., for permission to reprint poems and excerpts from poems from COMPLETE POEMS OF ROBERT FROST, Copyright, 1930, 1939, 1943, 1947, 1949, by Henry Holt and Company, Inc.; Copyright, 1936, 1942, 1945, 1948, by Robert Frost.

Published simultaneously in Canada by
Clarke, Irwin & Company, Ltd., Toronto

To Nita and her mother

And in memory of

Juan Centeno

INTERLOCUTOR: "Our aim is to get you right, isn't it?"
ROBERT FROST: "To get it *understood* right—how I mean it."

At Bread Loaf, Vermont. July 28, 1955

We dance round in a ring and suppose,
But the Secret sits in the middle and knows.

FROST, *"The Secret Sits"*

Mask thy wisdom with delight,
Toy with the bow, yet hit the white.
Of all wit's uses, the main one
Is to live well with who has none.

EMERSON, *"Merlin's Song"*

Preface

Whatever Robert Frost is, he is at least a complex and sophisticated man. I do not know that there is any secret concerning him, but if there is it is open enough. He writes out of the heart of his material, neither spiritually and physically detached from nor superior to it. What is original in his response will be found in the fact that between Frost and life there is *rapport*. And there is euphoria! Poetry is for him a holiday and a gaiety of the spirit, and even when it is serious, the writing of it is still the most passionate fun imaginable.

If he had been born and bred in an urban settlement, this passion for poetry would have been equally strong. His genius—*furor poeticus* —has been a possessive daemon. All that he has lived—his anxiety, agony, laughter, wisdom, grief—has been turned into his art. Committed to an exciting adventure—the mastery of art as a vehicle of a vision—he has practised that art while wresting a living in a workaday world not primarily interested in poetry. What he has lived lights up the poetry. This is the root of the matter.

Self-described as "a plain citizen," he is about as plain as Biblical Joseph with his coat on. He is, according to the facts, an American of Scottish ancestry, impregnated with something more than passing interest in Greek and Latin culture; a man deriving what he has to say from contemplation of the directly observed; an uninhibited, tireless, penetrating talker; a principled realist, undeluded by phony ideas; a political and social conservative; an intransigent perfectionist in his art. There is warmth in him as there is in his poetry. Many like the warmth; many like the poetry. It is hard to realize how the one could be divided from the other. "There is in all great poets," says Emerson, "a wisdom of humanity which is superior to any talents they exercise. The author, the wit, the partisan, the fine gentleman, does not take place of the man." This can stand as written for Frost.

If we would understand poetry, let us be informed about a poet's experience and the crises out of which he speaks honestly if painfully. For at the heart of a poem is a poet's own heart. Awareness of the personal element in poetry does not imply that the poem cannot be appreciated for other, impersonal qualities. Nor does it mean that the obligation of the critic or reader is anything less than the attempt to pluck the heart of a poet's mystery. It means, simply, that we should be imaginative enough to realize that biographical details are of the utmost importance in the analysis of the poem and in understanding the psychology of the poet. You can be only partially accurate when you say that it is possible to test poetry thoroughly by the simple expedient of ignoring the poet. A poem is a threshold into a poet's mind as well as a window looking out upon reality.

In attitudes, beliefs and concepts the poet is part of the poem's meaning, and the thrust of that meaning vibrates with every push of the pen. Sainte-Beuve counseled readers that criticism which expects to get down to fundamentals must concern itself with a writer's life as well as his art, and Amy Lowell shrewdly pointed out in one of her numerous discussions of Imagism that "criticism is not merely an interpretation of technique: it is a tracking of mental bias, a tracking of angles of thought to their starting points, a realization of the roots from which the flowers spring." Literary criticism is, of course, more pertinently concerned with the qualities of poems, and less with biographical details. Just enough of the poet's life and traits, then, to give us a sense of his temperament and experience, and just enough of his theory of form and subject matter to give us a sense of his objectives.

Most of the materials recorded in this book have been picked up directly from the poet—by listening thirty years. Anyone familiar with Frost knows that he does the talking. And why not? Since his mind is germinal, he takes immense pleasure in talking. It enables him to try out his ideas, and it gives him a chance to burnish his wit. His full powers are released by the vocal chords, not in muscular action. We learn about Frost by studying the craft in his poems, for in the poems is hidden the secret of what, if not who, he is. But consider also the intrinsic value of the quotations which appear in this book, not chiefly as examples of his style of thinking, but rather as documents whose importance is reflected in the light they throw on the craft of poetry.

If I listened well—if I heard accurately—if I followed the hints, then I ought to come close to his center as a poet, at once a poet of the people and an independent spokesman.

So long as *Complete Poems* is available on the reader's shelf of books, the poet is always within earshot. Since his poetry grew out through the voice, he is an audible poet. "Why, then, do you propose to write about him? What is it you would like to say?" I would like to trace the development of Frost's original response, showing when he found it, how he nourished and conserved it, made it purposive, gave it direction, renewed it by absorptive interest in his native soil, and made both speech and idea communicable by association with the world about him. His poetry expresses a human personality. The test of this effort—a large order, granted—is to show how deeply his poetry reflects the heart and mind of man. This is the main aim in the book.

When, in 1950, *The Dimensions of Robert Frost* first took shape, Dr. Viola C. White, Curator Emeritus of the Abernethy Library at Middlebury College, helped by examining critically the first draft. Professor Howard M. Munford assisted greatly in making the text compact. The Wales Hawkins Collection of Robert Frost, an invaluable part of the Abernethy Library of American Literature at Middlebury College, was useful. I have also found very stimulating the talks about Robert Frost with my friends and colleagues at Middlebury College and the Bread Loaf School of English. My thanks to the President and Fellows of Middlebury College for granting two "leaves" during which the book was written, and to Theodore Amussen, Ranald Hobbs, Henry Carlisle and the staff at Rinehart and Company who assisted in preparing the book for publication. But to my wife, who patiently and devotedly typed the many notes and revisions, go deservedly the greatest thanks. I want also to acknowledge the use of brief passages or quotations from my own articles on Robert Frost, which have appeared previously in *College English, Accent, Vermont Life, Yankee,* and the *Quarterly Journal of Speech*. For permission to quote from manuscript sources and from copyrighted materials, I am indebted to Henry Holt and Company and the Henry E. Huntington Library at San Marino, California.

Contents

I

LOCAL AND PERSONAL
DIMENSIONS

He showed me that the lines of a good helve
Were native to the grain before the knife
Expressed them, and its curves were no false curves
Put on it from without.

ROBERT FROST

1. A Foreground Fact

The first foreground fact in Robert Frost's life is the time of his birth, in San Francisco, California, March 26, 1874, during the post-Civil War period of reconstruction, and his growing up in the East. His attachment to California is still strong, and when he reads from his poems he is careful to identify the California ones—"A Peck of Gold," "Once by the Pacific," "At Woodward's Gardens," or "A Record Stride." He recalls that his father, whose sympathies had been with the Copperheads during the Civil War, once spread a map of the United States before him and pointed out that the nation would inevitably become divided into seven sections. This way, William Prescott Frost, Jr., contended, America might better realize strength through diversity. Frost refers to his father as a "sep-a-ra-tist," and he adds drily that, if his father's notion had been realized, we wouldn't all be eating Shredded Wheat for breakfast. It is possible that Frost's independence comes directly by inheritance. As a foreground fact the early years in California make cherishable the memory of his mother, Belle Moodie Frost. In a sense more historical, of course, than pomological, he is a Western pippin grafted on a Yankee greening.

The irregularity of his education in the East intensified his individualism. He was not deflected into any conventional grooves, nor did he succumb to professionalism in American life. "Some men lead professional lives," Whitman told Traubel. "Some men just live." The unliterary part is to the literary part as the soil is to the flower, and the unliterary part of Frost's life—the youthful occupations of bobbin-boy in a textile mill, teaching in his mother's school, making shoes, editing a weekly newspaper, and farming—is a soil in which his imagination struck root.

Still the literary part should not be disparaged. Frost's discipline and taste took their rigor and influence from his time, the chief fore-

3

ground fact in his literary education. The rigor in the discipline came from his study of the classics while his taste was influenced by the strong current of native realism as well as by the genteel tradition and the Victorians. In both lecture and conversation, the notable fact is the prominent reference which he makes to the Pre-Raphaelites, the Victorian Lions, the decadent aesthetes of the yellow-nineties, and the *exotiques* of the mauve decade. Christina Rossetti, Francis Thompson of "The Hound of Heaven," Coventry Patmore, Lionel Johnson, John Davidson of "A Ballad of Hell," Ernest Dowson, Ernest Clarence Stedman, Edward Rowland Sill and, of course, Shaw, Kipling, Chesterton and Wells, form a solid frame of reference in his mind.

The *fin de siècle* flickers in his nimble wit, and shows more broadly in the vagaries of his humor, which at times can be quaint as the mimicry in a Weber and Field show, or full of "corny," leg-pulling fun that reminds one more of the era of Bud Fisher and George B. McManus than of Chester Gould or Al Capp. Sometimes almost hidden in his poetry will be the snatch of a popular song from Music Hall days, like Keeper's in *A Masque of Mercy* (1947). "There's not much we can do till Martin gets here." Ah, Wilderness! Not to speak of Frost's low resistance to punning in the same Masque. "So you've been Bohning up on Thomism too," says Keeper, and, "It's been a commonplace/ Ever since Alexander Greeced the world," comments Paul in another passage. This humor evokes the natty linen dusters and leghorn hats.

Both Frost's moral temper and viewpoint have their source in the nineteenth century. His ethics reflect the high, purposeful, optimistic Victorian era, but it would be unfair to insist overly on this reminiscent tone. It is more accurate to say that he grew up with his times and consequently represents its positive, affirmative side.

His growth parallels important changes. Between 1874 and 1914 he saw the United States rise to a position of prestige in Western Europe. In the Massachusetts mills he experienced firsthand the growing disparity between political equality and economic opportunity. As a close follower of politics, he became interested in the phenomenon of Eugene V. Debs, and observed intently the modification of the conservative middle class by a nascent post-Civil War liberalism. The social implications of industrialism—the variety and attractiveness of material lures, the glorification of the businessman, the dominance of the machines—did not escape him. Aware of the increasing influence of scientific thought, the older he has grown, the more he has talked and written about science.

Yet Frost, unlike Pound, Sandburg, Masters, Dreiser, Anderson, Lewis, and many other writers of this era, has not been an insurgent critic. He has gone his own independent way. Because *A Boy's Will* (1913) and *North of Boston* (1914) came out of a rural rather than an urban environment, the former emphasizes the love of sensuous beauty, and the latter the tragic facts of poverty, loneliness, suffering, disaster and mental illness in the back country.

His moral impetus originated in an epoch not yet filled with the sense of impending menace. An affirmative thrust and stability come from a country, an atmosphere, a people and an epoch in which and in whom a democratic belief in man's potentialities transcends doubts and tensions. "They would not find me changed from him they knew,/ Only more sure of all I thought was true" is not a boast, it is a fact, and for Frost it has been the sweetest dream that self-belief knows. The source and impetus of such confidence is found prominently in the time factor, and this is one of the major factors in the epoch in which he grew up. So he says:

> I could give all to Time except—except
> What I myself have held. But why declare
> The things forbidden that while the Customs slept
> I have crossed to Safety with? For I am There,
> And what I would not part with I have kept.

2. A Sense of Identity

I come and go between the urban and rustic.
ROBERT FROST

In *The Lives of the Poets,* Johnson refers with approbation to what Temple described as a poet's "race," "a word which, applied to wines in its primitive sense, means the flavour of the soil." Burns had "race." The raciness of Ayrshire cottage and villager are in his songs. Wordsworth had it, and the raciness of Grasmere, Ullswater and Silver How are in the *Lyrical Ballads*. Hardy's flinty poems have the raciness of furzy Dorset downs and coombes, and Emily Brontë's raciness sweeps through *Wuthering Heights* like the wind across the bleak ridges and heather-streaked moors of Higher Withins. Similarly, Robert Frost has the raciness of a well-weathered quartz outcropping with a clear vein of gold seaming it. It is apparently this raciness that Ezra Pound sensed when he described Frost as "vurry Amur'k'n, with, I think, the seeds of grace."

His "race" consists in an inalienable affinity for the earth and its ways. He has an eye for a mountain, an ear for the song of a bird, and, like any countryman acquainted with nature, he draws his knowledge instinctually from its roots. He has a confederate's knowledge of husbandry and tillage, of flower-stations and geological formations. The device on his poetic coat-of-arms could well be (after Abraham Cowley) "the plough in a field arable." Emerson described Plato as keeping two vases at his side, one of "aether" (or ideas) and one of "pigment" (or experience), and expertly blending them. Just as capably Frost balances "the eternal politics" with butter and beans. Although he abjures the regionalist label—he calls himself "a realmist"—his raciness is partly geography, partly temperament. He has absorbed from the Northern landscape quite as responsively as Lanier drank in the soul of the oak in the marshes of Glynn, but here the similarity ends, for there is as much difference between the temperament and reaction of the Northern and the Southern poet as there is between a Vermont sugar bush and a scuppernong arbor.

Twenty-five years ago Robert Frost said with a chuckle that he never went to a place to live unless it lay north of Boston. He laid a ruler on a map to be safe. Since, he has often been caught out of bounds, but he remains the *genius loci* of upper New England. A ruler laid across a map of New England shows that Amherst, Massachusetts, on the southwest, and Sugar Hill, New Hampshire, on the northeast, bound the heart of a country in which he is as much the tutelary spirit as Walt Whitman was of Paumanok or Jeffers of the Monterey Peninsula.

Not at all imaginary, like Cabell's Poictesme, or Lewis's Mid-American Winnemac, the Frost country is geographically identifiable names on the land and places on the map, like Lawrence and Methuen, Derry and West Running Brook, Franconia and Hanover, South Shaftsbury and Ripton, Amherst and Cambridge. It is Frost's point of vantage, its folk his subject matter, its idiom his kinspeech, its landscape his daily observation.

"Literature," he once said, "begins with geography." He does his thinking, in his own words, "out of the local." His materials are an abandoned cottage, a tuft of butterfly weed, a young birch, a hill wife, a Morgan colt, a hillside thaw. Yet locality is more than the subject matter of Frost's poems; it is the source of deep affection. He has enjoyed what Horace included among his prayers—"a portion of land, not so big, a garden and near the house a spring of never-failing water, and a little wood beyond." Woodchuck runways thread his fields and birches cluster in the upper pastures. In his line of vision there is usually a mountain—Lafayette, Lincoln, Equinox, or Bread Loaf—by which to gauge the upper weather.

He has never, like Emily Dickinson, hugged one hearthstone, or, like Thoreau, lived chiefly in one village. His dwelling places are "strategic retreats," like The Gulley in South Shaftsbury, Vermont, or the Homer Noble farm in Ripton, Vermont, where, at present, he summers. He is surrounded by mountains that add dimensional reality. Geologically it is an old land, and like Thoreau he can thrust a stick "many aeons deep into its surface," or with his heel "make a deeper furrow than the elements have plowed here for a thousand years." Because the mountains in New Hampshire were once recorded as ten instead of five thousand feet high, Frost wishes the peaks now were higher. He "cannot rest from planning day and night/ How high (he'd) thrust the peaks in summer snow/ To tap the upper sky and draw a flow/ Of frosty night air in the vale below/ Down from the stars to freeze the dew as starry."

Francis Higginson, seventeenth-century teacher of the Puritan Church at Salem, thought "a sup of New-England's Aire is better than a whole draft of old England's Ale." This is true enough in both Green and White mountain areas. When the atmosphere thickens and the air stales, a cooling north wind scatters the overcast, crisps a spring day, freshens a summer one, edges a fall day, and in winter powders the mountains with snow. The atmosphere becomes crystal clear, and the mountain ranges form three-dimensional solid blue masses. Cotton Mather thought "our winds blow not such razors as in the days of our fathers, when the hands of the good men would freeze unto the bread upon their tables, and the strongest wine there would in a few minutes be hardly to be swallowed for its congelation. . . ." Mather never felt the rugged wind out of Canada, cutting athwart the Champlain Valley, or he would have been forced to alter his words. In *The Farmer's Almanack,* Robert Thomas is more accurate when he refers to "searching, saucy and pitiless winds."

North of Boston season passes rapidly into season. Hardly is the song of the spring birds heard vibrating in the sky before the hot midsummer sun has tanned the spring grasses. Just as brief is the glimpse of the pipe-smoke blue haze of Indian Summer. The region has a low-pressure weakness. As changeable during the day as it is seasonal, the temperature indicates a variable but invigorating climate. In "Two Tramps in Mud-Time," Frost reminds us:

> You know how it is with an April day
> When the sun is out and the wind is still,
> You're one month on in the middle of May.
> But if you so much as dare to speak,
> A cloud comes over the sunlit arch,
> A wind comes off a frozen peak,
> And you're two months back in the middle of March.

Heavy precipitation keeps the glacial soil arable. Vegetation is abundant and on a moderately short midsummer walk the hiker will see Chicory, wild Asparagus, purplish blue Vetch, Indian Paintbrush licking the pastures with soundless flame, Tiger Lilies, Goldenrod and Black-eyed Susans, Joe-pye Weed, Steeplebush, Orchids, Meadow Rue, Fireweed and Indian-pipes. Not only are the flowers abundant, but among the upland stands a devotee of shades and sizes, foliage and form of trees will always find blue spruces, pin oaks, shagbark hickories, white pines, arbor vitae, wineglass elms, sugar maples and canoe birches within sight.

Frost is on terms of amiable intimacy with the natural world. His affection for nature is warm and sympathetic. The bluebird arouses his whimsy, the ovenbird stirs him to reflection, the hermit thrush touches his deeper moods. His bears are philosophical; his woodchucks are circumspect; his deer unaggressive. The lesser "minims of nature," like the hornets, are self-tormented and the grasshoppers waggish. Nothing in this region is sinister although it may be perplexing; nothing is terrible although it might be annoying. To satisfy Frost it could be wilder. Nature's claws are undrawn but not long.

Hidden beyond the gaps in the foothills are lonely upland farms. A generation ago the folk who lived in the hills were more severely oppressed by monotony of effort and by remoteness from their fellow man than they are now. Loneliness worked into the grain, gnarled the flesh, withered the spirit. Those who were by temperament reserved and taciturn became morose and aberrant. The generous natural beauty with its satisfying stretch of the earth to the eye was not enough. In later years the telephone, radio, television and automobile have made the lot of the country folk easier. Although few have made money on these upland acres, many live less lonely lives.

North of Boston the people are just as varied as in the industrial areas of lower New England. The Scotch-Irish have long been settled around Londonderry, New Hampshire. The Canucks have worked down from Canada into the farming areas of Vermont. The Italians quarry granite and marble. Finns work upland farms around Ludlow, Vermont, and there is a small Spanish settlement at Barre. The folk Frost writes about—loggers, farmers, store keepers, millhands, ox drivers, orchid hunters, water dowsers, witches, star gazers, gum gatherers, and a preacher of the Racker Sect—are mainly old Yankee stock. In his poetry they resemble Dr. Magoun, provincially suspicious of Lafe in "A Hundred Collars"; the farm woman with her unreasonable timidity in "The Fear"; Loren shrewdly taciturn about the good berry-picking in Patterson's pasture in "Blueberries"; the hired man proclaiming his rural declaration of independence in "The Code"; and the diffident ox driver in "The Mountain." These are unexceptional folk, neither exalted nor underestimated. They are to be taken as they are.

From this stock plantings were made on the Western frontier. They gave the Mormons an initial impulse and provided leadership.

Among their members are Shakers, Jehovah's Witnesses, Townsendites, but few New Dealers. Many vote a straight party ticket, keep up their village church, attend town-meeting, gather at county fairs in the fall, fish the streams, hunt the woods, read the local weekly or daily papers, go to the Grange meetings, promote the 4-H clubs, work their farms. They are not embarrassed by the necessity, as Calvin Coolidge long ago pointed out, to raise what they need, "wear it out, eat it up, do without." They are a conservative people, stronger in tradition than in innovation. In spite of the increasing number of filling stations and hot-dog stands that dot the main highways, they stand pat when it comes to protecting their wilderness areas against the incursions of strangers from the cities. What goes for Vermont holds for New Hampshire. It is as true now as when Frost first said years ago the two states are "yoke-fellows in the sap-yoke from of old."

3. Traits

My object has been to hold my own with, not against, other things.

ROBERT FROST

A man is more than the sum of his qualities, and Frost is not different from other men in this respect. To isolate and describe his qualities will not give a rounded picture, but it will give us an impression of the kind of human being he is. In a personal record such as this it is important to feel the humanness of the man before determining what characterizes him as a poet. There have been subtle changes over the years, yet they indicate not a difference in but an intensification of personal traits. Friendliness and cordial warmth are compounded in his camaraderie, the vigorous, virile companionableness of a man for his own kind. In his presence one feels something salutary and restorative. He attracts the young like a bright light, and not only the young but others, too, for someone of prominence—an editor, or former student, or friend, or neighbor—is always beating a path to his door, seeking him out.

His camaraderie is an intrinsic part of his personal raciness. No matter where you meet him, whether in his Cambridge study, on a lecture platform, in the local grocery store, in a suburban street, in his mountain cabin, whether in the pasture grazing a horse on tether, or among the tall poles in a garden where the broad-leafed bean flowers, or in a thicket with axe and long-handled cutting hook, the special quality of his raciness is apparent. There is no pose, no pretentiousness, no mask. Such bonhomie seemed incredible to a Spanish friend reared in the formal tradition of Madrid and Salamanca. He was fairly bowled over when he met Frost in a jumper and overalls, and blue canvas-topped shoes, dressed simply but comfortably, and completely relaxed. It is almost too much for the European, who apparently expects the guard of a notable writer to be up and his mask to be well fitted. Frost is genuine enough to be very natural, and this is the essence of his charm. He is what he is. The European "genius" has a reputation at stake. The democratic American poet is only like the rest of us; his difference is his genius.

Physically, Frost has the solidity of the close-sodded native soil. He stands about five feet nine, and you are aware at once of his strong-armed, full-chested, rugged build. In his old clothes he looks bigger than he actually is. When approached in the garden, he appears to loom; but when dressed up, he shrinks to medium height. Close up you notice the full, thick, muscular, workmanlike hands, the backs of them rough, the thumb large, the fingers long, the tips blunt, the nails wide and thick—firm fingers to grasp an ax, strong shoulders to start the swing, muscular forearms to follow through. His practical truths are the tougher, you think, recalling Thoreau, for the calluses on the broad, well-lined palms. His blue eyes, which are rarely measuring, nevertheless take you in. He looks, listens, appraises. And he sizes up memorably, saying, "I see what I see." His nose is strong and aggressive. His lips are full but not sensual; the chin is firm. Altogether, the quality of raciness is in the big-framed, shaggy-headed appearance. It is in manner, carriage and speech. It is in his manner which is neighborly, but not unurban; in his carriage which is not to be distinguished from any city dweller's; in his speech which is not gauche or clumsy, and not identifiable with rustic voices.

He describes himself as lazy, but this is hardly the word that characterizes a relaxed calmness. He is relaxed, not lazy, because he has known how to economize energy. His so-called "laziness" and "evasiveness" have protected him, enabled him to get the important work done. He is always active about the real work, which is writing poetry, and, in a sense, his talking contributes to the writing, for it is while talking he tries out the ideas and expressions that go into making a poem. In his talk a process is always going on: it is the reflection upon ideas in experience and the conversion of experience into ideas. This is the nub of it. He turns interior meditation inside out and lengthens a thought in conversation.

What Henry James said of Ivan Turgenev is certainly true of Frost. "He was the richest, the most delightful, of talkers, and his face, his person, his temper, the thoroughness with which he had been equipped with human intercourse, make, in the memory of his friends, an image which is completed, but not thrown into the shade by his literary distinction." Frost is one of the readiest of the vanishing tribe of original talkers in the twentieth century, a tribe that includes William Butler Yeats, James Stephens, Paul Claudel, George Santayana and D. H. Lawrence. He belongs with them; not, perhaps, with Coleridge whose monologues were said to ascend, in De Quincey's description, "like Jacob's ladder, by just gradations, into the Heaven of Heavens and the thrones of the Trinity." Nor yet with Swinburne, whose spellbinding talk, the exhilarated Henry Adams described as a "wild Walpurgis-night." Frost's talk is not pyrotechnic or febrile. On the contrary, it is social, genial and expansive. There are few unintended pauses in it. One thought starts another, and he rambles on while the deep-set blue eyes, the blunt nose, the expressive lips, the formidable chin and the shock of white hair all help to pin a point down.

Best in a small group, preferably man to man, it is true, as a friend says, in idiom, "He'll stay there talking until the last dog is dead." Yet what he says makes good listening. Where all of it comes from, different almost every time, is a wonder. He is hard to corner, and you soon learn to watch both holes for his appearance. His manoeuvrability is positively ingenious. He always seems at random like a bluebottle fly on a hot midsummer day. "I have an endless resourcefulness to change my ground," he says, and it is this endless resourcefulness

which animates the conversation. Almost any topic trips the trigger of
his loaded memory. He talks about twelfth-century jongleurs as readily
as about witchcraft, about Ezra Pound and the Bollingen Award as
sharply as about submarginal economy, about Bohr's atom as informa-
tively as about T. S. Eliot's *Four Quartets*. At any given time he may
make allusions to the Mormons and their art, the Mayas in Yucatan,
Swedenborgianism, the Parmenidean idea of identity, the Nietzschean
Will to Power, glass shirts, water witches or Morgan horses.

Although he mentions simple, natural things—a fresh flower found
in an upper pasture, or the white-throated sparrows at the field's edge,
or a cornered fox—there is a wide sweep to his conversational interests, which include internationalism (like Thoreau, he's a "home-
cosmographer"), politics (he's an independent Democrat), athletics
(usually baseball), literature (chiefly poetry), America (notably Vermont), teaching (as "performance"), philosophy (out of the grass
roots), and people (individuals, not types). Ranging the humanities, he
explores rather than exploits his reading. Using it as a man does who
makes it a part of himself, he is Bacon's ready man and brandishes like
trophies quotations from the classics and his contemporaries. He talks
nimbly at the surface, but he arrives there from a distance. It is the
very fact that he has this surface which makes him a ready talker.
Edwin Arlington Robinson lacked it and envied Frost the satisfying
gift of being a conversable man.

Playing superbly, he touches nimbly the keys of many moods and
ranges with agility from banter to seriousness. His voice is medium in
pitch, rather low than high, but not guttural; and it registers sensitively
shades of feeling—elation or scorn, exultance or sadness. Just as the
charm of the man comes to focus in his talk, so the total force of the
poet comes to focus in the resonant voice. It is the voice of a man who
is readily able to reproduce the brogue of Irish speech tones, or nuances
in colloquial idiom and the accent of a countryman, or blank-verse
paragraphs of Miltonic eloquence. Those with whom we talk usually
have a control of language only at the level of sense, and even at this
level usage may lapse into slang or stiffen into formal phrasing as in a
book. There is another level—the tonal—that comes from the arrange-
ment of words in sequences of sound. In Frost's poetry the meaning
is partly in the tone. Similarly, in his conversation one has to hear the

voice intonate the thought to catch the total meaning. His habitual speech is idiomatic. Whether in letter or poem, reading, preface or introduction, the phrasing has an idiosyncratic intonation.

Sauntering along at an unhurried clip, his voice not only expresses an amiable and sensitive personality, it also expresses the phonetics of thought—the way a thought sounds. His thoughts have the creative touch of personal language. In the native tradition he uses a concrete illustration, a homely allusion or a folksy story to make a point. But the style is the man himself. Strongest and most enkindling is the explorative thrust of the mind. He is always reacting, and always unpredictably, for his mind is refractive as well as reactive. Anyone would have difficulty outguessing him. The natural variability of his weathered mind is its life. Fluently, he ranges from the speech of common sense to lyrical eloquence. Quite unexpectedly there will be a run of speech that has the lilt of poetry in it. So I have heard it often as the poet's aroused sensibility raised the listener as by verbal levitation on a sequence of metaphor, or released in him by flashes of phrase the rich joy of *The Odyssey* or *Walden*.

II

Another salient trait is Frost's passion for poetry. Very early in life he accepted the conditions of an exacting art, serving the muse of writing, "who is," in Flaubert's exciting recommendation to de Maupassant, "still the best bitch of all." Like Cellini, when he poured the mold for the statue of Perseus, Frost has also tossed in everything to build up a fire hot enough for the performance in poetry by which he would stand. In him the fire that creates, not the fire that consumes, has burned fiercely. This should never be forgotten: so much poetry, so much life.

Yet there is nothing solemn about Frost's passion. His vocation was not a forced or imperative choice. He did not take a stand to die or win out by his poetry. As a young man, he turned from one thing to another—from making shoes to editing a weekly newspaper, from farming to teaching. Admittedly, there is nothing particularly heroic in his attitude. At the time his choice of a vocation was, in his phrase, a "catch-as-catch-can" kind of rambling, as it often is. He simply took chances, and tried this job and then that. Being a poet was neither an act of consecration, nor an escape to Bohemia. He simply turned from one occupation to another before any one of them swallowed him down. When he began to write, he remembered his grandfather, William Prescott Frost, saying, "I give you a year"—that is, a year in which to see the light and quit this nonsense and turn to something else. Frost replied, "Give me twenty." He has been deflected from his goal about as much as a migratory bird is when it starts down the autumn flyways. Yet this is not to suggest that he had a moment of great and disturbing decision. The agony of finding out what to do with oneself is usually so prolonged, involved and inescapable that it is impossible to name any day, hour or minute when the decision is made.

It is an open secret that Frost is as deeply attached to poetry as Thoreau was to nature. The latter could say, "I go and come with a strange liberty in nature, a part of herself." Frost tells us, "I'm an unprincipled schemer. Writing poems is all that matters." A schemer, it might be added, who schemes to husband his time so that out of the unhurried enterprise of his effort he can write good poems. Whatever else may have contributed to the success with which he has wooed "the best bitch," discrimination weighs heavily. His refusal of many things has made him "ruthless" in some, but his refusal to be lured by the practical gains in the workaday world is always this side of folly. He is canny in getting the pennyworth of his time. "I'll talk for nothing, but I won't lecture for nothing," he will remind you. And he likes to tell about the editor of one of the "quality" magazines who, in 1915, meeting him on the street, asked if he had any poems ready for publication. He whisked a manuscript from his pocket and told the editor he could have some poems right now; they were all his. When the editor consulted a college teacher for professional advice, the latter suggested returning the manuscript. The editor called Frost and in their conversation used the word "submission" of manuscripts. "No," replied Frost, "I didn't submit the poems. I don't submit. I sold them to you, and you've got to take them. Submission! No! I'm inexorable." The editor was "stuck" with three poems, and they appeared later in the year with no loss of prestige to the magazine.

It took Frost a longer time to arrive than it took him to find himself. For the first twenty years of writing he earned two hundred dollars. He thought it might take a lifetime to realize one's passion for poetry; it has not taken less. Yet because his interest in poetry has been passionate rather than obsessive, he has not been so rapt he does not know what is going on around him. On the contrary, he has taken wise counsel and avoided the enervating society of arty groups. "I keep far enough away from the crowd (of fellow writers) so that I don't have to get mixed up with that sort of insincerity," he explains. He has tried "to know something," and he has tried "to know how to swing" the knowledge he has. "You know," he says, "some try swinging things aimlessly, like dumbells, or some find the weight too heavy to swing and have to sit down on it. I've never written about sewing machines. I don't know anything about sewing machines. But Amy Lowell wrote about carpenters shingling a roof and got it all wrong." Poetry is what he "swings" with deftness; it is the root of his passionate devotion.

III

What has enabled Frost to transmute Gerard Manley Hopkins's "deep down things" into communicable experience is a charged sensibility, a further salient trait. No less than Keats, his senses directly relay nerve-tip experience of the natural world. "Let's go slow so I can see the flowers," is his enjoinder before starting out on a ride through the countryside. He will point out a cluster of flowering milkweed by the doorstoop of his Ripton cabin. "Sometimes I see a hundred butterflies out here," he says half apologetically, and at once the drab little patch comes alive. Of his vegetable garden below the cabin, he says without sententiousness, "I like to feel the corn grow." Or, of a clump of fireweed, "I like to have something growing without my help."

Once another poet quoted Frost's "the slow smokeless burning of decay" and pointed out what difficulty a translator would have in putting this into French or Italian or Russian. Frost agreed. The magic of it is in the phrase—"smokeless burning." Then he added, "the magic of the thing is the lucky snatches you take as you go." The phrase might have originated, he suggested, in smokeless powder, a phrase then current in advertisements when he wrote the poem. True! But where does the sensibility come in? Directly in the center. It is the sensibility that picks up these details and makes possible the lucky snatches in the mind. Every writer knows it is the quickened sensibility that takes the lucky snatches in art. When Flaubert referred to "those thrusts of power beyond the reach of conscious art," or when Walter Pater referred to the impulse behind da Vinci's effort actualized in Mona Lisa as "some puissance of nature," it is the sensibility that is— that must be—involved. When Frost, unboastfully, says of *Complete Poems:* "I have a thrust of power that comes out in the book," he is only compounding Flaubert and Pater. The thrust of power may have its source in the behest of his daemon, but the daemon that literally "infuriates" the poet and drives him on to poetic *katharsis* is a sensibility as responsive as a hairspring.

Imagination is the drop of transforming ichor in an otherwise human blood stream. For without imagination, which is so much involved in memory, there would not be the play of mind with the deep stock pile of stuff which the senses have procured. Frost believes "a poem is a connection of two things in the universe," and we can readily see how metaphor effects the connection between things which the senses have gathered. But it takes imagination to see the latent connection. In the pocket of the mind must be the materials which memory uses and which imagination fuses in metaphor. In the *Prelude* Wordsworth clarifies the activity of the sensibility:

> Nor is it I who play the part,
> But a shy spirit in my heart,
> That comes and goes—will sometimes leap
> From hiding places ten years deep;
> Or haunts me with familiar face,
> Returning, like a ghost unlaid,
> Until the debt I owe be paid.

The part the poet plays in the creative process is that of a sentient being who feels the sudden leap of the shy spirit. What arouses the shy spirit is recognition of something not identical but similar in experience, and the insight that connects smokeless powder with the "slow smokeless burning of decay." Usually Frost's memory deals more with ideas than with chronological data—is more philosophical than opportunistic.

Here, then, we have the first meaning usually associated with a sensibility—the objective response of the senses feeding the creative energies of the writer at the instinctual level. His senses are probably not more intense than the next man's; it is the purpose to which he puts them that marks the difference. His experience pressures the lively images, and mental gravitation assists his patient watchfulness of life in all "its antagonisms, conflicts, iridescences"—the antagonisms that grow out of human relationships, the conflicts that are seen in the poet's sensitive awareness, the iridescences that leap out of natural observation.

There is a second meaning of sensibility—the subjective response of the poet's sensibility—how he reacts to the immediate world of men and nature, and in this response is a measure of his sophistication. Frost, as we know him, is no common countryman but one who has learned a great deal about what goes on in the world of human thought and feeling. Knowing very well this world outside himself—being, as it were, a kind of commuter between the simple and the sophisticated, he reflects both negative and positive aspects in his reaction. Sometimes, when he is deeply moved by the hatreds and rancors of worldly society, he seems to inhabit a world of real enemies and imaginary friends. He is, indeed, complex as simplicity usually is when it is compounded of many simples. The strong forces have affected him as corrosive not attritive energies; they have bitten into his ruggedness, but they have not worn it away. He has contained them. In the years when Amy Lowell and Ezra Pound carried on a typically twentieth-century aesthetic warfare in acerb tongue, he stayed out of it, avoiding the savagery of the poet's ego world where envy is sharp as the serpent's tooth. And blessed with a highly developed wit, he has been able to hold his own against critics like those who in the early nineteenth century impaled Keats on their lethal weapons. Of these literary squabbles which make bad blood, Frost says, "I was smart. I never tried to draw any man's fire."

On the positive side, we may be sure that humanistic values are safest where a human being is no ingenuous backcountryman, hoodwinked by the subterfuges in a devious world. Frost, who is well acquainted with the world of men and affairs, is better equipped to fight for these humanistic values than a great many retiring writers and, in the sincerity and courage of his convictions, we have the assurance that these values will never be deserted or temporized. When asked, "We never tell the real things, do we?" he replied without hesitation, "No, we never tell the real things." He might have added, that as a poet it is not good form to tell them. It is expected that you will show them in your art. In one of the subtlest and most exacting arts, implication is the art of arts. In his relationship to his fellow man, Frost's sensibility is acutely intensified. "We never get over being hurt," he says, when recalling the reaction of people to him when he was young and just starting out in life. His father-in-law once said grimly to him, citing another man as a success, "You'll never earn a thousands dollars a year." This is the challenge by which he was supposed to stand or fall—the challenge of worldly success by which his reputation in the eyes of his fellow man was to be tested.

It is doubtful if the range of his sensibility extends as broadly as, let us say, Henry Adams's did, but it is far warmer and the expression of it is a lot funnier. He mentions music little, except ballads and folk tunes. Visual art has probably little influenced him, although one of Alma Tadema's paintings contributed to his conception of the messenger approaching the king in the Himalayan narrative, "The Bearer of Evil Tidings." He looks approvingly at Van Gogh's Sailing Boats at St.-Maries, but it is to be doubted if he has ever walked voluntarily through the Metropolitan Museum of Art. The cinema he dismisses bluntly; ballet he ignores; sculpture like Mahroni Young's he regards with a patriotic interest.

IV

Two more traits, which have stood Frost in good stead, are courage and independence; the former toughening his sensibility and the latter forthrightly expressing it. Man, in one way or another, makes a declaration of independence which reflects the degree of his personal freedom, formulates a bill of rights which signifies his rights and duties, and issues an emancipation proclamation by which he seeks to liberate the slaves in his own mind. Frost says the two big moments in his growth as a poet occurred when first he found he understood what the words on the page really meant in his studies; and second, when he found what "stance" to take and hold. The first moment is the discovery that not only has man an intellect, but that he can use it. The second moment is one of decisiveness when he takes his stand and declares his purpose.

It is stimulating to hear Emerson utter his declaration of purpose in 1834, two years before *Nature* appeared. "Henceforth I design not to utter any speech, poem, or book that is not entirely and peculiarly my work." The important decision about a career of the other equal but opposite force in American letters, Walt Whitman, actually came after the newspaper world had rejected the first edition of *Leaves of Grass*. "When the book aroused such a tempest of anger and condemnation everywhere," said Whitman, "I went off to the east end of Long Island and Peconic Bay. Then came back to New York with the confirmed resolution—from which I never afterward wavered—to go on with my poetic enterprise in my own way and finish it as well as I could." As close as Frost can come to telling, "My November Guest" is the first of the poems of which he could say, "This is mine and from now on all the others must be mine." And the lines in "My Butterfly" which confirmed his belief are:

> The gray grass is scarce dappled with the snow;
> Its two banks have not shut upon the river;

In describing the emotion he felt when he knew that he had "come through" in these lines, he says, "It's a funny feeling—like tears inside."

Frost's independence is a very personal quality. It is at once in and of the grain; he is assertive. When aroused, he is a formidable opponent who rakes his antagonist with devastating raillery and reproof, mockery and slow quip, sly banter and trouncing wit. The vivid vigor of his attacking mind—tough, virile, sensitive and longheaded—is a thing to behold! Like the rest of us, he has antipathies and distastes, prejudices and *bêtes noires*. He is a tormentingly aggressive opponent. Whoever has known him will never forget the rascally gay cackle of his laughter in which little icicles sometimes form.

He is also a fearless independent. A stubborn and spinal man, where his own rights and convictions are concerned, he is uncowed by mob appeal and sensitive to inferior standards. Only the arts can "scare" him; but scare him, as he says, into some "disciplined response." He shares the prejudices of an average man, the fears of a big one. Moreover, his independence is part of the tactic in his "strategic retreat." As he says, "I sneaked some of my time. And like a man I took some. And some was given me." This defensive independence has enabled him to get his work done in spite of "the system." "A furtive worker" is the way he describes himself. Only those who know how to manage their independence can be furtive workers. I doubt whether he has ever been caught wriggling in the hair shirt of duty. Yet I do not detect in his attitude any self-righteous assertion of individualism over the sense of community. He is a good neighbor who likes good fences in their proper place, with swinging gates for the unintrusive friend.

His self-defensive independence has enabled him to withstand the coy little groups of self-approving writers. He did not whirl haplessly in one of these eddies, or crawl into the snug cocoon of an educational institution and go asleep. He has earned and paid his own way. Consider what might have happened when he first started to write—*circa* 1890—had he succumbed to the New York group, of which Maurice Thompson and Susan Hayes Ward were prominent members. Such an easy acceptance would have put him off twenty years. He encountered this group when he was mature enough to resist their dominance. Had he met them earlier in his career or had he been more pliant in temperament, he might have found their attraction irresistible, but with his growing technical assurance and with his subject matter in hand, I do not think they could have stopped him, although they might have distracted or interrupted him. Because his independence doesn't capitulate readily to influences, he broke into modern poetry by withstanding the lesser genteel traditionalists.

He admires taking a big risk for *mortal* stakes. This kind of courage does not bolster the bravado of the fearful. "We live by fears," he says. "Like a snail, we move our feelers this way and that way. We fear death, poverty, the jail." For himself, as if in repudiation of the uncourageous, he adds, "I take an awfully dim view of them [the fears]." His fearlessness extends to social relations of the upper upper class as well as to the arts. "No big front door ever bothered me" is no idle boast. In the sports field the virtue he applauds is *performance*— the courage an athlete shows in prowess. In the arts prowess is the thing! "The skill one has in danger—that is prowess." Courage and skill are attributes of the artist that "go on together."

A vigorous courage has its roots deep in his life. Frail and sickly as a small child, survival was the most immediate problem. As an older man he likes to say that he has grown more rugged. And this is the truth of it. When he was in his early twenties he had a peculiar pain across the chest that the doctors couldn't diagnose. The pain had started after he had gone down to clean out a well on the place where he lived in Lawrence. "We used to put a can of milk down the well to cool the milk and some of the milk slopped out. So I went down to clean out the well. It was dark and restricted down there. And that's where the pain started. Probably a touch of consumption. Not until I went on the farm at Derry [New Hampshire] did it disappear." His courage was sorely taxed to survive and make a go of things.

As a child he was poor. His worldly and brilliant father was not a good provider and the burden fell heavily on a gentle, nature-loving and religious mother. After his father's death, when the family lived in Lawrence and Methuen, Massachusetts, it was continuously debt-ridden and, in consequence, looked down on by the neighbors. Frost remembers bringing eggs to market to sell at fifteen cents a dozen. The insolent grocer, to whom the Frosts were in arrears, said he would take the eggs and break the dozen, and if none of the eggs were rotten, he would pay for them.

When, in 1900, his grandfather staked him to a farm at Derry in the West Running Brook country of southern New Hampshire, he had a great time the first few months putting up chicken houses "all over the place." "I wrote some," he explains, "but I was careful because I didn't want to become too facile. Later (1905–11), when I taught school—sometimes thirty-five periods a week—I didn't write at all, not for two years. Take the new volume—*Complete Poems* (1949)—how many pages is it? About six hundred. Well, I've been publishing for nearly sixty years. This makes an output of about ten pages a year and say I destroyed as much again, but I doubt it. This isn't usually very much writing in a lifetime. I sent out a few poems. When I got the rejection slips, it made me angry, and I burned them." Here is independence—in plenty—and abundant courage. The independence shows, too, in his rejection of Hamlin Garland's advice to "bulk it," that is, to write a lot of poetry, and in the rejection of Professor George Herbert Palmer's counsel to make his poetry "big and serious."

When it is understood how deep the iron entered the soul of Frost in his encounters with hard, bitter onsets, it is not surprising that he is concerned—some would say obsessed—with frustration, denial and difficulties of the past; and that he erects careful defenses as a protection from further onsets. There is a good deal of the stoic in him. Once, in his presence, Mrs. Kathleen Morrison said, "War *is* cruel." Quick as a flash he replied, almost involuntarily, "Life is more cruel." On another occasion we had been discussing the comparative merits of the sports page and the front page of the daily newspaper. I told him I turned to the sports page to forget what was going on in the grim World War II days. He replied laconically, "I can take both." What really sums up his independence and courage is his saying once, "I wouldn't lie down on the floor [that is, give up] because I wouldn't move if I got down, but if I'm up I'll stand up and go my way." It is necessary to know the background of a man's life to catch the nuances in this reaction.

V

Frost's formal education, such as it was, did not curb his intellectual curiosity. He has not a fact-stuffed mind, such as one might acquire in a conventionally formal education. The "genteel traditionalists"—Emerson and Longfellow, Lowell and Holmes—had minds that were like well-furnished libraries. They were well-educated writers, but an education such as each of them had might have proved a liability to a young poet full of growing like Frost. He is lucky to have been footloose and literally fancy free, yet the chance he took in growth by self-education is a great one. Most do not survive its temptations. That Frost has is attributable in part to his curiosity. What Whitehead calls "a touch of genius arising from vivid apprehensions stimulating originality of thought," can stand as Frost's formula. What touched his genius awake, like God's hand touching the tips of Adam's fingers in Michelangelo's "Creation of Adam," is vivid apprehensions which spring from a vitalized curiosity.

What constantly amuses and delights all those who read his poetry or know him is—and there is no other word for it—the "play" of his mind in fun. The play is the flexibility of a mind which readily perceives interrelationships with great clarity. The play's the thing, and his mind always seems in movement, restlessly looking into, turning over —"Education," he says, "is turning things over in the mind"—inspecting, appraising, revising; in effect, meditating and seeking an inevitable fusion or connection in metaphor. In the latter we find originality of thought, which Whitehead ascribes as an exponent in the genius formula.

This active, venturing inquiry operates in the world of ideas by sensitive recall and combination. In September, 1935, I visited Frost at The Gulley in South Shaftsbury, Vermont. As we sat talking, he mentioned a recent ride over the mountain with a friend—a college teacher—during which he called to his friend's attention that *King Lear* is not to be taught or read as a piece of research, or a chronicle or a saga or an epic or even as "a work." It is none of these things; it is, in fact, just exactly what Shakespeare, who ought to know about such things, had called it, "a play." For it had been written in the spirit of playcraft. Shakespeare had not let down all the bars into his inmost soul. He had kept himself well in hand and written plays in the play spirit. There is the life Shakespeare lived in and out of his family and the life within the plays. Part of the one spilled into the other. *Lear* is a play and that Shakespeare did not make it a confessional is apparent. He wrote to delight us, emotionally and intellectually. "He only is the master," says Dr. Johnson, "who keeps the mind in pleasing captivity." And Shakespeare, a master of the revels, exhibits this mastery of the play spirit. How relevant this is to Frost's own attitude! "I'm never serious except when I'm fooling," he confides revealingly.

Then Frost picked up from the table a brown paper-bound composition book with ruled lines, and after telling of a meeting with Edwin Arlington Robinson, he read from a bold longhand script the introduction to *King Jasper,* which Macmillan had invited him to do. Here again was the play idea set down—this time for keeps. But where had it come from? How is it associated with his poetry? What light does this incident reflect on the curiosity of Robert Frost? The germ of the play idea was in the life of a professional big-league baseball pitcher—"Ted" Lewis—who later became president of the University of New Hampshire. Frost had long known Lewis, who had told him that his first delight in victory had not come in athletics, where he had pitched brilliantly in the National League, but from poetry—one of the playing fields of the arts.

A little later—during the fourth in the Charles Eliot Norton series of lectures at Harvard University, on March 25, 1936—Frost said that it was in baseball he discovered the idea that poetry has always been something like play. One of the important things in poetry is prowess which, in athletics, is the play spirit in action. What makes the poem "an adventure" is the play of ideas, images, sounds, rhymes; to see if the poet can "pull it off," as the phrase is. In life the play is for mortal stakes; in art presumably for immortal stakes. This is the difference! How deep this play attitude penetrates Frost's own thinking and action is apparent when he says, "My life has been such a gamble. I have enjoyed so much the uncertainty of things. I couldn't live without it." The growth of this idea shows his curiosity. His curious, probing intellect establishes a connection between the sports world and the world of art, and the association is a fresh insight. That *Lear* is a play is perfectly obvious. That there is a spirit of play involved in the art of writing poetry is not quite so obvious.

Curiosity is also demonstrable in the multiple things a man is curious about. Poetry, philosophy, education, politics and people are endless sources of interest to Frost, and, to borrow a figure from Henry Adams, he uses his talks as an anvil on which to hammer his ideas. Talking is "making" ideas; it is not, in his own wisecrack, "all opinionation." His curiosity is boundless. Curious about any new thing, he will hurry out of a parked car to watch the operation of a new rocker jack installed in a nearby service station. It is the same trait that stimulates him to see if he can make the redbud and dogwood grow in Ripton, Vermont, and to experiment with rhyme in poems and try old words in the context of fresh thoughts. What is impressive is his comprehensive curiosity, absorbing a detail from a newspaper or a deed of conveyance, from the stanza in an otherwise commonplace poem, or a passage from a little-known book, or a thing said or seen in passing. And he seems to have remembered everything important to him.

Frost's intellectual inquiry is like that of the polygonal Americans of the eighteenth century—those inquiring men—Jefferson and Franklin and Paine. He deserves this comparison if only for his general culture which, in view of his self-education, only a curious man would have acquired. When he discovered a strange kind of fungi on an ascending strip of the Long Trail in Vermont—a tender, exposed rootlet, with a small snakelike head and long runners—he loosened the earth around the roots and probed the round brown pellets. He kept at it, saying, "We'll follow it up the mountain." So curious, he grubbed for specimens, and those he dropped in his front overall pocket, until he had a dozen of the runners and seed pods and heads. He kept ruminating about the plant. Was it a parasite? How deep did the roots go? Was it to be found far off the trail? Did it grow higher up? He thought there were people who had once lived around here who could tell us what this plant was—its name, history and associations. He would look it up himself. Days later at the Ripton cabin I asked him what he had discovered about the enigmatic plant, and although he couldn't name it yet, he was looking. Big botanical tomes were lying on the floor by his old Morris chair.

His poems are filled with references which suggest two avocational interests. The later poetry has shown a gradual expansion in his archaeological interest—one of philosophic range. The stars also attract him as he distinguishes Venus and Jupiter burning in the early evening sky or traces the constellations on a clear night. And his inquiry extends to the object of his admiration—to the Greeks. For the boldness of the Ionian philosophers in initiating hypotheses and challenging the authority and hold of the hieratic gods over the minds of the Hellenes, Frost has, as he says, "been moved to the pleasure of tears." Of Xenophanes, Heraclitus and Parmenides, he wonders, "But where did they get their stimulus?" And he recalls, with commendation, the Inca who stood out from his people and challenged the claim that the Incas were descended from a God—a God-chosen people. The epigram of the Cynic philosophers—"Mint your own coins"—that is, think your own thoughts, is one of which he would approve. He says, "Having thoughts of your own is the only freedom."

Similarly, he prefers Epicurus and Lucretius because of their boldness in facing the bleak infinities. In the staunch little band of Ionian thinkers, who were not dissuaded in their intellectual ventures by Eleusinian mysteries, and in the redoubtable Lucretius, he finds inspiration to a latter-day boldness. "What is more interesting than to be original—daring into the unknown?" And he says feelingly, "What I like in people is a bold newness."

Frost's curiosity is psychological as well as literary. He is as interested in man's behavior as he is in man's thoughts. The people who interest him are handlers of horses and master artisans in the rural communities, or youngsters like the apprentice in the graphic arts he discovered, who, at twenty-two, had found the one thing that meant everything to him. "With his big thick fingers," says Frost, "he can make penguins start up from ice cakes. He's that deft. He's infected and how rare it is to find them so." He is interested in men like an Orford, New Hampshire, basketmaker, tinkerer and ballad singer, who makes baskets of split oak and swamp ash so expertly that when someone tells him they don't leak grain, his pride is touched, and he remonstrates, "Damn it all, they won't leak *flour*." Thirty years ago I recall hearing Frost speak about a friend, a mail clerk on a railway train—owner of a triangle farm with roads all round it—who considered his bees and family and home as "so much velvet." This man, who thought there wasn't any more that he had coming to him, Frost contemplated with interest. He had just enough to get the virtue of a thing; just enough alcohol or money or love or apples; in effect, he was "a sampler." "What do you want more than enough of things to get the virtue of them?" was the way Frost put it. Here we discover an amplification of his doctrine of "synechdoche."

Just as Thoreau had his notion of the right kind of man, so has Frost. What he likes is the upstanding, able, natural man who can do things for himself—the independent and versatile man. These are his Reuben Rices, Edmund Hosmers, George Minotts, not of Concord, but of the upland New England country he knows best. There are also the men of energy—the pioneering type—who scramble to the top of the pile by dint of initiative, character and intelligence. Frost never makes the mistake of denigrating the successful man to build up the common man. He also likes the rebels, and distinguishes carefully between real rebels and "semi-rebels." Emerson can stand as a representative of the real rebel. "A great disturber of the peace," he calls Emerson, whose "Uriel" is a "bugaboo poem that is meant to scare people." Emerson, like Jefferson, is a revolutionary whose rebellion is not far this side of incendiary; a rebel who is not establishing but breaking away from the established. Who can stand as his representative hero? In ancient Greece would it be Miltiades, Pericles, Demosthenes, Socrates, Plato? Perhaps Pericles or Themistocles—the Pericles of the great speech; or Themistocles, the shrewd, wise, articulate statesman who saved the Greeks from the Persians; not the later Themistocles, intimate of the Persian Xerxes's son. And certainly Socrates, whose great loyalty to Athens was unremitted even to the end. In the Bible it is probably Nehemiah who most impresses Frost, the man who gave up his career as a courtier at the Persian court of Artaxerxes to vitalize his people and regenerate Jerusalem. Among the Romans whom shall it be? Men of ideas like the Gracchi; or a reformer and man of the people like Marius; or a Scipio Africanus, the Younger, popular champion of the Italians; or a reactionary like Sulla; or the eloquent, honest, ambitious Cicero; or the anxious egoist Pompey; or the bold, big-natured, large-minded Julius Caesar? Perhaps it would be Marcus Porcius Cato whose action springs from moral motives for the common welfare rather than Scipio Africanus whose behavior represents the self-assertion of individual personality. For Cato was one of the Romans of whom Ennius's declaration might be truthfully said, *Moribus antiquis stat res Romana virisque.* (On men and characters antique Rome stands.)

In American history Washington and Grant would take precedence over Lincoln and Lee. "The people I want to hear about," Frost says, "are the people who take risks." So he praises the big, awkward George Washington—*Pater Patriae*—"the greatest of the great," he calls him, who risked everything and won, and who refused dictatorship. He admires Washington's love of the land and his great, righteous anger, and he recalls the two letters he wrote to Ethan Allen, warning the Green Mountain Boys not to exceed themselves in their reach for power. And Grant and Lee! What he likes about Lee is his refusal to go North after the war to curry favor. He took his beating like a man and, quietly minding his own affairs, retired gracefully from the public eye. But Grant, the greater general, as a strategist, planned the whole war from the Atlantic to the Mississippi. Lee, the tactician, was too much the Virginian, scarcely aware of the West. He had not been able to win the important battles—Sharpsburg, Gettysburg, Richmond. "Courtesy keeps us praising Lee, but Grant was a real great general, like Marlborough."

Although, as a discerning friend of Frost's says, "he doesn't operate from books," it would be a mistake to underrate his acquaintance with them. He reads the classics, but not always in the original. "I'm a great

deal happier," he says, "in my own language." He disclaims being a
scholar, but he is curious about the truth of things. As for the scholarly
or "thorough" books, he thinks such fare only grazing in thistly pastures. Independent in his curiosity about books as in everything else,
he describes himself as "a reckless reader." The crux of his theory about
reading is contained in the coinage "readatability." He doesn't try to
cover everything in a book; he always leaves a little for the return trip.
His motto in reading is, "We'll be back." In his "recklessness" he reads
a little in *Arabia Deserta*, Plutarch's *Lives,* the *Bible, The Voyage of
the Beagle, Walden, The Decline and Fall of the Roman Empire,
Typee, The Oregon Trail,* Thucydides, or Herodotus.

"The two things a reader can do in reading a book or poem are to
think it [see what it says and what ideas it imparts], and to think about
it [that is, be aware of what ideas it generates in your own mind]," says
Frost. "It's like the ground forces and the air forces." He is careful not
to get overthorough about his reading. What he takes from a book is
"fresh pleasure from old pages." He has an eye and an ear for oddities
in literature. So it is that he constantly sprinkles his talk with neat,
unusual allusions and uncommon and off-tangent references—to Enoch
Lincoln's *The Village* or Longfellow's *Keramos,* to one of Abraham
Cowley's Anacreontics or Max Beerbohm's *Seven Men,* to Hawthorne's
Mr. Higginbotham's Catastrophe (which is regarded highly by him as
a detective story), and John Russell's *The Last Man,* to *Middlemarch*
and *The Bottle Imp,* to Olaf Stapledon and William Cobbett. I think
he takes most delight in discovering and circulating some little-known
writer or neglected writing out of the centuries now casting a pinched
shadow. Somehow he has found time to mark where these shadows fell
on ancient walls. By using them he vitalizes the past in the present.
The past well read is a continuous now. Because of his intellectual
curiosity his memory is full and tenacious, and he quotes captivatingly
far-off remembered phrases and poetic passages.

VI

Another characteristic trait is his sense of humor. Once Mark Van
Doren said genially to him, "You're a comic genius." He puckered up
and brushed off "the genius." He likes nothing better than to antic like
Puck on Parnassus, and although he antics with less inhibition in al-

fresco talk, his humor has been no liability on the lecture platform. Here is where he puts over ideas and poems, and the way he does it is one of the keys to the special quality of his humor. Often it is a kind of mellow, musing humor—the starting loose of something funny to him—a surprise that it is there or that it looks so droll when mentioned. It does not pounce upon the listener; the inflected voice releases it. How he says what he is saying; aye, there's the leverage of his humor. Because life is seriocomic he has learned how to ride easily the contiguous moods of gaiety and gravity. His light manner usually belies a serious intent. If he is seemingly serious, he is probably inwardly gay, and if outwardly gay, inwardly grave.

I've never seen Frost when he was as funny as Oliver Wendell Holmes's "funnyman." That is, he never killed anyone with a convulsing joke or destroyed them with a devastating burst of wit. Not quite. Nevertheless, he can be irrepressibly comic. One evening at a lecture he warmed up with a casual quip about how writing free verse was like playing tennis with the net down. Then he launched into a technical distinction between free verse and regular meter. "In the Bay of Bengal/ I lost my all," he improvised. Now, that is regular verse, he was saying. He continued, "In the Bay of Bengal/ I lost my shirt." That's free verse for you, he implied. There was a murmur of laughter. "If I wanted to rhyme shirt," he added, "I'd say Mount Desert." This remark was good for a more moderate laugh. Then he started to play with the jingle. Each fresh improvisation increased the tempo and spontaneity of the laughter until, with the audience's imagination at tension pitch, he said abruptly—and with inflected tone—"In Paris, France," and then stopped. No one in the audience spoke out audibly, but every one there must have finished the couplet. It was risqué but neat; it scored a point and relaxed the audience. The evening was his. Such a gambit is not easy. You have to have a certain kind of risibility, and you have to impose that risibility upon others. You have to dominate. Twain could do it. Witness "The Golden Arm." Artemus Ward could. Witness his effect on the Savage Club in London. Will Rogers also could. Witness his appearances in the Ziegfeld Follies when, as he whirled a lariat, he lassoed humor from topical items in the morning newspaper. Frost is a natural showman, who knows how, in the vernacular, to set up the laughs. Often the repartee in his lectures, especially in the introduction to the poetry readings, is a kind of Mr. Gallagher and Mr. Sheean performance. He doubles as his own straight man.

This is what his humor is like in action, but to analyze the motivation for it and to distinguish it from the humor of others is more difficult. Cervantes and Twain, as well as Meredith and Bergson, have made us aware that humor is laughter evoked by a man in balance at things off balance. It may be that this is true of Frost: that his humor originates in the good temper of a man in balance, whose observing eye catches things incongruously off center. I'm sure of one thing: his humor is the inner man surfacing and its origin is in the sanity of the senses. For, in his humorous moods, he has the easy tolerance of a man whittling a shaving; the bite of anger is not in it, although pity and sympathy usually are. There is a story going the rounds, probably not apocryphal, of a friend who told Frost that he had spent all afternoon in the fields worrying what to do about lacking a sense of humor. Good, kind, wise, humorous Frost counselled, "I'd try getting along without one." As for a sense of humor—*ne plus ultra*. The important part of the story is in the inflection of the voice; it wasn't harsh, I am sure.

Frost's sense of humor has lifted the strain in personal stresses and tensions. Moreover, such a sense of humor is the natural accompaniment of an empirical attitude. Since the essence of humor consists in getting the jump on the object of our laughter—the incongruous, disequilibrated, off-center object—in Frost it is expressed by his cutting an abstraction down to size or in exaggerating the pretentious for the laugh it has coming to it. And since life can impose a continuous strain, his motto seems to be: he laughs longest who starts laughing first; a kind of quick-breaking, anticipatory humor, as it were.

He is a witty man and he insists on wit in any phase of life: in education, love, literature, politics, religion, science. By wit he means the perception and making of "unexpected connections" in thought, ideas or reactions. The wittiest person is the one who has "the freedom of unexpected connections," a characteristic he ascribes to Emerson. But wit is also the laughter of percipience; it is the *sense* of humor sharpened at a certain point to expose folly and stupidity. Usually his wit is pointed at savantism, bookfast scholars, demobilized intellects, whether in science, scholarship, business, or the military. He satirizes cozy thoughts, smug rejoinders and adherents of the simple life—unleavened enthusiasts whom he calls "Thorosians." He mints witty epigrams casually amid the chatter of people at cocktail parties or in conversation. He tosses them about with accomplished accuracy. And he uses this talent just as cleverly as he uses his humor: to protect the quick of his sensitivity, to brush aside gnattish annoyances, to whip in ideas.

His witticisms have been freely circulated. We all remember having read one or two in the newspapers and magazines. "When I'm asked if I'm an introvert or an extrovert, I just tell them I'm a plain vert from Vermont." Or, "I call myself a 'teacher' on my income tax report, but next year I'm going to put down 'resigned.' When they ask me, 'Resigned from what?' I'll say I'm resigned to everything." He has "gotten off" better, more spontaneous, ones than these. While Frost was lecturing in California, Chief Justice Earl Warren, then Governor, reminded him that he was a native Californian, born, as a matter of fact, in San Francisco, and asked, "Why did you leave California?" He remembered all right, but he couldn't resist confounding the local public-relations men in the busy Chamber of Commerce in a great state. Frost, who left San Francisco when he was two, told Mr. Warren, "I went out very young. I was carried out screaming." He thinks this is one of his ablest comebacks. I prefer a more profane one. It is in the free-for-all, give-and-take, no-holds-barred exchange where Frost rarely comes off second best. When he first met Reed Powell, a brilliant jurist and native son of Burlington, Vermont, the latter punched Frost right in the midribs: "You're a bastard Vermonter." Frost nailed the jurist with a haymaker: "And you're a Vermont bastard." "Our friendship," says Frost engagingly, "began right there."

Frost likes to circulate good wisecracks. "I like a quick answer," he will say. "They're often in self-defense." He revels in applied wit, his own or someone else's. One of his granddaughters, who attended a progressive school, said, "At the progressive school we learned to talk about everything. And now [at college] we have to find out what we were talking about." This kind of thing pleases him. Some of the stories he likes to tell are grubbed right out of the Vermont hills, like the one about the old-timer in Ripton who took a glassful of whiskey and gulped it down, making a wry face, and after a bit, remarked ingenuously, "I've digested it." Or the one where someone took the old Ripton patriarch into the anteroom and put in his hand a glass half filled with neat whiskey, and turned to get some water. "Here, let me fill it with water," said the friend. But the old man brushed him away, saying, "I ain't that thirsty." There's more than a visceral laugh in the much-publicized and oft-quoted story of Frost's reply to the inquiry of what most influenced his life. "When I was twelve," he says, "I worked in a little shoe shop and all summer I carried nails in my mouth. I owe everything to the fact that I neither swallowed nor inhaled."

The most acerbic and closest-cropped expressions of his wit are reserved for the analysts of literature who try to pick a poem clean or miss its intent. When a friendly critic asked if the last two lines in "Stopping by Woods" referred to going to Heaven, and, by implication, death, the poet replied, "No, all that means is to get the hell out of there." How often someone gets caught like an insect in the slip stream of his jet-propelled wit. For the manner of poets, like T. S. Eliot in *The Waste Land,* who scatter through their poems multiple quotations borrowed from other poets' works, he has nothing but scorn. He calls this tendency "scatteration." The nub of his sharp point comes when he says (with Eliot in mind), "You're obligated to make your own quotable lines or thoughts." In Pound's translations you find the poet working not directly from originals but from the original *plus* a lot of other translator's versions. To Pound he once said, "The witticisms [in my poetry] are mine; the *skittericisms* [in yours] are yours." What touches the quick of his risibility is pretense in any form, clerical or secular. The antics of contemporary poets offer a field day for his nipping wit. When Wallace Stevens accused him, "You don't face life; you write from subject matter," he replied quickly, "You write *bric-a-brac.*"

His humor tickles the viscera; his wit amuses the cerebral cortex. In baseball parlance his humor is all slow-breaking stuff, the kind that is native to the American tradition. But he mixes up his stuff and the play of his wit is "live" fast balls. I think I shall remember longest the marvellous rococo wit at play, even as Shaw's was, with the awareness of time running out on him and a world in the throes of political diablerie. It is wit laughing, not at death but standing directly in front of it. It is perhaps the most searching illustration of his affirmation that you will find. It is natural—with no grin-and-bear-it pose; nor a Browningesque up-heart response to the inevitable in human experience. It expresses a human being's freedom to be amused when and where it wills. Of the ironies and incongruities in life, it can truthfully be said that he ribbed them as much as they ribbed him. "Sometimes," as he says, "I am more amused than amusing." Laughter is one way he had of swinging his load; one way he had of keeping on top of tragic griefs.

VII

As commonly as wit and wisdom are paired in our speech, they are rare attributes of any person. We know wit when we hear it; it takes us by direct assault. We are never sure when we hear wisdom. Yet wisdom as a trait can be ascribed to Frost with justice. By characterizing it as we find it operative in him, we shall come a little closer to a definition of terms. Pindar, who considered that a man was gifted with genius when he knew much by natural talent, thus suggested a clue. For wisdom is not so much an acquisition of any social or intellectual class as a natural endowment, which experience either releases or inhibits. Frost helps us clarify the meaning wisdom has for him when he asks of a scholar, "What has he more than his knowledge?" Or, when he characterizes a classicist. "You know what a classicist is?" he inquires. "He is one who knows all the Greek irregular verbs."

Frost possesses what Socrates shows us, a quality of the human spirit which a Spanish friend called *sabiduria*. This Spanish word has no exact equivalent in the English language. Neither mother wit nor horse sense is quite comparable. It is an intimate personal wisdom, unranked and unrankable, which is sometimes apparent in people's speech and sayings. It may be felt in one's attitude or noticed in his expression. It is a profound, distinctive folk trait—a kind of preternatural awareness of experience. Wordsworth thought he detected a natural wisdom (*sabiduria*) among the Westmorland shepherds. He was probably more percipient than sentimental.

To talk in vague generalities about *sabiduria* is no help. Let us be specific. By way of illustration, my Spanish friend told me a little anecdote. When several Spanish huntsmen had returned to their headquarters after a day in the open, one of the hunters inquired of his host where the men were to place their guns, so that no accident would mar the occasion. "Where the body goes, goes death," remarked the host simply, expressing a truth common to the experience of the Spanish people. To an American, the host's *sabiduria* is essentially fatalism, the

inescapableness of death. What the host meant was, apparently, that if you are going to die, there is no getting away from it. The turn of the phrase is, however, even in translation like a folk saying and *sabiduria* is, in fact, like the wisdom of a people welling up in any one of its articulate members. My Spanish friend recalled meeting in Arizona a cowboy with whom he spent an evening—a long one, I gathered. For hours the cowboy talked only about horses and boots and cows, and noticeably without *sabiduria*. He was fenced in by his practicality. There was no wellspring in him.

It is possible to describe *sabiduria* as the subsidence of human experience that originates in living (not existing), and in awareness of (not insulation from) death. It is in Cervantes and Unamuno, Ortega and Federico Lorca; it is also common to the Spaniard in any province, in any activity, on any social level, and as much in women as in men. It is a wisdom that is no less wise for being modest and a popular possession. And it is in Frost just as it was in Socrates. And it is in a Greek like Heraclitus, or in Romans like Cato and Lucretius, of whom Frost in the temper of his thinking sometimes strongly reminds us. I think among historians it is also in Tacitus, and, among our native writers, in Thoreau and Emily Dickinson.

Frost's is a deep-set mind with a high-water level. It is full of little fountains. They jet up and bubble over into memorable sayings. *Complete Poems* is full of *sabiduria:*

> What we live by we die by.
>
> For to be social is to be forgiving.
>
> But inside in is where we've got to get.
>
> And what are wars but politics
> Transformed from chronic to acute and bloody?
>
> The ground work of all faith is human woe.
>
> Each knows his own discernment best.
>
> And there is always more than should be said.

When one of the contemporary critics of modern poetry referred to Frost's wisdom as "introspection," he corrected, "No, it's insight."

In Frost's conversation what is said never sounds like some Sinaitic truth. Nor is it mechanically produced like sounds from a musical instrument. He does not even take time to plane the rough corners of a homely thought, or set the bone of a fractured one. I do not think he is always aware of these insights until they are out. Certainly he doesn't fondle them. He is halfway through uttering another by the time you have rallied to catch the first. When he is "going good," it is like watching light pass through a prism and break into color:

Everyone's marked by his own craziness that he does not give way to. . . . Everyone should hold his own confusion.

I can curl up and go to sleep in a process.

If you're a Democrat, you'll believe the mob was right and Moses wrong.

Everyone is lost in his own age.

You can't improvise a background.

Democracy is power divided against itself.

Life is just a few removes from chaos and it is on the way up to art.

Observation covers both sight and insight.

Life is a pursuit of a pursuit of a pursuit.

There's no great unity but many little unities.

Intensity comes out of dormancy.

All great people did everything before they knew enough.

You can be a rank insider as well as a rank outsider.

It's right that we should be dedicated to revision, but I'm dedicated to vision.

These apothegms bear the unmistakable Frostian mark. They are not someone else's ideas riding pickaback; of this we can be sure. The quality of *sabiduria* is in them.

His speech is proverbial, a colloquial Yankee wisdom comparable to Lincoln's border wisdom. As Emerson says, "A man is only half himself; the other half is his expression." For it is possible to be so enraptured at the vision we have of life that we can find no adequate means to represent it. It is also possible to have the gift of words without an imperious vision. Neither the hand nor the tongue can make the vision, but the vision will go a long way in making acceptable the work of the hand and the tongue. Take Cezanne, for example. Wonderful it is to watch how he became strong by greatly solving the difficulties in his aesthetic dilemma. He did it by reaching down to the instinctual levels of the senses to find a way to evoke his vision on canvas. Similarly Frost has tapped the instinctual springs but with no such conscious effort as in Cezanne. Frost just does what comes naturally. His poetry is one of the most interesting examples of organic functioning in American poetry since Whitman's *Leaves of Grass*. The quality of instinctual awareness and tanginess is common to both Whitman and Frost. Yet Frost has the advantage of wit which he keeps burnished by sorties into the company of sophisticated people, and a wisdom which he keeps vitalized by contact with the instinctual world where sophistication is little known. The light of the former is refracted by the latter. Light always plays on the facets of his intellect. He is always fooling in a seemingly lighthearted but actually very wise way. He says himself, we recall, that he is never serious except when he is fooling.

Another characteristic of his wisdom is its critical intelligence. Lively as are his senses, he is never immersed in a stream of reverie and memory like Wordsworth or Proust. His sagacity tempers pity with a rough justice, sealing it off from sentimentality. He does not make the mistake, so far as I know, of praising the "common" man for virtues which are shared by the uncommon man. Furthermore, his wisdom consists in a delicate sense of balance. Mostly we exaggerate one way or another. When Frost was accused of lacking imagination, he asked, "You mean I don't exaggerate?" One needs, he contends, to know the difference between hyperbole *and* miosis. He is a careful adjuster, an Aristotelian who believes in the necessity of saying the thing right, getting the story accurate, seeing the thing as it is. In every relationship—to society, art, world problems, nature—his independent judgment is an important factor. For he is a poet with an independent stance, which reminds one of Melville's

> Yea and Nay—
> Each hath his say
> But God He keeps the Middle Way.

The middle way is Frost's way, too. Not too much of this; not too much of that—a middle-of-the-roader. So he objects when a Supreme Court Justice argues too personally in his liberalism. A justice of the highest court should, he thinks, take no sides personally; he should weigh and consider.

He balances the two chief ideas in Greek thought—*Being* and *Knowing,* or *Doing,* which represents change. He doesn't know with which he "takes sides"; perhaps the latter, with a small initial letter. The balance is so delicate. It is his art in philosophy, experience and poetry to swing naturally between extremes. In philosophy it is the difference between being and becoming. In experience it is the difference between supernaturalist and naturalist. In the tone of his poetry it is the difference between talking and intoning. Sometimes he is a little on one side; sometimes he leans a little toward the other. Characteristically, he says, "When poets like Sandburg say 'the people, yes'; I say, the people yes *and* no." Or when Franklin D. Roosevelt announced the Four Freedoms, Frost proposed "the four and twenty freedoms."

Frost praises Anaxagoras for saving Pericles, keeping the latter "of but not lost in his time." This is the nub of his relationship to his time: a little detached but with sufficient *simpático* to understand it. He knows that what we desire is a little fixity or stability in a dynamic universe. "At least the constellations in the sky haven't shifted their shapes very much since man took notice," he contends. "There's some fixity somewhere." In the Periclean age "confusion" was rampant, yet the Greeks had their moment of brilliance. Invariably people have to make clarity out of confusion; and all times are perhaps more confusing than orderly. Consequently, he may be critical of, but he is not dismayed at the present "age of anxiety."

"First-hand knowledge," says Whitehead, "is the ultimate basis of intellectual life. . . . The second-handedness of the learned world is the secret of its mediocrity. It is tame because it has never been scared by facts." Frost has this firsthand knowledge. The iron has entered his soul from terrific personal onsets. He has had to face the intractable facts of inter- intra- and extra-worlds—the psychological, political and astrophysical facts of experience. An amiable empiricist, his knowledge is derived directly from reality, and it is shot through with noble hints. What he starts from and what he tests a theory by is fact. In his passionate finiteness he is a specialist in the *sense* of life. An Austrian educator, listening to him during an afternoon's discussion, decided that the quality of intellection which is most distinctive of Frost is his quiet way of nailing down generalizations and deflating them by *specific* reference. When a young poet exclaims, "What I like in *Complete Poems* are the love poems," Frost quietly adds, "And there are ideas, too." When the young poet casually describes a prominent member of a highly regarded university faculty "as just a brilliant person," Frost reminds him, "Intelligence is also important." He does not let excited statements slip by unqualified. His carefulness in judgment, which is also a special quality of his wisdom, is reflected in his art where he watches words for their multiple associations, in his relation to people where he distinguishes particular characteristics, and in his personal attitude of cautious boldness.

Some of his critics have been greatly disturbed by his conservatism. They think he is an old fogy or a Tory because of his distrust of the radicalisms of our time. Yet he thinks he is a more valid radical than his critics and, by strict definition, he sometimes is. The opposite of valid he contends is in-valid, or, as we say "invalid." And the origin of radicalism is in the word "radicle," or the roots of a thing. If a man is a radical, in what sense is he one? If he is a Tory, according to whose definition? When I said to Frost, "They say you are a conservative," he replied, "No, I'm not; I'm more radical than they (the social thinkers) think. If I were one of the poor, I'd ruin the world to satisfy my needs."

A discriminating artist like John Marin knew that "in all things there exists the central power, the big force, the big movement, and to this central power all the smaller factors have relation." The big power to Frost is tradition in poetry and a belief in the confluence of poetry in our time with the great tradition of poetry. In relationship to this central power, he knows the important job is to get one's work done. In consequence, he has been interested only in the one thing that counts for him, and this is poetry. Such an attitude is pretty annoying to practical people, to "radicals," to the men of "higher treason," for he is no respecter of or apologist for their efforts. "I'm made," he says quite truly, "to brush things away—the inessentials, the petty technicalities." His pride in craft, which is concomitant with his belief in the dignity of the human spirit, makes him a redoubtable independent. From the vantage pont of his "strategic retreat," where he absorbs personal worries and works out the economic ones, he is one of the wise men of his time. Living inside his world, he ruminates its problems, observes its ways, speaks its language, feels its hopes and despairs in his bones, and with salutary humor laughs both at and with it.

II

ARS POETICA

THE BEEFEATER: What manner of thing is a cadence, sir.
I have not heard of it.
THE MAN: A thing to rule the world with, friend.
G. B. SHAW: *Dark Lady of the Sonnets*

1. A Theory of Poetry

Poetry as an art is the central passion of Frost's life, and the theory by which it is written originates in his own intimate experience. His comments on how this theory operates are important, just as Cezanne's *obiter dicta* is important in understanding the painter's art. How little we could spare Cezanne's statements—now that we know them! "I believe I become more lucid before nature." Or, "Everything we see is dispersed and disappears. Nature is always the same, but nothing remains of it, nothing of what we see. Our art should give to nature the thrill of continuance with the appearance of all its changes. It should enable us to feel nature as eternal." And, the simple, pregnant statement that clarifies Cezanne's technique: "When color has its richness, form has its plenitude." So little too can we spare Frost's statements— so eloquent and informative—on the art of poetry. For Frost is a thinker in his art as he is by direct evidence a craftsman.

His statements on his art often have an offhand, at-random air. Actually they represent the coherent and consistent but unsystematized doctrine of a sophisticated consciousness. When fused together, they inject into the practice of the art of poetry those refinements by which the poet exercises an innovative interest in his craft. Although the following dicta on the art of poetry have been fused into a whole, we should remember that "the separateness of the parts," as Frost himself says, "is just as important as the connection of the parts." Most of these statements, carefully selected and arranged, have not been wrenched from any written context; they are presented simply as I heard them *vivavoce*. Furthermore, Frost always expressed reluctance in closing a thought in form, which is easy to understand. When an idea is committed to paper, that marks an end to it for some writers. I doubt if his interest would so quickly evaporate, since he preferred to carry a poem in his head until it was well conceived before committing it to paper. But with his general ideas on poetry there was less reason to hesitate.

So he talked about them at large, the better to test their validity in the give-and-take of conversation. For there was no compelling necessity to commit them at once to paper to meet a newspaper or magazine deadline.

Another interesting side light is his way of thinking. He never answered important questions directly. He would appear to tuck an inquiry away on the upper shelf of his mind and discuss other things, and sometime later he would manoeuvre the talk around to the inquiry and give a highly characteristic reply. I suspect he is far more an intuitive thinker than a logician. In an afternoon's talk he might make an important reference to poetry; he might say a dozen relevant things about it, and often these important thoughts were tangential. The significant part about such talk is that when you start to think about what was said the ideas crystallize into an interesting relationship. The tentative and disparate statements are found to belong to the same family. This is one of the most exciting things about listening to him. He is not fuzzy on the principles of his art; neither is he inconsistent. His talk is creative like his poems and invariably releases an idea to significance.

They say that when Ictinus designed the Parthenon he made the general plan as simple as possible, so that it would effectively release the subtlety of the proportions and details. My task is to simplify the general plan of a poet's *ars poetica,* hoping that, as the parts slip into their places, I shall be lucky enough to release the subtlety of the proportions and details. Anything less will belie the method in Frost's art. First we shall discuss the meaning poetry had for him in relationship to literature. Then we shall discuss the aim, genesis, structure, qualities and tests of a poem.

2. Aim as Performance

Once, when he was discussing Gamaliel Bradford's *Saints and Sinners,* he told of a condescending college teacher snorting, "Do you suppose Bradford did all that work?" "You see," Frost commented drily, "the professor was looking in vain for footnotes. The book hadn't any footnotes; it wasn't authoritative. It lacked distinction or something." Then he added shrewdly, "Literature is a performance in words." Bradford's book was just such a performance and the psychographer had accomplished something without footnotes. Frost's definition of literature as performance is a recurrent theme whenever he talks about literature and life. *Performance* is one of his key words. Just as Bradford "performed" in his biographical sketches sans footnotes and sans authorities, so Frost makes his poetry a performance in words without footnotes and without the sanction of "authorities." (The notes in *Steeple Bush* satirize the use of explanatory notes in Eliot's *The Waste Land*.) We have already noted the relation of performance to athletics, and especially its connection with the idea of art as play.

In a Charles Eliot Norton lecture at Cambridge in 1936, he enumerated three factors which make a poem a performance. "The first thing in performance is evidence of self-surprise." Any prepared notes or outlines are suspect to him. "If it [the poem] is thought out first and expressed last, I dismiss it," he said. The second factor in performance is the difference between what he called "a cool morning clarity and a midnight auto-intoxication." He chuckled, "I suppose I know what the latter means. I've written both ways." "Cool morning clarity" is like the leaves on the tree proliferating in spring; it is the brightness and freshness of growing, expanding things. The third factor is when the poem "ramifies," branches out, and still keeps its direction; or, as he said, "When it shoots branches and still is a network." A single straightness, or concatenation, is not what he means by performance. To illustrate his idea of performance as the ramifying of thought, of shooting branches, like a tree, but still keeping the direction, he quotes John Philpot Curran's "Let Us Be Merry":

> If sadly thinking, with spirits sinking,
> Could, more than drinking, my cares compose
> A cure for sorrow from sighs I'd borrow,
> And hope tomorrow would end my woes.
> But as in wailing, there's nought availing,
> And Death unfailing will strike the blow;
> Then for that reason, and for a season,
> Let us be merry before we go.

To joy a stranger, a wayworn ranger,
In every danger my course I've run;
Now hope all ending, and death befriending,
His last aid lending, my cares are done.
No more a rover, or hapless lover,
My griefs are over—my glass runs low;
Then for that reason, and for a season,
Let us be merry before we go.

3. The Height of Poetry

The first dominant aspect in Frost's theory is a preference for the organic and the natural over the geometrical and the self-conscious. Here he agrees with Spenser's "for soul is form and doth the body make," and with Emerson's development of this idea in his essay on "The Poet," when the latter refers to "a thought so passionate and alive that, like the spirit of a plant or an animal it has an architecture of its own, and adorns nature with a new thing." Frost, whose first canon is self-surprise, would find no essential disagreement with Emerson's statement of the organic in art. He often recalls the metaphor which appears in the preface to the *Collected Poems* (1939), of the boulder-strewn pasture in Franconia, New Hampshire, where he used to cross the field, leaping from drift boulder to drift boulder in an irregular course, in "a straight crookedness." So it is with the poet; he senses his direction and reaches out in a Keatsian "trembling delicate and snail-horn perception of beauty." There is both surprise and wonder as the poet follows the path of straight crookedness rather than a surveyor's mechanical straight one.

In the making of form, he proceeds, in Benjamin Franklin's words, "regularly from things known to things unknown, distinctly and clearly without confusion." He does not try to wrench out the significance of the experience inherent in the poetic impulse; he tries only to release it to significance by suggestive detail and concrete object. From its origin in the vague mood, which committed the poet, until the last sentence is set down, the poem unfolds organically, like a leaf from a bud. When Frost sees (*e.g.,* "Desert Places") the snow falling in a field, he proceeds "distinctly and clearly without confusion," from the object seen to the feeling which it arouses in him, and the relation of personal loneliness to impersonal spatial vacancy. Or, he sees (*e.g.,* "Tree at My Window") a tree by his window, and "proceeds regularly from things known"—the tree and its outer weather—to the suggestion of the inner weather of a man. Or, he walks (*e.g.,* "Closed for Good") a road made by people now long gone, and proceeds regularly to his own thought of what he owes and pays (in his own private means) to those who unwittingly opened the road for such as come after them.

He doesn't keep a notebook. The tendency of the writer with a notebook is, he thinks, to put down his thought, finished or unfinished, and then conclude that there is an end to it. He depends upon memory and recall. The freedom that he would like to have, as he often says, is the freedom of his material, and he realizes this freedom by apt recalls from past experience. To make sure that he does not always turn backward, he welcomes enough of the new to freshen his thought. If what attracts his attention has any real significance, he believes that it will stay in his mind and that, by turning to it now and then, he can develop it further. "Inconsiderable things that happen to you that you don't realize are important often turn up in your writing," he has said. "I never really used anything I thought I was going to use. I don't live that way." Part of the pleasure of lecturing or conversing or writing is to take up one of these unfinished thoughts and unfold it a little further. It is as surprising and fresh to the poet as it is to the reader or listener.

He counsels "build soil." He turns thought back and back again, until the tilth of him is "sweating-full" and "drips" poetry and wisdom. The poems he writes are really produced from observed data that may go ten or twenty or more years deep in his life. Moreover, these poems are frequently "composites." "Many of the details," he will say of poems like "Departmental," "are out of poems that failed when I was young. Detritus! A tree builds its own soil." Poetry builds from its own waste, and "the only thing that isn't waste is the point in a poem or story." He tells how Wilfred Wilson Gibson, whom he had known in

England, used to search every nook and cranny for poetic materials in order to write a daily poem. That has not been Frost's *modus operandi*. He has not set out deliberately to write about this or that; he has not "worked up" something to write about. His contemplative glance picks up the material which the unhurried mind absorbs deliberately at leisure. He has been content to wait patiently for experience to settle. In consequence, his poems have not been the product of mere retinal observation. They have been the product of the longest necessary meditation. He has only written under a compelling and controlled impulse. Of three kinds of writers—those who write on assignment like journalists, on self-assignment like those who force out the stuff, or on one's own, waiting upon the mood—obviously he is to be associated with the last group. Until the composing mood comes, he is well satisfied "to gloat on things of this world."

One estimates the success of the organic method by the tenacity with which the poet clings to the coattails of his inspiration and by the depth of the mood in which the inspiration originates. To insure an effective poem there must be no letting go but a steady holding on. It is a dauntless and an exhilarating method, and has, among other advantages, suspense as well as surprise. Intense is the suspense as the poet follows through to a dimly perceived but ultimate fulfillment of his expression. "The best of a poem," Frost will tell you, "is when you first make it, the curve that it takes, the shape, the run, the flow, and then you can come back to it."

The curve that it takes! The shape! The run! The flow! Here we have the second dominant characteristic in Frost's theory. It is what William Blake, who surely was a poet in the tradition of the organic method, called "the bounding line," a phrase to be clearly distinguished in meaning from Gerard Manley Hopkins's "running" rhythm, the rhythm common to English verse. Blake's bounding line is the element of suggestibility. "The great and golden rule of art, as well as of life, is this: that the more distinct, sharp and wiry the bounding line, the more perfect the work of art, and the less keen and sharp, the greater is the evidence of weak imagination, plagiarising and bungling. . . ." Suggestibility in poetry is secured by the selective word; in painting, by the economical line.

Underscoring the significance of suggestibility, Frost says, "I'd hate

to have to speak right out—a verse being straight out." It is by elim-
inating many words and impressions, and by making the exact choice
that the virtue of the poet as artist is most apparent. The essence of
suggestibility is the uninsisted—the quiet, unobtrusive but casually
exact reference. In painting, the line summarizes; in poetry, the selective word implies. When the poetic sentence expresses its own autonomous joy, then it may be said to leap and bound, in Blake's sense of
the phrase. And it leaps and bounds toward the completion of its
idea and form. One of Frost's favorite poems, which illustrates the
bounding line, is the old and anonymous "Hey Nonny No":

> Hey nonny no!
> Men are fools that wish to die!
> Is't not fine to dance and sing
> When the bells of death do ring?
> Is't not fine to swim in wine,
> And turn upon the toe,
> And sing hey nonny no!
> When the winds blow and the seas flow?
> Hey nonny no!

He quotes with gusto places in a poem where it "blazes" or "lights up";
for example, the song of Callicles in Arnold's "Empedocles on Etna":

> Far, far from here,
> The Adriatic breaks in a warm bay
> Among the green Illyrian hills;

or, the following stanzas of Christopher Smart's "A Song to David":

> Strong is the lion—like a coal
> His eyeball,—like a bastion's mole
>   His chest against the foes;
> Strong the gier-eagle on his sail;
> Strong against the tide th' enormous whale
>   Emerges as he goes.
>
> But stronger still, in earth and air,
> And in the sea, the man of prayer,
> And far beneath the tide!
> And in the seat to faith assigned,

> Where ask is have, where seek is find,
> Where knock is open wide.

What he finds to praise in Christopher Smart's sentences is really the
bounding line. What he likes is the way Smart makes "free with the
English language"; "his cavalierliness with words." "The height of
poetry," he thinks, is "a kind of mischief." As he says of the lines
"Where ask is have, where seek is find,/ Where knock is open wide,"
this is not "an obfuscation," but "it's a nice way to say that." This kind
of mischief with idea and cavalierliness with words is in his own
poetry.

He cites the following passages as examples of what he looks for in
poetry. The first witch in *Macbeth:* Act I, Scene III:

> A sailor's wife had chestnuts in her lap
> And mounch'd and mounch'd and mounch'd.
> "Give me," quoth I,
> "Aroint thee, witch!" the rump-fed ronyon cries.
> Her husband's to Aleppo gone, master o' th' Tiger;
> But in a sieve I'll thither sail
> And, like a rat without a tail,
> I'll do, I'll do, and I'll do.

In "Kubla Khan":

> Where Alph, the sacred river, ran
> Through caverns measureless to man
> Down to a sunless sea.

In Louis MacNeice's "Bagpipe Music":

> It's no go the merry-go-round, it's no go the rickshaw,
> All we want is a limousine and a ticket for the peepshow.

"Those are the top places in poetry," he says. "Every word does something to the other words." He continues, "There are two kinds of peaks
in poetry—the imaginative kind to the eye and to the ear." The latter
has to do with "something in the voice speaking." Then he quotes
Keats' "Charm'd magic casements, opening on the foam/ Of perilous
seas, in faery lands forlorn," and says, "that adds up to another peak
of spiritual insight too."

4. A Renewal of Words

Since literature is "a performance in words," what distinguishes the poet's performance, Frost thinks, is "the renewal of words," a renewal that takes place when the poet feels the deep, vague mood in which poems are gestated. There is "a suggestion of making" in the words. Words are, of course, "renewed" by the prose writer, so at these times his writing approaches poetry. *Moby Dick* is charged with poetic language; so, too, are Thoreau's writings, and there are many others. Frost describes metaphorically what happens in the renewal of words. In the laboratory we sometimes see a crucible of quicksilver upon which gathers a leaden scum, and we notice that when it is shaken it crackles like lightning. "That's what happens," he says, "when the words in a poem come alive." They crackle like lightning. Hardy, for example, renews in his poems older English words which he uses in a fresh context—words like *ken, unscanted, westering, bruit, broach, lours*. In "At Lulworth Cove" he writes, "And as the evening light scants less and less," or "I have fifteen miles to vamp across the lea." In "Why Do I?" he says, "Where no pain is: Then shall I hush this dinning gear," and in "According to the Mighty Working" he uses several old-fashioned words in an interesting way.

> When moiling seems at cease
> In the vague void of night-time,
> And heaven's wide roomage stormless
> Between the dusk and light-time,
> And fear at last is formless,
> We call the allurement Peace.

And so, too, does Frost use effectively words and phrases common to man's speech, words like *beholden, daunted, wonted to, the lay of, to fetch*. An illustration of Frost's use of the common speech is the following idiomatic passage from "The Mountain":

"I don't advise your trying from this side.
There is no proper path, but those that *have*
Been up, I understand, have climbed from Ladd's.
That's five miles back. You can't mistake the place:
They logged it there last winter some way up.
I'd take you, but I'm bound the other way."

He cherishes words and ruminates on such phrases as "poring over," so close to "pouring over" that he thinks both must have a common basis in Middle English speech—in a sense that when one pored over the page of a book one poured over it, too, with one's eyes and head; literally, poured one's mind over it. Time and again he will examine a word; for example, one like "vicissitude," which he had once thought meant "irregular," but which he later discovered interestingly enough marked a regular change. Often he uses common words in their etymological sense, playing with them—words like *extrication, cant, extravagance, conformance, frist, prowess, adventure, confluence.* He is visibly annoyed after reading poems submitted by college students when he finds carelessness, ignorance and misunderstanding of etymological meaning in simple words. He knows "it takes years to have the right feeling about words," but without that feeling the writer can be no true poet.

Poetry is, then, for him a renewal of words, and the poet is "a renewer." This is one of many definitions of poetry which he thinks up; a new one each year, he says with a twinkle, but this definition is basic. It is one to which he returns frequently over the years. Degas, who tried his hand at sonnets as well as painting, once complained to Mallarmé that the art of versification is most hateful of all arts. "And yet, Heaven knows, I have ideas enough!" "But, Degas," Mallarmé said, "You don't make poems with ideas, you make them with words." This is true—practically true—but it is what happens to those words in the cauldron of the poet's creative imagination that distinguishes poetry from prose. As Emerson tells us:

To clothe the fiery thought
In simple words succeeds,
For still the craft of genius is
To mask a king in weeds.

5. Composing a Poem

What is the mood for the poem? Is there an optimum condition? "When I write," says Frost, "I must be free of all sense of rivalry— away from it and a part of the life of the spirit where it is non-competitive." At these times he is insulated from the grinding of one ego on another, which fines nerves to a breaking point.

How do poems start? Not with ideas; not with the love of words. In his mood the poet picks up ideas; and the words rally to the mood. The poet throws ideas ahead of him like the giant (in Frost's recurring metaphor) throwing stones before him. To illustrate he quoted a sentence in his head at the time—"work that took me into the wood," which he will hold fast to until the poem is completed. He remembered a forest cutting where he had gone to look over the wood choppers' work. Because he looked for *something,* as the choppers most definitely had not looked for anything, he discovered some Whorled Pogonias. Work had taken him into the wood but the flowers, not the work, were his reward. And had it not been for his conscious awareness, he would have missed the flowers just as the myopic choppers had not noticed them. "I often start," he says of writing poems, "from some remembered spot. From something I understood, like the sight of Whorled Pogonias in a flower station." But when he talks much about these things, he finds he does not write about them.

He does not think a poem originates in an intuitive impulse. He shrugs off the word "intuitive" as too esoteric. He doesn't approve of ascribing mystifying terms to the writing of poems. When he has a good co-ordination of body, mind and spirit—an optimum condition, certainly—then he feels what he describes as "a funny sort of command" over words: "a nice kind of summons." In these moods the poem gets started, and develops from "ecstasy at some surprise in the mind" that the idea or emotion were already there and that he hadn't suspected its presence. It isn't external observation; it isn't the idea which starts the poem going; it is the vague mood that picks up the idea or emotion. Then he gets a "clew" and is drawn on by what he calls a "gatherer"—a thought or attitude toward something. Frost says, "Writing through a poem is being bold with caution, like creeping up on an enemy in a battle."

With Arnold's contention that a poet "should choose a fitting subject," E. M. W. Tillyard (in *Poetry: Direct and Oblique*) disagrees. "The pearl-making oyster does not choose the occasion of its pearl but is chosen by it," says Tillyard. "The poet's mind is a general mass of oysterdom. An alien grain of sand gets in, and the oysterdom seizes on it and grows round it till the pearl is formed and becomes autonomous." This is true in the light of Frost's reactions. He doesn't start by choosing a fitting subject. When the alien grain of an idea gets inside his mind, he seizes on it and holds it until incrementally it grows into an autonomous poem.

In the "black" pre-World War I days he was living at Dymock near Malvern Hill in England in a thatch cottage roofed with straw, four hundred years intact, and, disturbed by personal problems, he walked a floor in the dark room where the thatch roof ledge brushed his elbows. He remembers that in the night his brushing by and tramping about frightened birds that sheltered in the holes in the straw and scared them out into the strangeness of the dark. Frightening them out helped to settle his melancholy. Some other living thing had to face its kind of blackness while he faced his. This was a "clew," a "gatherer," "an alien grain," that finally took form in "The Thatch."

In composing he doesn't start with the end of the poem and proceed to make things fit in so it will come out satisfactorily. He brings to the creative effort the kind of "presence of mind" a tennis player brings to his game; he makes his play as he goes. The poem gets its destination in the first line, and goes on, with luck—in a kind of straight crookedness—to the conclusion. Each poem is a pure discovery—"a resolved perplexity" until, as he says further, there is "the pure emergence from the logic of the thing." In an apt simile, the poem "rides [like ice] on its melting." What he likes to do in a poem is "to touch in and strike out in form"; in effect, to get to the heart of something and clarify it in form.

Expression involves struggle; the "perplexity" must be resolved. The poet, like Jacob at Jabbok, wrestles for the blessing which is his form. There is, in the organic method, a dramatic tension or equilibrium between the contrary forces of sound and sense, metre and thought, matter and form, just as in life there is the constant struggle between liberty and authority, conduct and principle, body and spirit, grace and works. As Frost explains in "How Hard It Is to Keep from Being King," the poem's tune is the resultant of tensions: "Regular verse springs from the strain of rhythm/ Upon a metre, strict or loose iambic./ From that strain comes the expression *strains of music*./ The tune is not that metre, not that rhythm,/ But a resultant that arises from them."

The poet's virtue consists in being true to the idea. Hence, writing poetry, like teaching or any art, is a performance, a skill. Paul Klee clarifies the writer's process of creation: "The genesis, or process, of writing is a very good image of movement. The work of art, too, is experienced primarily as a process of formation, never as a product. A certain fire, coming to life, leaps up, runs through the hand, courses onto the paper, and flies back as a spark where it came from, thus completing the circle: back into the eye and on again." Frost's writing of a poem is not different from Paul Klee's description of the painter at his work. A certain fire of impulse whips a mood into life, the mood picks up its idea and the idea finds its form, running out at the hand on paper or at the lips in expression.

Once Frost explained the genesis of the poem "Departmental." "How did you come to write it?" I inquired. "You mean what it *rides* on?" And, without awaiting my reply, he continued, "A *queer* feeling or mood toward something, and then fulfils it." By *it* he means, of course, the mood toward something—the end of the straight crookedness. When he was living at Key West in the winter of 1935, the sight of an ant and a moth on a table stimulated "an alien grain" already latent in his mind. In a responsive mood he started his poem and went right through with it. In his manuscript copy, there were crossed-out lines and interlineations; nevertheless he had carried it to its conclusion. The greatest satisfaction comes when you can say, "Here is a poem that is a triumphal intention, that bore right through and dismissed itself."

•

6. Rhyming

Frost tests poetic form partly by its rhyming. He exults "when a man is upon his high horse rhyming easy." If the poet reaches for the rhyme rather than meet the challenge implicit in the poem's inception, then the poem wanders and the poet compromises his intention. He cites James Russell Lowell's "Aladdin" as an example of uncompromised rhyming:

> When I was a beggarly boy,
>   And lived in a cellar damp,
> I had not a friend nor a toy,
>   But I had Aladdin's lamp.
> When I could not sleep for the cold,
>   I had fire enough in my brain,
> And builded, with roofs of gold,
>   My beautiful castles in Spain!
>
> Since then I have toiled day and night,
>   I have money and power good store,
> But I'd give all my lamps of silver bright
>   For the one that is mine no more;
> Take, Fortune, whatever you choose,
>   You gave, and may snatch again;
> I have nothing 'twould pain me to lose
>   For I own no more castles in Spain!

"That's very good," he will say. "You couldn't get it better. No compromise there." He continues, "One of the great things in life is being true within the conventions. I deny in a good poem or a good life that there is compromise. When there is [in poetry] it is an attempt to so flex the lines that no suspicion can be cast upon what the poet does. Emily Dickinson's poems are examples of this. When the rhyme begins to bother, she says, 'Here I come with my truth. Let the rhyme take care of itself!' This makes me feel her strength." He takes pleasure in

Emily Dickinson's "The Mountains Grow Unnoticed," and he likes especially the first stanza as an illustration of how she lets the rhymes go in order to convince us by "the pervasive idea."

> The mountains grow unnoticed,
> Their purple figures rise
> Without attempt, exhaustion,
> Assistance or applause.
>
> In their eternal faces
> The sun with broad delight
> Looks long—and last—and golden
> For fellowship at night.

But there is a better strength than jettisoning the rhymes as Emily Dickinson does.

The truth within convention is what he has himself realized in "Stopping by Woods"—a poem that is, in his own words, "a series of almost reckless commitments." "I feel good in having guarded it so. It is my heavy-duty poem to be examined for the rhyme pairs." He tests the rhyming first, by whether it deflects the poem from its intention, and secondly, by the separate rhyme pairs. "Suspect the rhymes," he counsels. He says flatly, "If they govern the poems, they're no good." Another effective example of rhyming is "Departmental" of which he says, "Don't be too interested in it except for the rhyming pairs." He advises inspecting the rhyme pairs: cloth-moth; size-surprise; such-touch; formic-McCormic; Jerry-Janizary. Then he asks, "Did I do it?" (*i.e.,* Did I do the rhyming honestly?) He watches the rhymes to see "how valid they are." To be effective he thinks that they should not be more than five lines apart.

As an example of compromise, he cites Emerson's "Ode Sung in the Town Hall, Concord, July 4, 1857." "Watch Emerson go wrong here on freedom. He thought of the sun in the sky and he thought God would take the sun out of the sky before He would take freedom out of man." The suspect stanza reads:

> For He that worketh high and wise,
> Nor pauses in his plan
> Will take the sun out of the skies
> Ere freedom out of man.

Frost dismissed this stanza by saying, "It is a kind of cheap description. Too bad He has to be led up to by such scantling scaffolding." He contrasts Emerson's inartistic fumbling with Walter Savage Landor's technical excellence in rhyme in the famous quatrain "On His Seventy-Fifth Birthday":

> I strove with none; for none was worth my strife.
> Nature I loved and, next to Nature, Art;
> I warmed both hands before the fire of life;
> It sinks, and I am ready to depart.

"Suspect those rhymes as hard as you can. Try your darnedest. Did Landor like nature better than art? All poetry stands or falls by that kind of thing. It is the truth within convention."

7. Form

Frost thinks the advantage of a poem over any other literary form consists in its limited number of sentences. He prefers the compactness of integrated structure to the diffusiveness of Whitman, the "feminine shrillness" of Hopkins and Lanier, and the relaxation of free-verse writers. He remarks satirically, "We used to say that the beauty of poetry was that it [the form] helped in remembering it. Free verse is better; you can remake it." Once, while looking over some poems submitted in a contest, he kept saying, "What is it these poets have missed? What is it?" Among other things what he missed was finesse, "little twists of thinking," mental reactions. Then he noted the last stanzas of "The Coming of the King":

> Thus, if a king were coming, would we do;
> And 'twere good reason, too.
> For 'tis a duteous thing
> To show all honour to an earthly king,
> And after all our travail and our cost
> So he be pleased, to think no labour lost.

But, at the coming of the King of Heaven
All's set at six and seven;
We wallow in our sin.
Christ cannot find a chamber in the inn.
We entertain Him always like a stranger,
And, as at first, still lodge Him in the manger.

He kept exclaiming, "Neat as a pin! Neat as a pin!" Here the rhythm
is instinctive, like the swing of the batter in baseball, and the words
are entextured with the metronomic beat. "Everyone's got to have a
metronome in his head," he says. "Ezra Pound once said that everyone has a rhythm of his own and that's what he expresses. Once you
get it going you can adventure very far with it." Here is a sense of
form, wit and phrasing, and sentences that lie snugly in the poem "like
a set of boxes in a Japanese puzzle-box." These qualities in a poem
evoke his admiration, especially the finesse by which the verbal meaning dances on musical feet.

But what is a poetic sentence? It is "a thing caught whole by the
ear as spoken." And it is memorable when the ear hears "the singing
of the sentence into the form." There are poets, he remarks in a homely
metaphor, who tip the bottle so far the wine makes a glug, glug sound
coming out, and then there are those who know how to tip the bottle
just right so the wine flows smoothly. To write a poem is to go "a-
sentencing." Abraham Cowley's "The Swallow" is a good example of
the singing of the sentence into form:

Foolish prater, what do'st thou
So early at my window do
With thy tuneless serenade?

Cruel bird, thou'st ta'en away
A dream out of my arms today,
A dream that ne'er must equaled be
By all that waking eyes may see.
Thou this damage to repair,
Nothing half so sweet or fair,
Nothing half so good can'st bring
Though men say, "Thou bring'st the spring."

The sentences should never be stretched or squeezed. The worst is to
squeeze them. He prefers the natural, cursive quality and the easy flow

within the form in Shakespeare's sonnets to the "hot, tight and cramped" sonnets of Rossetti. In his own writing, he tries to find the point of balance between sluggishness, where, as he says, things "creak," and glibness where things are expressed too facilely. The poet should never "squeeze or cheat or do violence to the sentence." Nor should he alter it from what it should be "by nature." Since the poet is, after all, only human, he indulges a natural tendency to be "sweet" to himself, but the only hope for him is "to divest himself of the last ego." Too frequently he succumbs to self-deception. Addressing self-deceivers, he warns, "You've got to get the self-love out of a poem and transform the love into a bleak honesty."

"All inner form is metaphor," or, as he says, "the putting together of two things," and poetic sentences which together compose form originate in the poet's faculty for seeing likenesses. "All idea," he thinks, "in the last go-down is metaphor," and "a poem is the triumph of association" in metaphor. Metaphors grow out of things "cutting across one another and making a connection in the mind." Nothing is more characteristic of his thinking than his penchant for metaphor, and he discovers these aptly in homely associations. Something observed or recalled reminds a poet of a thing already known and perhaps long forgotten, and a connection is formed which gives a fresh vista by which something is seen literally in a new light. The poet's aim is to surprise and delight the reader "by trying to show a connection of two things in the universe" that the reader hadn't suspected existed. The expression of these "'little twists in thinking" in metaphor measures a poet's originality. The feelers of his mind vibrate perceptively. He divagates and exults in associative thought. In "Build Soil" he uses the metaphor of an artist's palette to clarify the interrelationship of man and society:

> My friends all know I'm interpersonal.
> But long before I'm interpersonal
> Away 'way down inside I'm personal.
> Just so before we're international
> We're national and act as nationals.
> The colors are kept unmixed on the palette,
> Or better on dish plates all around the room,
> So the effect when they are mixed on canvas
> May seem almost exclusively designed.

In "Two Leading Lights," he connects two historical figures from the Bible, King Solomon and the Queen of Sheba, with two natural objects, the sun and the moon, and points up the phenomenon of the moon's surface so often seen in daytime wanly reflecting the brilliant sun:

> The Moon for all her light and grace
> Has never learned to know her place.
> The notedest astronomers
> Have set the dark aside for hers.
> But there are many nights though clear
> She doesn't bother to appear.
> Some lunatic or lunar whim
> Will bring her out diminished dim
> To set herself beside the Sun
> As Sheba came to Solomon.

8. Tones of Voice

What Frost likes is "good sentencing"—easy rhyming and use of words, not as they usually are but as they can be used. Where did he first hear sentences of the kind he has in mind? Not on the lips of any upcountry man, not from Charley Hall of Windham, New Hampshire, as it has been said, but from John Milton in "Lycidas":

> Begin then, Sisters of the sacred well
> That from beneath the seat of Jove doth spring;
> Begin, and somewhat loudly sweep the string;

Or in the following passage:

> Alas! what boots it with uncessant care
> To tend the homely slighted shepherd's trade
> And strictly meditate the thankless Muse?
> Were it not better done, as others use,
> To sport with *Amaryllis* in the shade,
> Or with the tangles of *Neaera's* hair?

> *Fame* is the spur that the clear spirit doth raise
> (That last infirmity of noble mind)
> To scorn delights, and live laborious days;
> But the fair guerdon when we hope to find,
> And think to burst out into sudden blaze,
> Comes the blind *Fury* with th' abhorréd shears
> And slits the thin-spun life. "But not the praise,"
> *Phoebus* repli'd, and touch'd my trembling ears.
> *"Fame* is no plant that grows on mortal soil,
> Nor in the glistering foil
> Set off to th' world, nor in broad rumour lies:
> But lives and spreads aloft by those pure eyes
> And perfect witness of all-judging *Jove;*
> As he pronounces lastly on each deed,
> Of so much *fame* in heaven expect thy need."

"Here," says Frost, "the tones are all written in. They're all there. If they're not written in, I don't know about them."

What he has sought in his own poetry is the tone of voice. "When literature comes alive, it begins to speak" is a central canon in his *Ars Poetica.* But why tones of voice? "The thing that gives you variety in a poem is to vary in tone the phrases used. Why, think of the intensity of dramatic expression that would vary twenty end-stop lines!" Notice, he will say, that Milton "steps right into it: 'Fly, envious time, till thou run out thy race.'" Or how Shakespeare steps right into it with a minimum of statement; for example, "If music is the food of love, give me excess of it." He urges, "You've got to get dramatic." (Thus: "Where did you get that hat?" Or, "You would, would you?") Just as Frost's intellectual affinity is with the Lucretian inquirers, so he is in affinity with Shakespeare in the speaking, not the rhetorical use or language.

He distinguishes sharply between the rhetorical and the dramatic. "What we mean by rhetorical is what goes on without any of the dramatic to break it." This is the difference between an editorial and the writings of a great essayist like Charles Lamb. Lamb got the dramatic tones in the sentences of his essays. "Get the life of the sentence into the writing" is not only a suggestion to apprentice writers, it's the goal of Frost himself, for drama is the capstone of his *Ars Poetica.*

Time and again he expounds with care his theory of voice tones. Each live poetic sentence does double duty. It "conveys one meaning by word and syntax, another by the tone of voice it indicates. In irony, the tone indicated contradicts the words." A poem is "saying one thing and meaning another—a form of honest duplicity." Most writers have just one tone—a tone of statement. Others try to vary this tone by lengthening or shortening the poetic sentences. Frost varies the tone by using a dramatic image of speech, which is simply the precise tone of voice by which the meaning in a word is communicated. He illustrates by showing how many different ways there are of saying "Oh!"—ways, he points out, that are not personal to him but commonly used by men. As a matter of fact, he thinks, jestingly, that he would be able by inflection to make poetry out of "a, and, and the." In a humorous but very adequate example he dramatizes what he means by vocal images of speech. Compare the first version with the revitalized one, and hear literature come alive through voice tones:

Primer version: I see a dog.
                     The dog is in the house.
                     I will put him out.
                     He will come back.

Revitalized version: There's that dog again.
                     Get out of here, you brute!
                     Oh, what's the use! he'll come back.

Frost uses the regular metrical patterns. For him there are just two rhythms—loose and strict iambic. It has been his habitual skill to take the familiar iambic and give us effects as though he used a greater variety of metric. He does it by varying the regularity in the "tone of voice." These voice tones are not dialect; they are *accent*. Words he calls "a kind of notation and writing down of the voice." Style is picked up by the "observing ear," and he defines it as "the texture of the tones of the speaking voice. One has it as a visitation."

The thing to remark in the vocal imagery aspect of his theory is the fact that speech tones are not to be confused with dialect; they are the tones of the human voice whose range is very wide in pitch, tempo, stress and resonance. He would not have the poet limited to one way of saying a thing; he has *ways* of saying things. This should illumine his line: "But all the fun is in how you say a thing"—not over and over again in the same way, but repeated with variations in tone. "It is well known that a perfectly regular metre in verse is so monotonous as to become intolerable," writes Sir Herbert Read in *The Meaning of Art*. "Poets have therefore taken liberties with their measure, feet are reversed within the metre, and the whole rhythm may be counterpointed. The result is incomparably more beautiful." Frost uses a simile from the famous sword dance to illustrate how the poet can get variety within the convention of metre. The metre is a constant, but the poet's use of it varies, and dramatic images with their basis in tones of voice are one way the poet can vary it; it is Frost's way. "The metre," he will tell you, "is just as rigid as two crossed swords in the Sword Dance. It's after dancing that you get variety":

> The sentencing goes blithely on its way,
> And takes the playfully objected rhyme
> As surely as it keeps the stroke and time
> In having its undeviable say.

By using dramatic images of speech circumspectly the poet strikes a tone with many possible variations. Since the dramatic images of speech are involved in the context the poem is not only a set or assortment of sentences, it is also a set or assortment of speech images. But "too many [speech images]," he warns, "make the work coarse. Work can be coarse with them. One must use delicacy." The following examples show expert treatment of the vocal image. "Who dreamed that beauty passes like a dream?" inquires Yeats in "The Rose of the World," and in Christina Rossetti's "Uphill" she uses dramatic images of speech interestingly:

> Does the road wind uphill all the way?
> Yes, to the very end.
> Will the day's journey take the whole long day?
> From morn to night, my friend.

In "Blueberries" an effective vocal image appears in the last sentence:

> There *had* been some berries—but those were all gone.
> He didn't say where they had been. He went on:
> "I'm sure—I'm sure"—as polite as could be.

He says that the dramatic dialogues in *North of Boston* represent an extension of "something I used to think listening to people in another room. I could tell what was going on by the tone. That has had something to do with my art." This reminds me of Synge's penchant for eavesdropping on the speech tones of the servant girls in an old Wicklow house, which had something to do with his art in *In the Shadow of the Glen*. Think of the drama there is in the human voice! The height of poetry consists in this dramatic give-and-take. In the lyric, the give-and-take is within oneself; in the dialogues it is between two people. The kind of intensity a poet can achieve is different from the white-hot intensity of Faulkner and Wolfe. There is another kind of intensity—a cool intensity, the kind to be found in dramatic expression when the skillful poet varies the tones of phrase. "Why what intensity there is," exclaims Frost, "in the cool phrase!"

He calls his poems "talk-songs," and describes himself as being "on one of the scales between two things—intoning and talking. I bear a little more toward talking." "Mending Wall" and "Stopping by Woods" are on the talking level; "The Oven Bird," "Desert Places," "Acquainted with the Night," are on the intoning level. "The Mountain" combines both. So important is sound to him, he will sometimes inquire after reading a poem like "A Drumlin Woodchuck," "The tone's everything in it, isn't it?" A valid token of the poet as artist is his statement that "the reason you don't write every day is because you don't want to get in the rut of sound." The challenge he faces is the one he reveals in a little anecdote. "Why do you write poems?" inquired a reporter. He replied, "To see if I can make them all *sound* different." In Emerson's phrase, he is no "hack of routine." What the reader hears in his poems is the voice—sometimes lyrically as in "Stopping by Woods"; sometimes dramatically as in "The Black Cottage"; sometimes dialectically as in "The White-Tailed Hornet." But it is always a voice one hears, and it is never oratorical. In the longer dialogues the people seldom raise their voices, conversing quietly as though they didn't want to startle the sleeping mice in the wall. In the lyrics the voice is level, and the inflective tones vary the dramatic images of speech. The poet's moderate eloquence does not sensationalize either thought or feeling. All the drama is in the inflected voice!

What Burton, Sterne, Lamb, Mark Twain and Hemingway do with
voice tones in prose, Frost does within the straits of English metre.

9. Motives

What is the motive behind his effort as a poet? I have heard him
say many times that what he hankers after is following through in
form, like the golfer following through in his swing, or like the baseball pitcher who breaks off a curve sharply and catches the inside
corner of the plate for a called strike. The poet follows the clue in his
poem until "the little destiny is fulfilled." This is the rare creative
excitement he has; and in great measure it is also his reward. But there
must be something a little deeper than this in his effort. He might be
delighted simply at form for form's sake like Flaubert, which often
prompts a self-induced dilettantism. Frost stops short of dilettantism.
Suffice that he likes, as he says, "a pretty fine piece of doing," like the
ballad of Sir Patrick Spens, "the little rounded way" of certain stanzas
in Arthur O'Shaughnessy's poetry, Coventry Patmore's "The Bay," or
the grim little ballad called "Two Rivers." What he is really concerned
with is more than an appreciative delight in the poetry of others; it is
far more than this. Very humbly he explains, "All I know [about
things] is what I find to say sometimes. The highest nobility is in that."

He improvises a scale of order in the life of the mind, nature and
the universe. He starts with chaos and goes on to the organic development in the vegetable world, showing the ascent to the level of the
animal, and culminating with the spiritual where the fear of God
prevails. Then he quips that, if you are Gertrude Stein, you return
to chaos again. "What we try for in a piece of writing," he says edi-
torially, "is a little order," and the order he likes to see is the kind
which in art shows in form, like the form in the world of material
things; for example, in a diamond "with the play of light in its facets."
"What is the point of drive?" he asks. "What is the will back of it?"
The point of drive in his life is poetry, which consists in "making

form in little bits of clarity." The impetus back of the drive is communication, is victory—"to bring it off." This is why he has never written any practice pieces. "I haven't written any exercises in my life," he says. "I write the poems for keeps."

How does he evaluate the result? First, he must have a right kind of feeling that what he writes is good. He must feel "in form," like an athlete. Secondly, he examines the poem critically in order to make sure that he isn't being too nice to himself. He sets it against all he knows—against the master poets, technique, experience, to make sure that it is all right. What he likes to be able to say is "When I tap the poem, it rings like a bell." Then he leaves it to its fate and he enjoins the poet to remember the old song title, "Love Them and Leave Them." To love the poems and then to leave them when they are done takes "the nicest discretion." Since the poem must be interesting, the poet must be careful to distinguish between the objective interest of the poem and the lively interest which he has in himself. "We are more interesting to ourselves than we have a right to be," sums up Frost's attitude. Two characteristics in writing to be stressed are interest *and* accuracy, and the latter is especially to be enforced in the use of words. For to Frost, as to Coleridge, poetry is never less than "the best words in the best order." Two qualities of a good poem are honesty and integrity. Its tests are brilliance (in the sense of originality or "little twists of thinking") and validity (in the sense of strong and healthy, as opposed to the invalid). The height of the poet's performance consists in creating a poem "that can't be retold except in its own words exactly." Poetry's the thing! And it is its own excuse for being.

❧ III

THE ORGANIC

The poet . . . uses forms according to the life,
and not according to the form.

R. W. EMERSON: *The Poet*

1. Introductory

Distinguishing between the art of the Bushmen of Southern Rhodesia and Southwest Africa and the art of the Negro, Dr. Herbert Kühn, as quoted by Sir Herbert Read in *The Meaning of Art,* says, "The Bushman, more closely related to nature, experiences more strongly the plastic character of the object; its form, colour and movement. To him the object is reality, not symbolism or essential meaning, as it is to the animistically-inclined Negro." In this distinction Read detects the difference between the organic and the geometrical. In both the Bushman and the Negro the sensual faculty is strong, but in the latter, for whom the object is not reality but a stylized abstraction which stands for it, we find the symbolism of geometry. In the Bushman, for whom the object is most definitely reality, we find the organic. Moreover, it is thought that some relationship exists between these two opposed types and environment. It is possible that they are determined by the contrasting environment. "Where the forces of nature are felt to be inimical, as in the frozen north and the tropical desert," comments Read, "art takes the form of an escape not only from the flux of existence, but even from anything symbolical of it. The organic curve, to reduce it to its simplest element, is regarded as unsympathetic; the artist therefore geometricizes everything, makes everything as unnatural as possible. Nevertheless, a work of art must be dynamic—it must arrest the attention of the onlooker; move him, infect him. The geometry of this abstract art is therefore very agitated; it is mechanical, but it moves. The vital art of primitive people, on the other hand, is sympathetic toward nature. It adopts the organic curve, enhances its liveliness. It is the art of temperate shores and fruitful lands. It is the art of joy in living, or confidence in the world. Plants, animals, the human form itself, are portrayed with loving care, and in so far as art departs from exact imitation, it is in the direction of the enhancement of a vitalistic urge."

These contrasting types of art—the organic and the geometrical—recur throughout the history of man's self-expression. On one side there is the organic: the Palaeolithic and Bushman, Greek and early Christian, and a full flowering of the organic in the humanism and naturalism of the Italian Renaissance. The geometrical tendency appears in the Negro, in the Saracenic style of the Arabs in Spain and Egypt, in Byzantine and Romanesque art, in Peru, Mexico, Java, Japan, and in our time, in the Cubists. On occasion these two types have fused. Gothic and Oriental art represent this fusion. At the risk of oversimplification, this distinction between the organic and the geometrical can be applied rewardingly to poetry in our time. Certainly the strict symbolists, like Mallarmé and Paul Valery, and the poets who wrote "Hugh Selwyn Mauberley," *The Waste Land, The Bridge* and "Sailing to Byzantium" tend toward the geometrical, while the adherents of tradition who wrote "Renascence," "The Ballad of William Sycamore," "Piazza Piece," "Ben Jonson Entertains a Man from Stratford," and "The Death of the Hired Man" tend more toward the organic.

In no sense do we use the terms "organic" and "geometrical" as counters of evaluation. Neither is more significant than the other. And they may co-exist in the poetry of the same poet. To wit: "The Ballad of the Goodly Fere" is organic and any of the Pisan Cantos is geometrical. But the level at which the organic poem is experienced is quite as high as that where the geometrical impulse dominates. The sensuous language is renewed and informed by the highly articulate intellect and by an attuned sensibility. In T. S. Eliot, a good example of the geometrical impulse, the intellect is never quite at home on the sensory level—the violet hour and the cry of quail and whirling plover always seem either written in or written up. In Frost the sensuous level will not impress some as rising to the intellectual level; and yet poems like "Stopping by Woods" belie this. The aims of Frost and Eliot are dissimilar. The principles underlying their art differ little.

2. In the Poet

First, there is the organic within the poet; then there is the organic within the poem; and finally, there is the organic within the poetry as a whole.

In Frost, the man, the organic shows in his faculty of observation, so intrinsic a part of the sensibility. Several qualities characterize his sensibility in action, the most characteristic of which is the faculty of observation, whose chief quality is keenness. He sees sharply the significant detail. In "The Runaway" he points up the distinguishing characteristic of a little Morgan colt: "And all his tail that isn't hair up straight." Frost's observation suggests Flaubert's exemplary counsel as reported by his disciple Guy de Maupassant: " 'When you pass,' he used to say to me, 'before a grocer seated at his door, before a janitor who smokes his pipe, before a stand of coaches, show me this grocer and this janitor, their pose, their whole physical appearance, including also—indicated by the ingenuity of the picture—their whole moral nature, in such fashion that I cannot confuse them with any other grocer, or any other janitor; and make me see, by a single word in what respect one coach horse differs in appearance from fifty others that follow him or precede him.' " What is observed by Frost is seen, as John Marin says of himself, "With a looking eye of many lookings." Sight is doubled by insight. "Do you really see it?" Frost might ask of many of his poems. For he is a seer whose faculty of observation is tested by directness of vision, by how clearly a thing is seen in its relationships, and by the ability to restore to the human consciousness a sense of the beauty in T. E. Hulme's "small, dry things."

Another quality in his sensibility is reserve. To know him is to know the reserve—the unspoken comment, the withheld conviction, the abeyant judgment—which add a decisive weight and importance to his commitments. There is always more to the saying than he ever says. His art is a kind of hinting rather than a total releasure. When he described himself as "a synecdochist," he was on the target in self-description.

To ascribe reserve to Frost is not to imply a lack of delight. There is some lament and reverie, occasional gloating, and restrained delight. No delight is wanton, no grief flagrant in his poetry. For this reason he resembles a classicist for whom, as Hulme says, "even in the most imaginative flights there is always a holding back, a reservation. The classical poet never forgets this finiteness, this limit of man."

One difference between the classical and the romantic temperament is the distinction between inner and outer rapture. Enthusiasm, common to both temperaments, is restrained by the classical temperament, while the romantic gives the emotion exuberant expression. The outer rapture of the romantic temperament is like the play of a fountain in the sunlight, or the beating in the breeze of a brilliantly colored flag. The inner rapture of the classicist is like the strenuous pull of the tides, or the circulation of the blood in the body. Frost's enthusiasm is like the classicist's. It is disciplined to inner rapture, not to romantic abandon. It is a "gloating" on things of this world, but by careful discipline he keeps his emotion restrained. The feeling does not volatize in tremulous or inarticulate excitement. Nor does it startle us by a pouncing enthusiasm. There is no flurry of highly excited rhetoric, either in Frost's speech or in his poetry, but an easy flow of speech-cadences. Like Lao-tse, "he speaks the language of evidence."

This restrained delight shows in everything he does; it is organic in the man and his poetry. It shows in the way he starts with the perception of materials close at hand in which he takes delight, like unharvested apples lying on the ground, a mowing field, dark days of autumn rain, rose pogonias in a meadow, an alder swamp, a thawing wind, gathering autumn leaves, glimpsing a moth in winter. These are the facts by which sensibility alerts the mind. Yet the fact is first seen as the fact *per se*. It is not like an object in some paintings which is used to suggest an idea: a hill to suggest permanence, a flower fertility, or water the flux of things. Frost's perception of objects, like a runaway Morgan colt, or a dark stand of wood, or a young birch, does embody feeling, and although his poetry inheres in empirical experience, its substance is certainly not simply direct observation. It is some truth hardily won out of personal experience. He is certainly not so much interested in the facts of knowledge, which he respects, as he is in the truth of knowledge—a generalization that synthesizes many facts into a working plan.

The Imagist poet gives us the facts. Had Frost nothing more to reveal than the fact, he would not be greatly praised. It is by looking into what he looks at that he triumphs. Frost's observation is pragmatic; Henry James's is selective; Emerson's is ethical. Frost starts with the observable, and what it results in, tested by experience, is the important residue. James starts with a consciousness that receives experience, "like a fine-spun silken web." What is seen by James is identified, assimilated, comprehended, refined. Emerson's seeing is revelation—spiritual insight, which is an act of belief in a Beneficent Tendency.

3. In the Poem

Since nature holds the secret of forms, the term "organic" is significant. A poem is an artistic counterpart of the economy of natural forms. Just as form fits function in the flight quills of a bird's wing, the pincers of a crab, the filament of a milkweed seed, or the fins of a fish, so the sonnet or blank-verse monologue or stanzaic lyric fits a specific poetic function. Frost's poems function like nature. "A Young Birch," for example, is no more a copy of nature than Thoreau's reference to the polypody in his pitcher is a scientific description of a fern. "It was a thing of beauty," says Frost of the birch, signifying that, like Thoreau, he is primarily interested in the effect natural phenomena have upon him. But it is also true that the poem is in itself —in form and language—an illustration of *natura naturans*. It does not copy, it is a manifestation of the creative impulse active in nature. The organic poem is dynamic and represents a co-physical art, where man and nature interact. Frost's art consists in co-ordinating the world of natural phenomena and the world of human beings—the two chief sources of his material—fusing the fact in nature with the image in the mind. An effective illustration of this fusion appears in *A Masque of Mercy:*

> When a great tide of argument sweeps in
> My small fresh water spring gets drowned of course.
> But when the brine goes back as go it must
> I can count on my source to spring again
> Not even brackish from its salt experience.
> No true source can be poisoned.

What is significant here is the organic interaction. The metaphor is just as natural as any phenomena in a world where trees grow by nourishment surging through the cambium layer or where chambered nautiluses grow by spiralling their shells.

In the poem Frost starts with a feeling of the thing seen, and the eye—inner or outer—is always on the object. His basic method of organization is a logical flow of ideas in a series of events as they occurred, and not, as in *The Waste Land,* a sequence of associational ideas, thoughts and feelings. "A poem," says Frost, "is an idea dawning. If you have it before you write it, it will be like translating it into poetry; but if you feel it as it is making in your mind, then it is a poem. If it hasn't that freshness of dawn on it, it isn't a good poem." The associational method of Eliot is neither more nor less preferable to the method of organic unfolding. Method is all *de gustibus.* The lightning may be chain or it may be a single vertical stroke. All we are concerned with is where and what it strikes, and particularly with what velocity. In *The Recognition of Robert Frost,* Edwin Muir has shown how skillfully the poet reveals his theme in "The Ax-Helve," not in an instantaneous flash but gradually "in the whole movement." Frost's poems, as we have already noted, unfold. Probably a good deal of meditation aided the gestation of the idea. Certainly, a clear, rational observation contributed to sharpen the perceptions. A counter-tendency to the organic method is a writer's finding a general idea, after which he looks for evidence to make it stand up. Sandburg's *vers libre* strikes me as though written by this latter formula. "We seek too soon," says Thoreau, "to ally the perceptions of the mind to the experience of the hand, to prove our gossamer truths practical." So it is that in Frost's poems ideas fuse into composites, an idea joining another idea, and both finally coalescing in metaphor. It is not at all farfetched to describe Frost's poems as "composed." Perhaps it would be more accurate to say that his poems *compose*. They have cohesion because he is a competent craftsman. "There is," he puns, "nothing so composing as composition."

We have already seen how Frost thinks imagination is closely allied with memory and how it functions by perceiving relationships between things; a kind of "drawing in" what we read or what we write in metaphor. We have also seen how Wordsworth, in *The Prelude,* evoked the shy spirit in his heart "From hiding places ten years deep." This is not an uncommon approach among painters and poets and novelists. In Paris, Henri Rousseau painted his canvases from a memory stored with exotic images which he had picked up in Mexico twenty years before, and Marcel Proust, in his cork-lined room in Paris, restored to general experience the specific human events of his early life, conjured to reality from a vibrating, retentive memory. Frost's poems are like pyramids whose bases are broad extensions in experience: the present reaching into the past and the past reaching into the future. So sensitively felt are these facts upon which the poet meditates—"the love of bare November days," or a lonely ghost house where he dwells "with a strangely aching heart"—they find a suggestive extension later in a lyric like "Come In." There are the recurrent images and feelings of which we shall write later in greater fullness. You can follow the dark trees and the stars all through his poetry.

Genuineness in the adherence to the organic is the very chastity of art. This is, indeed, where the idea of a pure poem comes into the discussion. Frost's attitude toward a pure poem differs considerably from the commonly accepted viewpoint that a pure poem is one in which the poet's personality is eliminated from the vision which the poem suggests. The proponents of purism in poetry contend that disinterestedness is a great virtue. But if a poet is trying to express beauty or truth—and what else would he be trying to express?—can he then be wholly disinterested? Isn't one's vision personal? Surely; yet it is a matter of how this vision is presented. Frost thinks poetry is pure not from any attempt of the poet either to subordinate or eliminate himself, but in the organic quality of the poem. To be organic, then, a poem must grow according to the principle of its own nature. As Emerson explains, the organic poet "uses forms according to the life, and not according to the form." "Poetry," said Frost in a lecture at the New School for Social Research, "is pure by the way in which it starts, that is by where it takes its source. Don't begin a poem with the idea complete, but think it through as the work progresses. A thing thought through before the writer sets pencil to paper is distasteful to me." It is certain that his own poems are not *pièces de circonstance*.

So much for the poet and the organic, but what of the reader? The reader takes delight in riddling a meaning that ramifies. Lyrics like "Come In," "Acquainted with the Night," "My November Guest" are notably "pure" in Frost's sense. They were not thought through before the poet set pencil to paper. They surprise us in their possibilities as they surprised the poet in his venture while the idea unfolded. Frost likes to tell how he had been "all night working on a poem called 'New Hampshire' and went out in the daylight and looked into the sun at eight or nine o'clock and wrote this one"—"Stopping by Woods on a Snowy Evening." He says, laughing off the afflatus, "I always thought it was the result of auto-intoxication, that it came from tiredness." Probably the "purest" poetry is written while the poet is in a mood which Coleridge described as "impassioned meditation." Rumination refines the poem to unalloyed gold, and art transposes the theme to its purest form. The purer the organic art the more clearly it communicates experience and the more self-sufficient the individual poem is. It releases a story in a syllable ("And just the kind that kinsfolk can't abide") and a history book in a sonnet ("The Gift Outright").

"Stopping by Woods on a Snowy Evening," one of Frost's most familiar lyrics, is a good touchstone of the organic. Poetry's "constant symbol" is the form it takes in rhyme, metre and versification. But what are the versification or rhyme or metre symbols of? Frost starts out perfectly free in his poem. "I can have my first line any way I please," he says, and he is right. "But once I say a line I am committed. The first line *is* a commitment. *Whose woods these are I think I know.* Eight syllables, four beats—a line—we call it iambic. I'm not terribly

committed there. I can do a great many things. I did not choose the
metre. What we have in English is mostly iambic anyway. When most
of it is iambic, you just fall into that. *His house is in the village
though*—the second line. I might be committed to couplets. If I had
made another couplet beside that—a rhyme pair—I'd be in for it. I'd
have to have couplets all the way. I was dancing still. I was free. Then
I committed a stanza·

> Whose woods these are I think I know.
> His house is in the village though;
> He will not see me stopping here
> To watch his woods fill up with snow.

He will not see me stopping here is uncommitted. For the three rhymes
in the next stanza, I picked up the unrhymed line in the first stanza
and rhymed its end-rhyme 'here' with 'queer,' 'near' and 'year,' and
for the third stanza I picked up 'lake' from the unrhymed line in the
second stanza and rhymed it with 'shake,' 'mistake' and 'flake.' For
the fourth stanza I picked up 'sweep' from the unrhymed line in the
third stanza, to rhyme with 'deep' and 'sleep.'

"Every step you take is a further commitment. It is like going to
the North Pole. If you go, you have to bring back witnesses—some
Eskimos! How was I going to get out of that stanza? It's going to be
like the Arabian Nights—one story after another. By the third stanza
you have a sense of how long a poem is going to be. It's 'sweep' I'm
commited to:

> The woods are lovely, dark and deep.
> But I have promises to keep,
> And miles to go before I sleep,
> And miles to go before I sleep.

For my poem is a commitment to convention. That's what it's a symbol
of. The form of regular verse—Greek, Latin, English—is a symbol of
commitment.

"The interest is the quarrel with those commitments. When I read
a poem, I ask myself: What is the main point in the argument? Where
is the insincerity in the argument? Having committed ourselves to go
to the North Pole or to our love, we have to believe we have been to

the North Pole or that we have been in love. The modern poet who uses free verse or new experiments quarrels with the commitment to convention. His revolt is based on that, that all life goes false by its commitments. Consequently, I look at a poem very examiningly, very suspiciously. I don't want to think that the poem is a compromise with the rhyme."

Only a poet in love with his *métier* can write either "Stopping by Woods" or about it as Frost does with such conviction. In the poem there is an easy confidence in the rhythm, so composed it is almost lazy, but lazy like a running fox. The personal idiom flows out at the tip of the words, pivots on a phrase, and runs along the inflective cadence of the voice. The idiom, which is made up of common speech words, reads as though it was first aural before it was transcribed. By the discipline of art the poet achieves that inevitable rhyming whose charm is irresistible to the listening ear. The lyric appeals equally to the eye. And just as the appeal of eye and ear fuse in the fundamental emotion of cherishable affection, so also do "the logic" of the thing and "the sound" of the thing unite in one dominant effect. There is no sound for sound's sake, as in Swinburne or in Poe. The sound has meaning only in association. The content of such a poem distributes its weight evenly like a floating body. As a matter of fact, the quality of the poem is in its fusion of co-ordinates: the technical co-ordinates of traditional metre and idiomatic rhythm; the ethical co-ordinates of irrepressible lures; the recognition of obligation; and the aesthetic co-ordinates of logic and sound.

Qualities of simplicity and directness characterize the structure; sympathetic understanding characterizes the mood. But I notice that even if the art is habitually conservative and in technique traditional, in implication it is neither. The method is strictly organic and the form lies in the thought like the spruce in its seed-cone. The poet has tamped his experience—built his soil and in the rich soil the seedling idea has germinated, struck deep roots, and come to fruition. But this weighs down by metaphor something whose natural magic is that wonder-filling and inexplicable quality of inspired simplicity. Nevertheless, here is that kind of transmutation of actuality, remembered or directly observed, the art of which consists in "the purification of one's quality"—the releasure not only of the transcribed experience but of its meaning.

One of the secrets of Frost's art is contemplative detachment. By detachment he is able to see not the image of himself and his desires but the image of the universal. "This is the essence of the artist's vision," says Jane Harrison in *Ancient Art and Ritual,* "that he sees things detached and therefore more vividly, more completely, and in a different light. This is the essence of the artist's emotion, that it is purified from personal desire." By burning the dross of egotism from the poetry, the poet purifies his quality.

Under the disarming pressure—what Frost has called "a nice kind of summons"—the words release their charge in an idea. Here the idea is the conflict between obligatory promises, a matter for the head to decide, and the enticements of the feelings. The poem balances the two. The head has its wits about it and resolutely holds the heart to its constancy. So the last sentence in "Stopping by Woods" suggests renewed activity after an enticing pause. In this lyric, form communicates what art embodies.

4. In the Poetry

Just as we have seen the organic within the poet and the poem, so there is an organic development in *Complete Poems* (1949). There is a seemingly large, free, loose, speculative atmosphere in *Complete Poems*. Yet on closer inspection an apparent casualness in details reflects subtle variations in the master idea, or, as Taine called it, *l'idée maîtresse*. Frost has not consciously written on fixed ideas or attitudes. He has written as the mood inspired him, and so we find several basic ideas and attitudes of which the poems are variations or extensions with which they have affinities. Ramifying in *Complete Poems* is a network of interrelationships but not necessarily in intellectual progression. The impression made upon the reader is of linear dimension and not mass effect. The linear dimension is seen in the extension of an idea, and its recurrence and variation in a later poem. This is natural to Frost who is a ruminative rather than a systematic poet. Symmetry in his poetry comes from the development of these ideas during a lifetime of experience. It is a natural symmetry and not a built-in one. It works according to the principle of its own nature like crystals forming.

The organic is a matter of fluctuations and foliations, fits and starts, progressions and regressions. The organic unfolding in *Complete Poems* reflects Frost's personal discoveries and intimate revelations. "Every poem," he says, "is like a straight line drawn across a piece of paper and under the sheet is a fifty-cent piece. And as you go back and forward, back and forward, you see an American eagle, and the figure comes out." In the poetry the figure that comes out is the figure a poet's life makes unconsciously; it is what he releases to significance of himself. "It all brings out something. It's more than saying," he comments. Just as there is something discovered through the poem, so, too, there is something of the poet brought out in the complete poems, lines of meaning, a design, a pattern. The figure the poet makes is like the eagle on the coin under the paper.

The organic operates in two ways: in the effort of the poet to express himself and in the effect experience has upon him. There *is,* for example, an organic relationship between "Directive" in *Steeple Bush* (1947) and "Into My Own" in *A Boy's Will* (1913). The poet who, in "Into My Own," struck out independently for himself, is, in "Directive," positive in a different way. "Directive" tells us about the adventure of the spirit which he began when he wrote "Into My Own." From an egocentric, subjective view he has moved to a sociocentric, objective one. No longer a Melvilleian "Isolato," he is now "a piece of mankind." "Into My Own" points to the future; "Directive" addresses the present. "Directive" is reflective and searching; "Into My Own" is assertive and perceptive. The point of drive in the former is salvation; in the latter it is self-justification. The movement in *Complete Poems* is a slow ascending one and "Directive" is an apex of ascent. Frost's progression is from subjective self-defensive assertion ("Into My Own") to objectivity in *North of Boston* (1914) and *Mountain Interval* (1916). From the latter to a sensitive musing on natural beauty in *New Hampshire* (1923) and meditation in *West-Running Brook* (1928). And then an increasingly marked interest in and contemplation of the topical in *A Further Range* (1936) and *A Witness Tree* (1942). Finally, the long look in the two *Masques* (1945–47), and a balancing of extremes—science and religion—in *Steeple Bush* (1947).

Moreover, the early dialogues show a dramatic involvement in the plight of particular individuals; the later longer poems, like "The Lesson for Today," "The Literate Farmer," "Build Soil," and "How Hard It Is to Keep from Being King" are more concerned with general ideas. There is a modest touch of humor in *A Boy's Will* (1913), where the poems are usually grave and earnest, but in *A Witness Tree* (1942) and *Steeple Bush* (1947) the laughter is both satirical and mocking. One of the most interesting organic changes is the development of the shy, tentative inquisitor in "Reluctance" ("The heart is still aching to seek,/ But the feet question 'whither?' ") to the sagacious counsellor ("Don't join too many gangs. Join few if any./ Join the United States and join the family—/ But not much in between unless a college.") in "Build Soil." It is a rare virtue when the poetry has grown more rugged and wise without sacrificing its tenderness and lyrical quality.

A distinguishing characteristic in the organic process is change, and a poet not only registers the impression experience makes upon him, he also exerts an effect upon it. "Life," says Santayana, "is an equilibrium which is maintained now by accepting modification and now by imposing it." Frost reflects this equilibrium in two ways—by inheriting the conditions of his craft and renewing them through the restatement of human values in imaginative terms *and* by presenting at different times varying aspects of a similar idea. In illustration, consider "The Tuft of Flowers" and its often-quoted lines, "Men work together," I told him from the heart/ "Whether they work together or apart," and compare these lines with his reference to "Men work alone, their lots plowed far apart" in "The Strong Are Saying Nothing." Experience which inclined him toward fellow feeling in the early poem modified the view in the later poem. But I would not unduly press the point. Here is no antithesis of the social man and the solitary. This is simply an awareness of varying points of vantage.

Another distinguishing characteristic, reflecting the organic in Frost's poetry, is the freedom he has of his subject matter. He is not cornered in a private world. Back country decadence, nature, love, tragedy, the humorous aspects as well as the tragic, are not dead ends about which he writes with a certain descriptive skill. They are only his material— aspects natural to him—and they form the background for the poems. For instance, take the nature poems. Frost is not trying to make nature addicts of us. Nature is his subject matter, and the content in the nature poems is the product of the natural background and the poet interacting at a point of intensity. No more a propagandist in the nature lyrics than in the dramatic monologues and dialogues, he is chiefly concerned with reacting to the world of reality as it appears to him. Stars, the dark woods, earth, woodland springs or flighting birds are tokens for cryptic analogies and poetic parables and sportive riddles. In their allusiveness inheres the poetry, a poetry that is saturated with the weather of the poet's mind. Frost is—simply and importantly—one for whom things have happened, for whom experience carries a charge; one who hoped to light fuses that would detonate charges in other people's minds. His poetry reflects the freedom he has had in his materials, developing this or that aspect a little further when the mood moves him.

It is a very human poetry about people as well as things; about children as well as older people; about love as well as loneliness; about machines as well as wagons; about heaven as well as earth. It has range as in Whitman and ideas as in Emerson. The center of his art is not single sight *or* double vision. It is now single sight as in "Lost in Heaven," now double vision as in "A Lone Striker." The ideas and attitudes are there and the poems embody their variation.

A further distinguishing characteristic, reflecting the organic in Frost's poetry, is the lay reader's relationship to the ideas and attitudes. Frost did what he could do best in his own way and he usually did it differently. The reader gets along best with him when he does not ask something different of the poet, attempting to appraise him by what he thinks he should have done rather than by what he did attempt. There is no obsessive quest in his poetry such as one finds, say, in Melville. To test Frost's poetry by a failure to reflect a passionate questing would be unfair. But if there is not questing, there is at least a confrontation of, a feeling for, a response and reaction to, experience. And here the reader has a perfectly legitimate right to test the poet in terms of what he does with experience. He can test him by what Edmund Burke called the "true standards of the artist," which are "in every man's power." As the boy and the bird know the blackberry, so should the reader also know in what experience consists, and, by virtue of his knowledge, he has a right to test the validity with which the poet uses his experience. Certainly the reader will find that Frost's attitudes and ideas are delicate indicators pointing to the stresses, penetrations and residues of intellectual, emotional and moral experience.

Before the ideas and attitudes are enumerated there is an aspect which should be underscored. The reader should be very wary before he ascribes a definite change or variation in Frost's viewpoint to any of the later poems. Early and late poems intermingle, appearing in the same volume. Sometimes Frost directs our attention to the poem's date; more often the poem stands on its own. "The Rabbit Hunter," which appears in *A Witness Tree,* is an early poem; and so, too, is "Design," which appears in *A Further Range.* The latter poem was written as early as 1912. It must give Frost wry amusement to find his genius made more effective by such shafts of light as some critics have beamed his way in illumination of these early poems as representing greater maturity. "The Rabbit Hunter," which was first entitled "Death" in the original manuscript, has the first six lines lopped off in its final form. But another poem which was written early, "To a Moth Seen in Winter," is considerably changed in its later form, and "Design" is decisively altered. "Design," which was originally called "In White," first appeared as follows:

A dented spider like a snow drop white
On a white Heal-all, holding up a moth
Like a white piece of lifeless satin cloth—
Saw ever curious eye so strange a sight?—
Portent in little, assorted death and blight
Like the ingredients of a witches' broth?—
The beady spider, the flower like a froth,
And the moth carried like a paper kite.

What had that flower to do with being white,
The blue prunella every child's delight.
What brought the kindred spider to that height?
(Make we no thesis of the miller's plight.)
What but design of darkness and of night?
Design, design! Do I use the word aright?

Frost's practice, then, of including early with later poems suggests the need to be cautious in ascribing development where only difference occurs. It is important to determine whether the difference is a change in form or in content. Frost, like Emerson and Emily Dickinson, can be elliptical and oblique. We can expect this tendency toward obliqueness anywhere in the poetry, but if he is criticized, as he has been wrongly, for perverse evasiveness and obscurantism, it is uncertain at exactly what date he is so. It is easier to describe general tendencies than to date a poem to which the critic ascribes vagueness or incoherency or tenuousness. There is a chord of sadness in the poetry and it is not perceptibly more intense in *Steeple Bush* than in *A Boy's Will*. He strikes a spiritual note, too, and this is neither more nor less solemn or anguished from beginning to end of *Complete Poems*. The note is muscular, humorous and resolute. There are one or two other tendencies. The tragic note so frequently struck in the earlier poetry, notably in *North of Boston,* is not so reverberant in the later poetry, although it is still to be heard. And I note few references to downright failure in human effort. Standout exceptions are "A Roadside Stand," "Provide, Provide," and "The Discovery of the Madeiras."

Perspective is one of Frost's recurrent attitudes. In "The Vantage Point" he reclines unseen "amid lolling juniper" in an upper pasture and looks at the homes of the living and the graves of the dead "on an opposing hill." Close to him is "the sun-burned hillside," ant craters and bluets, where, indeed, the consubstantiality of man and nature is intimately realized and where life and death are seen objectively. In "The Road Not Taken" the point of perspective is where two roads bifurcate in a yellow wood. And of the two roads he takes the one that "was grassy and wanted wear"; for perspective ultimately involves decision and action as well as detachment. In "For Once, Then, Something," he is the chidden one whose point of perspective is a well-curb where he looks inward and downward, until he sees *something,* either the abstract truth or the concrete pebble of quartz. In "The Freedom of the Moon," the perspective point is as experimental as the eye that, looking skywards at night, tries the new moon "tilted in the air" from several angles "as you might try a jewel in your hair." In "The Master Speed," he feels a power in standing off and appraising the past as well as the immediacy of historical time; "the power of standing still"—"off any still or moving thing you say." In "One Step Backward Taken," when his standpoint is shaken "in the universal crisis," he makes a saving withdrawal.

The problem is, of course, what to do amid the distracting confusion of things—what stand to take, what point of perspective; whether to go with the drift of things, like Dos Passos' feckless people in *U.S.A.,* or like Thoreau, to fish for reality in the stream; whether, like Hemingway's Nick, to fish the big-two-hearted river in *joie de vivre,* or to head for the brook, as Frost suggests in "Directive," where we can "drink and be whole again beyond confusion." But of one thing we can be sure in *Complete Poems*: we pass from strategic perspective point to point.

Another recurrent attitude is the reality that seems like a dream. The reality of the scythe whispering to the ground in "Mowing" is "the sweetest dream that labor knows." Swinging birches ("One could do worse than be a swinger of birches"), gathering spruce gum ("I told him this is a pleasant life"), blue butterflies ("But these are flowers that fly and all but sing"), spring pools (that "still reflect/The total sky almost without defect"), and the smell of sweetness from the unharvested apples ("A scent of ripeness from over a wall") are realities which the contemplative poet cherishes, even as he does the dream that seems like a reality. When he drowses off after apple-picking, the reality returns to animate his dream. "Magnified apples appear and disappear,/ Stem end and blossom end,/ And every fleck of russet showing clear." And in "Never Again Would Birds' Song Be the Same," the underlying idea of the poem is the dreamlike supposition that the voice of Eve had influenced the song of birds "he would declare and could himself believe." "A Cabin in the Clearing" (1951), a colloquy between a groundmist and smoke from a cabin hearth, discussing the interior of a human habitation, is another form which the poet's awareness of reality takes when it is inverted and the dream resembles it.

Frost is a man of defenses and the symbol of these defenses is sometimes a wall as in "Mending Wall," sometimes a burrow as in "A Drumlin Woodchuck," sometimes a "porthole's slab of glass" as in "Assurance." The wall can be good for neighborly relationship, the good fences helping to make good neighbors. And the burrow is a strategic retreat like Henry Thoreau's cabin at Walden Pond. It is not by any means a symbol of rejection, and the tone of Frost's "defense" poems implies that what he has in mind is a place where he can, as he once said, "secrete in order to secrete." "Bees," Carlyle once said, "work only in silence." Similarly poets like Frost; hence the crevice and burrow about which he has been "so instinctively thorough." And the porthole of the ocean liner is only a token of assurance to hold off the great force upon whose sufferance we continue to live. In "Triple Bronze" Frost has developed the idea further. He identifies three boundaries—physical, social and political—as buffers "between too much and me." The tone of the poem is personal satisfaction with these buffers, and if there is any doubt, it is possible to add for good measure "A Mood Apart" where the poet, while singing at his work in the garden, feels the eyes of some schoolboys on him. "I stopped my song and almost heart,/ For any eye is an evil eye/ That looks in on to a mood apart." Defense is in this instance against the supererogation of man—callous interferences, indiscriminate gregariousness, unthinking impositions. Frost must know more than most the truth in one of Blake's proverbs of Hell in *The Marriage of Heaven and Hell*. "He who has suffer'd you to impose on him knows you." He has had to build defenses against excessive curiosity, critical barbs, victimizing sympathy, for how else would he ever have got his work done?

The most insistent emphasis on this defense theme is in the poems describing the necessity of defense to withstand the elements. There is the nipping cold that takes the life of the orchard tree ("There Are Roughly Zones"); the relentless assault of the menacing storm ("Storm Fear"); the violent rain flensing the top soil ("One Step Backward Taken"); the ocean water shattering on the shore ("Once by the Pacific"). And, most effective of all, the snow creeping up the windowpane in "Snow," sure evidence that Meserve has his work cut out for him, to battle the rising snow line over field and wall and fence and window sill.

> "But let me raise this curtain on a scene,
> And show you how it's piling up against you.
> You see the snow-white through the white of frost?"

Perspectives, defenses and dreamlike realities are recurrent in the poems, and so too are the contrary pairs like laughter and tears, self-indulgence and resistance, or, technically, the strain of rhythm and the demands of metre. Writers find their drama in antitheses; it sharpens the issue. In the early Dos Passos there are "haves" and "have nots"; in Hemingway the brave and the cowardly; in Edwin Arlington Robinson the successful and the failures (an alarming majority); in Faulkner the Sartorises and the Snopes; in Frost it is an awareness of the claims of the head and the demands of the heart; in short, the juxtaposition of reason and love.

In "Reluctance" when "the heart is still aching to seek" the question the head puts is "whither?" But this is not a satisfactory answer to the heart. With reluctance it accepts the end of the event, in the inner or outer world. "Ah," says the poet:

> Ah, when to the heart of man
>   Was it ever less than a treason
> To go with the drift of things,
>   To yield with a grace to reason,
> And bow and accept the end
>   Of a love or a season?

Frost returns to this dramatic conflict in "Bond and Free," and this time the situations of heart and reason are somewhat reversed. Love, or heart, has earth "to which she clings"; thought or reason, "cleaves the interstellar gloom/ And sits in Sirius' disc all night." Far-ranging, imaginative thought has its own personal gains, but the poet implies that earth-thrall love "possesses all/ In several beauty that Thought fares far/ To find fused in another star." The girl in "Wild Grapes" who, while trying to get wild grapes from vines tangled in a birch tree, doesn't know how to let go. Her plight poses a moral situation. Is it possible to let go with the mind without letting go with the heart? Can we balance the head and heart coexistently but not necessarily commit both at the same time? It is as perplexing as the resolution of Melville's chronometricals and horologicals, but for Frost there is apparently a healthy distinction between the needs and responsibilities of each. Sensibly the girl resolves her dilemma by deciding that there is no need for her to let go with the heart. She doesn't confuse the issue. "The mind—is not the heart." It is her head that strengthens her conviction. She says:

> I may yet live, as I know others live,
> To wish in vain to let go with the mind—
> Of cares, at night, to sleep; but nothing tells me
> That I need learn to let go with the heart.

In "On the Heart's Beginning to Cloud the Mind," the poet resists the heart when it begins to sentimentalize the apparent plight of solitary desert-dwelling Utah folk. "Life," the head tells the heart, "is not so sinister-grave." Matter of fact makes people brave. Endurance of what is may not necessarily be abject resignation. To paraphrase the poet, it's getting inured to things that counts. The point is, as Frost suggests in "To a Thinker," the best way is "to use the gift you do possess,/ And sway with reason more or less." But he certainly doesn't advocate, as it were, a foolish *in*consistency. Frost's own behavior is the best evidence we have of the balance of head and heart. When he attacks, it is invariably an idea or attitude, not a person. In "A Considerable Speck," he is not angry at the heart so much as distressed at the incompetence of the head when it lacks clarity and force in thinking:

> I have a mind myself and recognize
> Mind when I meet with it in any guise.
> No one can know how glad I am to find
> On any sheet the least display of mind.

We notice, finally, that in "Come In," when he could readily indulge the heart in lament, he resists it and sticks to his stars. In more ways than one he is not put off his aim whether by itinerant wood choppers or by "collectivistic regimenting love."

Frost's attitude toward time shares with these preceding attitudes an important place in his poetry. Our attitude toward time depends upon temperament. While the nervous man generally anticipates time, the relaxed man is usually anticipated by it. It hasn't been sufficiently stressed that one of Frost's qualities is wise patience. While Thoreau could with equanimity spend twelve hours "of congenial and familiar converse with the leopard frog," Frost could spend a comparable interval waiting for the impression experience makes upon the mind. Yet his patience is a means to a dissimilar end. It is a *wise* patience. He doesn't force any impression by anticipation or wrench it crudely and disastrously by manipular effort. It is the paradoxical patience, in

Thoreau's metaphor, of the dog who circles round and round his master's buggy: the patience of delight and attraction. Frost is playing with the experience that impresses him.

Objectively he sees and feels what he sees and feels—dark and light, joy and despair, woods and stars—and what he suggests deeply is the inevitable flux in things, the possible transformation, the universal change. The latter may be spiral; it is usually cyclical. It may be the little brown wave in the steady current that catches on a rock and rides back again on itself, or it may be simply run down—"a sigh for every so many breath,/ And for every so many a sigh a death." But time is of the essence.

The time idea has its symbol in the house. In "Black Cottage," it is the abandoned house, embodying the memories of the past. In "The Cocoon," it is the house enveloped in its own smoke, sans past and with no hint of the future but significantly implying the circumstantial presence of people as much as if they shouted or sang; they are somewhere present and self-contained. In "Directive," the house has disappeared but interestingly here at the brook, source of the house's water, the past and present meet to renew the future. So do we also find renewal in "The Generations of Men" when the present meets the past at the "old cellar hole in a by-road" where the Stark clan gathered to celebrate their origin. Two young Starks, out of the past, indulge the present with seats on the cellar wall, their feet dangling among the raspberry vines. Here they conjure a fantasy of the past—Grandsir and Granny Stark, their pipe and brown cider jug and the little boy "groping in the cellar after jam." And here they plight their apparent future troth.

> "Where shall we meet again?"
> "Nowhere but here
> Once more before we meet elsewhere."

Time is many things. It is chiefly change; it may be loss; it can be renewal. Or simply evanescence, a flicker, but in "Nothing Gold Can Stay" it is irrevocable. In nature it is part of eternal recurrence, absolute for the season only. But it is irretrievable in concepts like Eden. "They Were Welcome to Their Belief" emphasizes the stealthy and definitive aspect of time; and here it is the physical not the psychological or emotional fact. It is not grief or care that whitened the couple's hair. Time

is, moreover, limitary. Here is the artifact—"Two round dots and a rip-
ple streak" in "A Missive Missile"—which teases the archaeologically
minded poet, for it has come down as an inexplicable symbol of the
craftsman in ancient Mas d'Azil. But between him and the poet there
is a hiatus nothing can bridge:

> Far as we aim our signs to reach,
> Far as we often make them reach,
> Across the soul-from-soul abyss,
> There is an aeon-limit set
> Beyond which they are doomed to miss.

"I Could Give All to Time" evokes the idea of competitive time
found in Andrew Marvell's "To His Coy Mistress."—Since "Time's
wingéd chariot [is always] hurrying near," what we would save we must
tear "with rough strife/ Through the iron gates of life." Frost could give
all to time except what he has held; in short, all but the human values he
has saved by withholding them from time. In the same volume, "Carpe
Diem," a detached and contemplative poem, says because the present
is "too much for the senses,/ Too crowding, too confusing—/ Too
present to imagine" people tend to live more in the past than in either
the present or future. If this is an attitude commonly shared by man, it
is not necessarily Frost's personal viewpoint. The impression he makes
is not that of a time-spent man but of one who meets time realistically
on its own terms.

His dimensional sense of time differs from what Sartre calls "the
pure intuition of the moment," such as we find in Virginia Woolf and
Marcel Proust, and from obsession with the past as in Hardy and
Faulkner, whose characters are foredoomed by crippling behavioristic
mechanisms, and from T. S. Eliot's sense of time as the divine order of
things in eternity. Frost expresses his sense of time continuum—past,
present and future—in terms of human possibility, the fate of man
resting, as he thinks, on such variables as the exercise of will, and the
kinds of and opportunities for choice.

In sum, although *Complete Poems* was not initially conceived as a
"project," it does represent a drama of ideas in which the particular
poems are the poetic acts in the growth of the mind. It is a total experience in the sense in which each poem has genetically a life of its

own and in which cumulatively the poems embody a fulfillment of personal experience. Like the sigillation of plants, there is a common idiomatic seal. If we were to look for a metaphor by which to characterize the common idiomatic seal, that metaphor would somehow have to take in account the organic which we have discovered within the poet, within the particular poems, and within the poetry as a whole.

❦ IV

THE PARABLIST

Parables justify themselves but dogmas call for an apologist.

GEORGE SANTAYANA: *The Life of Reason*

If a man grasps the particular vividly, he also grasps the general, without being aware of it at the time; or he may make the discovery long afterwards.

GOETHE

1. Ulteriority

> The poet is entitled to everything the reader can find in his poem.
>
> ROBERT FROST

Frost's direct connection with such sources of power as a love of nature, an interest in people, profound personal experience and the tensions of a lively epoch, lie back of his steady growth. Together they contribute to an effective identification with the traditions of his people, country and time. Consequently, there is an impression in reading his poetry of something that comes up, as Melville says of the sounding whale, from several storeys deep. In *Complete Poems* we are aware of "ulteriority," to use an awkward word of Frost's own coinage. This ulteriority is as organic as the man, although, in his deceptive simplicity, he imposes upon us, as some one said about Sterne, "the odium of the obvious interpretation." What is expressed simply is not always so simply understood.

By fusing a speculative tone ("What was it it whispered? I knew not well myself;") with impassioned simplicity ("The fact is the sweetest dream that labor knows."), Frost raises the apparently flat or literal statements to the level of ulteriority. But even so the reader requires a relatively low intensity threshold. Frost is not commonly either direct in expressing ideas or exuberant in communicating emotion. The image of the thing evoked is not so surely seen as apprehended. Such indirection in strategy often disarms a didactic reader.

In pointing out the ulteriority I shall not "grub around" and I shall try not to translate the poems into "other and worse English." We don't need to know everything about Frost to understand any one of the commonly anthologized poems, but all the knowledge we can bring helps to understand the poems a little less superficially. The risk taken in attempting an interpretive reading of Frost is not in under-reading or in over-reading, it is in bringing to the discussion exactly the right

temper, tact, judgment and verbal accuracy, all of which are necessary
if the quality of his ulteriority is to be shown and justice is to be done
the poetry. Each critic has a right to praise or dispraise a poet by his
own definition, but he is restrained to interpret a poet by the poet's own
counters.

Frost's "pleasure of ulteriority"—of saying one thing and meaning
another—is immense. It is in the texture of the two New England
Biblicals—*A Masque of Reason* and *A Masque of Mercy*—and, among
many other poems, it is in "The Grindstone," "The Lockless Door,"
"The Demiurge's Laugh," "The Bear," "Directive," "The Egg and the
Machine," and "For Once, Then, Something." These poems represent
the extension of the literal to the plane of the imaginative: the bridge
is hint; the art is implication. What is significant is the shadow of the
unseen cast by reality, as though he wrote in particular about something
in general. "Everything (in poetry) is hinting," he says. Like the delicate tension in friendship, you have to know how to take a hint. Because poetry means what it says, there is no reason to assume it says *all*
that it means. The pleasure for the reader consists in seeing implications
—a kind of intimacy plus intimation. Frost will counsel satirically,
"Just take the surface of it as I do other people's poetry." He will warn
ruefully, "Poems can be pressed too hard for meaning." He will suggest
hopefully, "All that I ask is that you apply what you bring to the reading of the poems." In *A Further Range,* obviously with tongue in cheek,
he distinguishes betwen the poems to be taken "singly," and those to be
taken "doubly." He knows only too well there are readers who hover

> . . . for a moment near discovery,
> Figurative enough to see the symbol,
> But lacking faith in anything to mean
> The same at different times to different people.

He knows that those who read him perceptively are those who
know the difference between poems that are meant to have only one
meaning and those that are meant to have double meaning. Presumably
a reader ought to come to know a poet's work well enough never to
mistake the difference. In *Poetry: Direct and Oblique,* Tillyard distinguishes between one-meaning or direct and double-meaning or in-

direct poetry. Direct poetry is the poetry of observation and record in which the sense of the poem is stated. Indirect poetry is the poetry of implication in which the implied sense of the poem is diffused through all the poem. The implied sense can be apprehended only through the synthesis of all the parts, and the abstract idea is embodied in concrete form; it is not stated. This is very clear and helpful. It will enable us to see that the difference between "Mowing" and "The Grindstone" is, as Tillyard points out, the difference between direct and indirect or oblique poetry. Both kinds have their partisans. Those who prefer the former, to reapply Frost's thought about reading, think *the* poem, and those who prefer the latter, think *about* the poem. What is admirable about the latter kind of poetry is to observe in operation the highly developed faculty of verbalization and the vitalized sensibility by which the poet animates the materials at the point where symbol and vision are concomitantly realized.

Once Frost remarked, "I have written poetry ever since I was fifteen years old, and there come to be quite a number of people who know how to take me in my wry way, in my twisted way, with the words cocked a little like a cocked hat, like a cocked feather. That is poetry. The large strain of poetry is a little shifted from the straight-out, a little curved from the straight. Within the large thing itself are the lesser personal twists. One belongs to me; one belongs to someone else." He illustrated his point by quoting Emily Dickinson's figure, "The lightning skipped like mice." "Can you imagine some people taking that?" he inquired. "Can't you imagine some people not accepting that kind of play at all?" Again he illustrated, and this time from Browning: "And the startled little waves that leap/ In fiery ringlets from their sleep." And he added, "It is a very out-of-the-way sort of speech, isn't it?" The originality is sometimes the verbal twist that clarifies a perception; it is also in the "fresh insights" and penetrations he makes. Frost's own style is verbally and orally distinctive. Although it is exact, it can also be cryptic. What is cryptic in it is the obliqueness that comes from hesitancy in speaking straight out. "It's never straight out for me," he will say. "I've never versified politics or religion or philosophy." Of course he hasn't; not when it is possible to suggest or hint or imply or embody ideas, observations, thoughts and feelings.

Many lines in *Complete Poems* illustrate a personal twist in expression. "Midsummer is to spring as one to ten," he says in "The Oven Bird," and "The land was ours before we were the land's," he says in "The Gift Outright." Often the twist originates when he detects a relationship between apparently dissimilar things and associates them in metaphor. There is the road, now abandoned and closed for good, where he walks as he will, musingly. He projects his thought into the next season as into the future:

> And so on into winter
> Till even I have ceased
> To come as a foot printer,
> And only some slight beast
> So mousy or so foxy
> Shall print there as my proxy.

Or, in "Unharvested" he writes of an apple tree which "had eased itself of its summer load,/ And of all but its trivial foliage free,/ Now breathed as light as a lady's fan." A supple-limbed tree, shed of its crop and foliage, breathing "as light as a lady's fan" is an analogical triumph. Tree and fan apparently so dissimilar are associated in kindred lightness. But the kind of poetic metaphor Frost prefers is usually more philosophical than linguistic or rhetorical. He likes to commit, as he says, "honest duplicity" by saying one thing and meaning another. It is interesting to see how he commits honest duplicity in parable-like poems.

Although he comes late in expounding the theory by which his poetry has long been written, nevertheless, in private talk and public address, he urges education by metaphor as the responsibility of the poet in any age. The metaphorist is akin to the parablist since a parable is a story told in metaphor, like the parables that recall the metaphors embodying Christ's stories—the mustard seed, the talents, the stony and the good ground, the Last Supper, the vineyard. Frost has a natural storytelling ability, an impulse toward the dramatic, a strong tendency toward analogizing. In "Brown's Descent" or "Paul's Wife," he narrates with humor and whimsy. The latter is a "just so" story. You take it as it is, without analysis or double meaning. "Home Burial" and

"The Death of the Hired Man," are told dramatically, as in a play. But, in "The White-Tailed Hornet," an analogizing tendency is linked with storytelling ability, and the result is a parable. The parable co-ordinates the analogy and the story in an extended metaphor. It is the poem within the narrative. Frost's personal storytelling gift, which combines with an ability to perceive and join hidden relationship in metaphor, is a particular contribution to American literature.

Emerson says there is "poetry which, without aiming to be allegorical, is so. Which, striking close to its subject, and that perhaps trivial, can yet be applied to the life of man and the government of God and be found to hold." In testing Frost's poetry by this dictum the two words "allegorical" and "trivial" are open to challenge. Some of his poems can be called poetic parables—"The Grindstone," for example—but to describe them as allegory, like "The Faerie Queene," would be inexact. The parable embodies its interpretation in the narrative; the allegory emphasizes ideas as abstractions. Frost's poetic parables more nearly resemble the symbolic than the linguistic metaphor. Like the latter, they are basically analogical, but they differ from it in their general reference and in their subtle allusiveness. They are, in effect, considerably more than amplified figures of speech.

2. Double Vision

Unlike Walt Whitman, Frost does not hook you round the waist with his left arm while his right hand points to continental landscapes or the varied vistas of the public roads. Frost's elbows do not rest in sea-gaps; his palms do not cover continents. Nor does he fly the flights of a fluid and swallowing soul. Whitman's identification with the multi-dimensional world appears exaggerated and self-intoxicated beside Frost's self-restricted actualism. Neither does he, like Emerson, shadow-box with big, bland, transcendental abstractions. Of late, he is like one who, ascending foothills, looks toward higher and further ranges of the mind and spirit. A kneeler at well-curbs, a stargazer, a fatigued apple-picker, a leaf-treader, it never has been his intent to transcend the finite or the specific, the concrete or the common. He is sufficiently satisfied in "setting the thing that is supreme."

His literalness is an asset because it makes cherishable what lies in the line of vision. Doubtless, he would agree with Thoreau that "a true account of the actual is the purest poetry," but he would emphasize the "true account," which would mean to him neither photographic description nor idealized action. He distinguishes between the realist who likes his potato with the dirt on it and the one who likes the potato brushed clean. He believes that "the thing that art does for life is to clean it, to strip it to form." He says:

> Let chaos storm!
> Let cloud shapes swarm!
> I wait for form.

Possessing a classicist's devotion to form and a realist's interest in the quality of life inhering in concrete experience, his observing eye selects facts common in experience. By making the facts yield their essence, he eludes their domination, and this is why, for him, the fact is not the most imperious, but rather "the sweetest dream that labor knows." He would not agree with Wordsworth's "Peter Bell":

> A primrose by a river's brim
> A yellow primrose was to him,
> And it was nothing more.

Peter Bell's perception of the primrose is retinal. Frost grasps the particular fact in an effort to suggest the universal to which it is related as the part is related to the whole. To quote Wordsworth again, Frost is one

> Who looks
> In steadiness, who hath among least things
> An undersense of the greatest; sees the parts
> As parts, but with a feeling of the whole.

He knows that by refining a thought to its essentials you multiply the levels of meaning.

Recognizing the importance of the realistic fact tethered in human experience, he has never abandoned himself to the romantic dream of a "wild dedication of yourself/ To unpath'd waters, undreamed shores." Poe's heart-wrenching questioning of science:

> Has thou not torn the Naiad from her flood,
> The Elfin from the green grass, and from me
> The summer dream beneath the tamarind tree?

is the antithesis of Frost's assertion that "the sweetest dream" that labor knows is what "the fact" suggests. Frost gives us the fact *plus* its overtone, presented without undue strain. In "The Armful" we gather by implication he is an equilibrist, a balancer: one who takes time out to stack his armful of "extremes too hard to comprehend at once" in a better load. The poem accurately describes an intimate experience, and it implies more than the actual fact. In "The Tuft of Flowers," he not only presents a little pastoral scene, but he also suggests man's alliance with others in co-operative enterprise. A butterfly draws the eye of a solitary haymaker to "a leaping tongue of bloom" beside a reedy brook, in consequence of which he feels a sensibility kindred to his own in the mower who spared the tuft of flowers. The poet says:

> "Men work together," I told him from the heart,
> "Whether they work together or apart."

This is the overtone which the fact suggests, the intimation that the experience evokes.

In "Leaves Compared with Flowers" he says:

> Leaves and bark, leaves and bark,
> To lean against and hear in the dark.
> Petals I may have once pursued.
> Leaves are all my darker mood.

"Leaves are all my darker mood," he tells us. The smoothness of the leaves and the roughness of the bark have a special significance for him. Ardent desires of earlier years give way before sober and enduring satisfactions. Here again the common fact suggests the overtone.

3. Parables

In *Modern Poetry and the Tradition,* Cleanth Brooks is well aware of Frost's inclination to parable, although he discusses it in different terms. After noting how the elements used by Frost in the poem are usually anecdote, incident, character sketch, Brooks remarks that "as poet, he employs them for purposes of indirection." Discussing "The Woodpile," Brooks shows that the poem takes its form from the seeming directionless walker. The walker comes upon a woodpile, long abandoned by some wood chopper who apparently has turned to other tasks. The walker may surmise why, but comparatively more important is the fact that "nature has," as Brooks points out, "picked up the abandoned task and is completing it. Nothing is lost." The poem is a parable of the absorptive aspect of organic nature at work.

"After Apple-Picking" is similar to "The Wood-Pile" in "metaphorical extension." The apple-picker has completed an appointed seasonal task. His ladder is still in the tree and empty barrels stand nearby. Perhaps a few apples remain on the boughs. But the picker is finished with his task; he has gathered the crop. The suggestion is quiet and unforced, but nevertheless apparent. The poem opens with the ladder pointing toward heaven; it closes with the overpowering but not oppressive sleep that settles upon the picker. The sleep might be like the woodchuck's hibernative sleep, or just a human sleep, where tomorrow brings other tasks. But something has been done, and sleep represents either completion of responsibilities or interruption of activity, like the sleep we call death. At least the ladder, pointing in a significant direction, is "sticking through a tree/ Toward heaven still." This parable is one of accomplishment, told with casual simplicity. The analogy is suggested discreetly; it is not imposed upon the poem but remains implicit in the context, as it always does in Frost's effective double-meaning poems.

If there is any secret in his power, it must consist in the fact that what he has written has little to do with reactions to other men's lives and thoughts, and a lot to do with his own inner struggles. "Poetry," he has said, "is a still, small eloquence." The parable-like poems compound inner tensions in which intensity is controlled, not muted. The voice tones are low-pitched. They must be listened for stilly, like the cricket's throb from the grasses in the fall. When the inobvious sound is once heard it is as intense as the belling of a hound on a live trail. Frost has disciplined his art to release his feelings, simply and genuinely. Being genuinely moved, the poet moves us.

Frost shows no tendency to skid off into thin air. It is chiefly man's ways on earth that concern him. If earth's the right place for love, as he contends, then it is the right place for other things, and he knows of no place where things are likely to go better this side of Utopia. Of course, this does not mean that he hasn't a feeling for ideal aims implicit in man's desiring. Earthfast as his parables are, now and again the poet takes an oblique glance at the starscape. As a matter of fact, it is possible to divide the poems into those that are horizontal, like "The Middleness of the Road" and "Mowing," concerned chiefly with the far and near, and those that are vertical like "Birches," and "All Revelation" and "Astrometaphysical," that are concerned with height and depth.

Most of his parables are either dramatic lyrics like "The Lockless Door," or expository bucolics like "The Grindstone." The former is a parable of self-escape. It dramatizes the mysterious but definite force in human experience—the knock at the door—that scares some men into escaping from the indulgent solitude of self-inclosure. The "knock" compels them to pursue their destiny in the outer world where, although they may still "hide" their essential self and alter with age, they are in a better position to measure their quality with other men and circumstances.

In form "The Grindstone" is a deceptively rambling blank-verse narrative, the germ of which is an experience evoked by the sight of a grindstone standing under an apple tree. The poem breaks naturally into three parts. In the first part, the poet visually identifies the inanimate, neglected, place-bound grindstone with a boyhood experience when, on a summer day, he had to turn it unconscionably long. The second part recounts the tension that existed between the boy, whose task it was to keep the stone turning, and the old bespectacled gaffer, who ground a scythe blade with the assiduity of a disinterested perfectionist. The third part resolves the tension by releasing the incident to significance. For, in the boy's concern that too much grinding might overdo the job, the poet implies the Aristotelian mean—*meden agan*—in all things, rural or otherwise, whether sharpening a scythe, painting a picture or making a point. It is a parable, in short, of judgment and the recognition of limits.

Frost's wit, slow-breaking like a tricky curve ball, inobvious and idiosyncratic, pervades this rural parable. "I was for leaving something to the whetter" takes on meaning in the New England tradition out of which these poems come. The whetter can be depended upon to fulfil his responsibilities no less than the scythe-sharpener. The vivid particular situation saves the poet from the "danger of a turn too much."

One of the characteristics of his poetry, as we have noted, is speculativeness. It is particularly apparent in the parables and its origin seems to be in the poet's "perspectival" (a Nietzschean word) familiarity with his material. He not only feels sympathy with material common in experience, he also views it from the vantage ground of generalized experience. For example, "Design" (to whose early version we referred in part three, section four) has a metaphysical implication, and "Acquainted with the Night" has a psychological one.

In the close-textured arachnidan web of "Design," Frost recounts a nature adventure:

> I found a dimpled spider, fat and white,
> On a white heal-all, holding up a moth
> Like a white piece of rigid satin cloth—
> Assorted characters of death and blight
> Mixed ready to begin the morning right,
> Like the ingredients of a witches' broth—
> A snow-drop spider, a flower like a froth,
> And dead wings carried like a paper kite.
>
> What had that flower to do with being white,
> The wayside blue and innocent heal-all?
> What brought the kindred spider to that height,
> Then steered the white moth thither in the night?
> What but design of darkness to appall?—
> If design govern in a thing so small.

One morning, having found a fat, white spider clutching the dead wings of a white moth on a *white* heal-all, Frost evokes the grim nocturnal event in which the white spider nabbed an unwary moth that blundered into a cunning web stretched on a blighted heal-all. These "assorted characters of death and blight"—the off-color heal-all, the lethal spider, the vulnerable, misdirected moth—start the poet ruminating on what motivated this fateful encounter—design or chance? "What," he thinks at any rate, "but design of darkness to appall?" And to this rhetorical question, he adds an interjectory Parthian shot, "If design govern in a thing so small." His conjectural inquiry not only implies a subtle but a malefic force at work. And if design operates on the lower level in nature—if it is in the ruck of little things— then, by extension, it must also operate generally in the human sphere of activity since man cannot be separated from the complex, inter-related destiny of the natural universe.

It is a shrewd gambit on the poet's part to start with the specific rather than with the abstract. This method sharpens the logic of the poem and heightens the imaginative element, which consists in what the particular suggests of the universal, the physical of the meta-physical. He submits to a sharp scrutiny the assumption that if God's in his heaven all should be well in earthly as well as heavenly affairs. How is it possible to reconcile this appalling scene of a very minor tragic event in nature with the orthodox picture of design controlled by an omniscient and omnipotent, loving and redemptive divinity? The poet's relationship to the argument in the poem is interesting. He shows no sudden ingenuous surprise that creative design should include the malefic, and, even more significantly, he gives no indication of a sentimental wish that it were otherwise. Simply looking at and into he re-enforces factual observation by an ironic reflective comment in the last line. Certainly "if design govern in a thing so small"— if in God's kingdom of special providence no sparrow falls unnoticed— why is the white moth "steered" so unprovidentially to the fatal ambush on a *white* heal-all by a shrewd divine guiding force? At least, the poet is suggesting, this deed of nocturnal violence is not too insignificant to pass unremarked upon and unquestioned.

In "Acquainted with the Night," Frost particularizes the night of the human spirit by the enveloping darkness, the persistent rain, the rejected artificial city light, the sad city lane, the guilt-arousing watchman, the sudden disconcerting human cry, and finally, the temporal neutrality of the tower clock:

> I have been one acquainted with the night.
> I have walked out in rain—and back in rain.
> I have outwalked the furthest city light.
>
> I have looked down the saddest city lane.
> I have passed by the watchman on his beat
> And dropped my eyes, unwilling to explain.
>
> I have stood still and stopped the sound of feet
> When far away an interrupted cry
> Came over houses from another street,
>
> But not to call me back or say good-by;
> And further still at an unearthly height,
> One luminary clock against the sky
>
> Proclaimed the time was neither wrong nor right.
> I have been one acquainted with the night.

The poem evokes a sense of man's confrontation of elemental, sociological, personal and impersonal factors. The experience is symbolic and generalized, its cumulative effects are dark and depressive, unfriendly and detached. But counterbalancing this psychological oppressiveness is an absence of self-pity, and there is not the faintest trace of callousness or cynicism in facing the forbidding in human experience. The poem communicates a feeling of confidence that attends the initiated. The poet, who is revealing his experience in a parabolic statement, is fully acquainted with all that is implied by the nighttime of the spirit. Here, too, as in "Design," the particular is raised to the universal. Surely in his reference to the "unearthly height" or the lighted face of the clock against the sky, Frost is implying that there should be no expectation of man's finding either external help or solace *sub specie temporis*. Moreover, he implies that even if there is no moral sign or possibility of superhuman intervention to help mitigate the suffering in man's plight, there is still the formidable fact of man's self-dependence. Man is prepared to go it alone *sub specie aeternitatis,* and the assertion of his will counterpoises even as it intensifies the pathos of his situation.

In "The White-Tailed Hornet" the materials for a parable are similar in quality with those in "The Grindstone," but instead of an empirical parable we have a homily on skepticism, or what Frost subtitles "The Revision of Theories." "Trust my instinct," the poet says, "I'm a bard," and his sense of fun steals the didacticism out of an otherwise pedantic parable. First, he describes the hornet's shelter, manoeuvrability and attacking power as commonly experienced. Next, he shows the hornet in action: less aggressive, more woefully weak in instinctive identification of its foes than we had supposed possible. The white-tailed hornet, witlessly swooping, pouncing and striking nail-heads and huckleberries to no avail and trying vainly for a fly, invites derision. Finally, the poet squares off without any attempt to embody his point, as he did in "The Grindstone," and queries openly: "Won't this whole instinct matter bear revision?" Explicitly he tells us that befuddlement comes from making downward rather than upward comparisons. Man has ascribed too much infallibility to the animals and insects. The result of close investigation proves inquiring people to be wrong, and consequently their disillusionment is more intense.

"Birches" is an idyll in which the idyllist settles his coulter in the fieldsward, lines the furrow with his eye, and runs a direct course. It is a brilliantly spontaneous performance—a *tour de force* you would say if there weren't other idylls of comparable brilliance in *Complete Poems*. The theme is love—devotion to objects and actions cherishable to the human spirit. "Earth's the right place for love:/ I don't know where it's likely to go better" is the key line. When the poet reads "Birches" in public, he sometimes says, "This is one I am very fond of," or, "I lean on that," as much as to say, "Well, I haven't done it better. You can take me or leave me after hearing 'Birches.'" For a blank-verse monologue, it is fast-moving; it rollicks. And its effect is just as moving as its pace. Yet with all the facility in expression at no point does it succumb to artfulness. One reason for this is that the poet doesn't use a gaudy rhetorical vocabulary like Hart Crane, nor does he try to use words in unnaturally arresting contexts like Wallace Stevens. Accuracy and precision, not novelty and rhetoric, are what count with him. "Cut these words, and they would bleed; they are vascular and alive." Emerson was writing about Montaigne. It can with justice be said of "Birches":

> He learned all there was
> To learn about not launching out too soon
> And so not carrying the tree away
> Clear to the ground. He always kept his poise
> To the top branches, climbing carefully
> With the same pains you use to fill a cup
> Up to the brim, and even above the brim.
> Then he flung outward, feet first, with a swish,
> Kicking his way down through the air to the ground.
> So was I once myself a swinger of birches.
> And so I dream of going back to be.

I would not like to try to paraphrase or translate this Frost-flavored idiom. The speech is as natively American as Emily Brontë's phrases and words (*nab of heath, wisht, thrang, canty, sackless*) were natively Yorkshire West Riding.

"The part of poetry I like best is the part that cannot be translated," says Frost. How would you translate "Birches" and retain the speech cadences? When the poetic sentence can be easily translated idea dominates. I suppose "Tears from the depths of some divine despair" might be approximated in French or German, but I think the translator would work up quite a blood pressure with "Flits by the sea-blue bird of March," or with "Where the long dun wolds are ribbed with snow." A translator of Frost would find "Yankees are what they always were" perhaps simple enough. He would throw up his hands after trying to render in idiom (there is no other word for it) "I'll own it's cold for such a fall of snow." When an idea dominates in the line it is possible to translate the meaning, but where the idiom is inseparable from the idea there is no identical phrase (in this last "I'll own") in any foreign language. In a very real sense the most untranslatable part of a poem is the most idiomatic. Frost co-ordinates word and idea like sound and syllable. You can paraphrase but you cannot translate this kind of poetry without sacrificing the idiom native to the poet's race.

Frost possesses as acutely as I imagine it can be found in the poets of our time the conscience of the superior artist. A responsible man all the way round, he is committed to the words he puts into action as he is in his personal behavior. Any carelessness in writing, or speech for

that matter, can, he knows, lead to irresponsibility in action somewhere, sometime. He writes, therefore, as one primarily concerned
with clarity. No putterer with words, he is a pin-point verbal pre-
cisionist who avoids being finical. The weight of the word is felt; its
precision is thought:

> One by one he subdued his father's trees
> By riding them down over and over again
> Until he took the stiffness out of them,
> And not one but hung limp, not one was left
> For him to conquer.

Suppose "conquer" and "subdued" were transposed, or suppose "rigidity" was substituted for "stiffness." For example, "Until he removed
their rigidity." This would be anticlimactic in the first instance and
pompous in the second.

The imagery is also noteworthy. Here are no images lonely like
Arnold's "Breath/ Of the night-wind down the vast edges drear/
And naked shingles of the world." Or, reverential as Keats's "moving
waters at their priestlike task/ Of pure ablution round earth's human
shores." Frost's images are bright and well defined as the crystal shells
of the birches glittering in the strong winter sunlight. They are unblurred—the birches curved "Across the lines of straighter darker
trees." They are homely and appealing—"climbing carefully/ With
the same pains you use to fill a cup/ Up to the brim." They are
familiar—"like a pathless wood/ Where your face burns and tickles
with the cobwebs/ Broken across it." And they are memorable—"And
climb black branches up a snow-white trunk"—which suggests the
doubleness, the parable in the poem.

When we say that there are singing poets and interpreting poets,
we oversimplify. Yet the effect of the early Yeats and of Poe, Swinburne, Tennyson and the early Walter de la Mare depends more upon
incantatory sound than upon idea. They are more hypnotic than the
cerebral Arnold, Emerson and Eliot. Where does Frost come in here?
Is he what Longfellow called Emerson—"a singer of ideas"? He leans
a little toward the interpreter. In "Birches" we have his accomplishment, which is not the enchantment of Walter de la Mare, but "the
sound of sense." What is important in "Birches" is not only what the

poem sounds like; it is what the poem says and most emphatically it is
saying something from the beginning—"When I see birches bend to
left and right" to its last line—"One could do worse than be a swinger
of birches." It isn't a poet's materials but his point of view that gives
us the impression of penetration and clarity. Frost's viewpoint is self-
restricted. He hasn't tried to look everywhere at once. He looks into the
heart of a memory long enough to see and feel what is to be totally
seen and wholly felt. This is the undressing process; this is the fulfillment of Flaubert's counsel to Guy de Maupassant. The result is that
the Goethean particular expands into a general conception, and the
extension in meaning is as natural as light lengthening day. *Rapport*
with environment is established in the sympathetic relationship of the
poet with his material. The oneness is released by embodying his sympathy in the poem. In this sense it is a subjective poem, expressing
Frost's ideals and reflections. But it only starts with the subjective; the
ripples move out and out until they touch everyman.

So "Birches" is as fine a parable as Frost has ever written. It is a
parable of knowing and doing; of experience and education by life.
The poet recalls the boyhood passion of swinging birches when the
swinger learned about "not launching out too soon," and he acquired
the necessary poise—"to the top branches, climbing carefully." At the
top of the heavenward climb, he launched out, swung down, and so
touched earth again. "That would be good both going and coming
back" since experience consists in the *total* effort: the aspiring, the
release, and the return to the substantial earth. Life's a two-way experience, Frost is saying, the co-ordination of the ideal and the actual.
"Our strength is transitional, alternating; or, shall I say, a thread of
two strands," says Emerson, and Frost surely would agree.

4. Parablist and Symbolist

These parables suggest that Frost, like Gautier, the Parnassian, is
"a man for whom the exterior world exists." He is not, like Rimbaud,

at the other extreme, one who explains "magical sophisms with the hallucinations of words." Conceiving of reality as existing in neither the world inside man nor in the exterior world impersonally observed, he creates his poetry from the interaction of the two worlds, joining them to evoke the mood or emotion or idea in which the poem's meaning inheres. One of the impressive things about Frost's judgment is the fact that he never makes the mistake of the extreme Symbolists who turned for inner reality to the transcendent which lies *outside* the everyday world. Frost locates reality *inside* the everyday world, and this is at once the substance and meaning of his parables. They take their form in the natural mysteries of experience.

Unlike the Symbolists, Frost does not use language in a peculiarly private speech. His idiom is his own, certainly, but we are aware that he is trying to establish a correspondence with us, as though our reaction were important to him. His language is natural in its personal directness and intelligibility. Although the metre is traditional the language is unliterary. One only has to compare Robinson's phrase "futile as regret" with Frost's "But behind's behind" to catch the difference between the literary and the colloquial use of language. Each statement is laconic; both are telling. But they are as different as a rose and a spike of steeplebush. Finical poets and critics will not always find Frost's friendly correspondence to their liking. They are less stimulated by the intelligible use of language than by novelties in self-expression and *extra*-ordinary associational use of words, as in the poetry of Crane, Stevens, Eliot, Pound, or Cummings; such, for example, as the following stanza from Hart Crane's "Voyage: II":

> Bind us in time, O seasons clear, and awe.
> O minstrel galleons of Carib fire,
> Bequeath us to no earthly shore until
> Is answered in the vortex of our grave
> The seal's wide spindrift gaze toward paradise.

Or the following lines of Eliot's in *The Waste Land:* What the Thunder Said:

> Only a cock stood on the rooftree
> Co co rico co co rico
> In a flash of lightning.

Frost is also aware that words soon become devitalized when carelessly used. This realization has not impelled him to try to vitalize language by liberating words from their normal associations as Hart Crane has done. He renews words by selection and precision, and, like Wordsworth before him, by the tonal rhythm of man speaking to men. He renews words in a more conventional, the Symbolists in a more unconventional, way. If his language is rarely rhetorical, neither is it strained and tortured as Hart Crane's so frequently is. "Good writers are those who keep the language efficient," says Pound. "That is to say, keep it accurate, keep it clear." True, but the penalty for clarity is sometimes commonplaceness, a penalty which is annulled when mood, idea and feeling are evoked with intensity.

Through accuracy in usage of speech rhythms Frost touches off the imagination of the listening ear. Every Yankee ear catches the familiar tone in "A Blue Ribbon at Amesbury" when Frost says, "The night is setting in to blow." Northeasters, winter, illness and death—all familiarly "set in." And the Yankee, adept by experience at contesting with a rugged climate, meets the onset with hard-bitten resignation. What sets in can be sat out—even the imminence of death, sometimes. "The West was getting out of gold" is the way a farmer, who knows what it means to have to harness a horse and drive to the village store because he is "getting out of" salt, potatoes, or kerosene, or baking powder, might describe the fading light at sundown. The reader collaborates with Frost and fills out the description of the sunset for himself; while, let us say, in Shakespeare, where bees are described at work as "the singing masons building roofs of gold," and where Cleopatra's barge "like a burnish'd throne,/ Burn'd on the water, the poop was beaten gold;/ Purple the sails, and so perfumed that/ The winds were love-sick with them . . ." the brilliant word-pictures are imposed upon the reader as the poet dominates. Frost's undercoloring pays the reader's imagination the compliment of expecting it to rise to the occasion of poetry. It is as though the poetry came out of the reader's experience.

In his parables Frost uses the descriptive method to evoke the idea. The Symbolists, rejecting the descriptive method and the literal level, evoke the mood or idea or feeling through language used in a suggestive way. There is a greater range of communication in the former.

The latter is restricted since the aim is to communicate unique personal feelings in nuanced, not exact, language. *"Oh! la nuance seule fiance,"* exclaimed Verlaine. *"Le rêve au rêve et la flûte au cor!"* But it is doubtful if greatness can be ascribed to poetry which has only a technical expertness for the effort may be sheer *tour de force,* and certainly it cannot be ascribed to writing when the poet as bard or *vates* (like Lindsay on occasion) inflates the lungs and sounds off in bursts of sententious rhetoric. I think there is a greatness in poetry which is produced when the poet trusts intuitive impulses that rise independent of reason and whose eloquence is afterwards justified by reason. Such a trust is felt and such an eloquence is expressed time and again in Frost's parables. "Birches" is a continuous wave of intuitive impulse and eloquence.

The pride he takes in his poems is in both subject matter and form. "In making a poem you have no right to think of anything but the subject matter," he says. "After making it, no right to boast of anything but the form." Art is of the imagination; reality is of nature. The energy is similar not identical in each. And poetry is what the imagination does with phenomena of reality. In "Birches" an idea sets up a chain reaction, and the intellectual radiation which follows depends upon the effectiveness of the fusion of poet and reality. When Blake says, "Nature has no Outline, but Imagination has," he is saying what Frost also knows, that art orders chaos—makes, as it were, little bits of radio-active clarity. "Order," says Thomas Traherne, "the beauty even of beauty is." Such is the beauty of Frost's poetical parables.

❧ V

DIMENSION IN ART

Art is the point at which the growth of
the mind reveals itself.

I. A. RICHARDS

1. Themes

The conditions of genius are an open secret. Sensibility, skill and vision are incontestable factors by which a poet shows genius. Yet to name these factors does not explain them. "Art comes out of *theoria,* contemplation, steady looking at, but never out of theory," Jane Harrison reminds us in *Ancient Art and Ritual.* "Theory can neither engender nor finally support it." So at least Frost's poetry has come out of *theoria,* rather than theory. The intellectual or contemplative element is discoverable not only in one place—in a writer's *Weltanschauung.* It should be there, surely, but it should also show in the skill by which a poet does what he sets out to do. Technique *is* the figure in the poet's carpet. I. A. Richards seems everlastingly right. "Art is the point at which the growth of the mind reveals itself." The skill in technique is one of the important places where the mind shows its quality, the way a Cezanne landscape on close inspection shows its strength in the geometrical design. Leonardo da Vinci believed that painting was intellectual because technique calls for subtlety in its effects and because of the extensive scope it offers to invention and imagination. Poetry is similar to painting in these two respects. When the intellectual element is co-ordinated with the poet's sensibility, then art flows naturally from its instinctual springs, and the thought grows with the feeling, twins it.

By careful analysis we can detect the subtlety of a poet's effects. In the discussion of Frost's themes the subtlety of the effect will be apparent. A representative poem has been selected to interpret each of his themes. That I have chosen certain themes arbitrarily is less true than that I have arbitrarily selected the poem to illustrate the theme. The representative poem will be discussed for the light it sheds on the theme and the poet's art. The idea is to link the craftsmanship of the poet with the thematic development of the poem. Upon first reading a poem it may be assumed too readily that it has given up its secret. Yet here are some poems that are to be read once, and some twice. The poet says himself that those who really know his poetry know when to make the distinction between first and second "layers." "Stopping by Woods" and "Departmental" are first-layer poems; and so is "The Witch of Coös." "The Death of the Hired Man," "A Winter Eden," and "One Step Backward Taken" are second-layer poems. A competent reader will know a poet's work well enough never to mistake the difference between the "straight" poems and those with "double hints." It matters little to Frost if the reader doesn't get the second layer, but he ought at least to be aware that more is implied than said.

Of seven major themes the first is the theme that reflects his interest in the world of man. Love poems like "To Earthward" and "Love and a Question" belong in this category, and poems of intra-human concern like "An Old Man's Winter Night," "Birches," "The Tuft of Flowers" and "On the Heart's Beginning to Cloud the Mind." "Two Tramps in Mud Time" will represent this theme. A second theme reflects the tragic sense. "The Hill Wife," "The Death of the Hired Man," "Acquainted with the Night," "The Housekeeper," "A Servant to Servants," "The Self-Seeker" are poems in this group. "Home Burial" will stand as its representative. Thirdly—and in no order of rank—there are the multiple poems that show a strong, sensitive, restrained feeling for the non-human world of nature. "Mowing," "The Exposed Nest," "Good-By and Keep Cold," "To a Moth Seen in Winter," "Lodged," "The Quest of the Purple-Fringed," and "A Young Birch" are among the poems in this category. "Spring Pools" will represent this theme. A fourth theme is peculiarly Frostian; it is retreat (not escape). "A Drumlin Woodchuck," "One Step Backward Taken," "A Lone Striker" are examples. "Directive" will represent the theme. Fifthly, there is the theme of fatefulness. "Bereft," "The Peaceful Shepherd," "The Flood," "Acceptance," "Stars," "In Time of Cloudburst" show Frost's philosophical awareness of the inevitable. "Once by the Pacific" is selected to represent this awareness.

The sixth major theme is trust, which has three main aspects. There is trust in oneself, as in "Into My Own," "The Armful," "On a Tree Fallen Across the Road." There is trust in one's fellow man, as in "Something for Hope," "Sand Dunes," "The Courage to Be New."

And there is trust in the future, and purposive design in "On Looking Up by Chance at the Constellations," "What Fifty Said," "Too Anxious for Rivers," "West-Running Brook," "On Making Certain Anything Has Happened," "In the Long Night," "Neither Out Far Nor In Deep." Variants of this theme include affirmation ("The Lesson for Today"), reverence and humility ("The Fear of God"), and religious emotion ("Sitting by a Bush in Broad Sunlight"). "Willful Homing" is selected to represent this theme—a poem of self-trust and self-will.

The seventh theme, which is Yankee comedy, includes "The Gold Hesperidee," "A Blue Ribbon at Amesbury," "Brown's Descent," "The Cow in Apple Time," "A Hundred Collars," as well as "Haec Fabula Docet," "Departmental," "Astrometaphysical," "Why Wait for Science," "Etherealizing," "No Holy Wars for Them," and "A Wish to Comply." *A Masque of Reason,* a poem of higher comedy, will represent this theme. Obviously there is a good deal of overlapping in these themes and poems. "Tree at My Window" fits just as snugly in either of two categories and I suspect a good many other poems do. But we are interested to learn what the separateness of the parts can show us. A little later we shall hope to see more clearly the connection of the parts.

2. Relationship to Fellow Man

There is no key poem in *Complete Poems.* There are only key poems which illustrate general themes or moods. That I have chosen "Two Tramps in Mud Time" to illustrate the theme of Frost's relationship to his fellow man should not preclude the consideration of any other similar poem as a prime example of the theme. A more comprehensive statement of this theme would require the close examination of several other poems. My motive in selecting the poem is a dual one. "Two Tramps" will represent one of the chief themes, and it will also be a touchstone of the poet's technique. "The proper Method for studying poetry and good letters is the method of contemporary biologists," recommends Pound, "that is careful first-hand examination of the matter, and continual comparison of one 'slide' or specimen with another." Pound's suggestion is a sensible one and I shall apply it throughout the discussion of themes.

An effective illustration of the movement and temper of Frost's mind, "Two Tramps in Mud Time" starts characteristically with the particular and ends with the general. The play of the poet's mind as the poem unfolds indicates a considerable range of mood from affection to irony and also a spread of awareness, which includes awareness of self, others and the world of nature. In structure its nine stanzas present a logical flow of reactions. The first stanza satisfies the three unities of time, place and action. The second stanza is concerned with self-justification. The third, fourth and fifth stanzas amplify the vagaries of New England seasonal climate. The sixth stanza embodies the chopper's euphoria. The seventh stanza shifts the point of view from the interrupted chopper to the appraising lumberjacks. The eighth stanza points up the situation of the man who chops for love and the needy wayfarers who eye him in their extremity. The ninth stanza fuses the co-ordinates of love and need, and reconciles the tension which is psychological as well as economic.

It is characteristic of Frost's thinking to attempt to resolve the contradictions in a complex situation, especially when the situation affects his independence, and, by extension, when it affects the problem of the independence of all men. The distinguishing quality in his own thinking comes out in his effort to build a defense against the encroachments of the world of man and nature, such a defense as he mentions in "Triple Bronze"; and such an awareness of encroachment as he mentions in the last stanza of "Skeptic"; and which, by inference, he warns of in "Build Soil" ("We're to unseparate out among each other—/ With goods to sell and notions to impart.") He has always been concerned about interposing something between man "And too much world at once."

The underlying theme is a defense of the individual against the "gang security" of those who would without examining the situation suppress his effort because they think they know better how to regiment security. In effect, it is a political poem and embodies the core of an important problem. When does a man's self-selected independent effort impinge on, interfere with, or violate the welfare of others? In converse the problem is, what justifies another man's appropriation of one's honorably and competently performed self-selected task? Frost reconciles the tension between heart and need when he says:

> Only where love and need are one,
> And the work is play for mortal stakes,
> Is the deed ever really done
> For Heaven and the future's sakes.

The keyword here is the penultimate word "mortal" in the second line. For the poet isn't sentimental; he knows we have no right to exercise a personal indulgence willfully, arrogantly and sportively when others are in dire need or distress. When we unite our love and need in work that is play for *mortal* stakes, then the motive is pure and the act is justified. His relationship to his fellow man is one of sympathetic understanding. Moreover, it is ruggedly independent and coolly philosophical. It will take more than Steinbeck's Joads or the combined rationalization of labor leaders to outsmart this tough logic. But this is not a political poem in the usual sense. It has nothing to do with voting the Republican or Democratic ticket. It is at once more specific in its personal psychological approach to the problem of living one's life, and more general in its advocacy, like Emerson and Thoreau, of the higher, more conscientious individualism. Individualism sans conscience is amoral Nietzscheanism and leads to *Machpolitik*. Such individualism is the opposite of Frost's belief.

Although the subject matter of "Two Tramps" is familiarly rural, the point it makes transcends locality. Frost is really a sophisticated poet with a knowledgeable eye, who happened to grow up on the borderline between rural and urban environments. If his subject matter were strictly within city limits, his poetry would be just as discerning and philosophical. It is merely coincidental that "two hulking tramps" are the people about whom he writes. In using them as background figures in his poem he is not conforming to any literary tradition of which I know. These are neither lonely leech-gatherers nor Shropshire lads. In the beginning the authority in his early "talk-songs" came from material which he found for himself, and from a desire to create a poem in his own way. The actions in the "talk-songs" arose from the passions of the people and from their being who and what and where they were. Of these pastorals the reader does not inquire, "What does the poet say?" Rather, he inquires, "What does the self-seeker say, or the hill wife, or Silas, or the housekeeper?"

In the later eclogues, like "Build Soil," "The Lesson for Today," "From Plane to Plane," and in the *Masques,* the reader hears the voice of the poet editorializing for better or for worse, as he agrees or disagrees with the poet's opinions on the state of the world. When the idea is forced to stretch over a protracted narrative, attenuation results, as in "How Hard It Is to Keep from Being King." Dialectically, Frost appears to win his victories in these polemical poems, but when we examine in an historical light his resolution of the problems posed, the victories are less certain. The poet gives "opinion-judgments," always open to controversy. In direct poetry, of which "Two Tramps" is a valid example, the idea is embedded in the poem like the clingstone in the peach; it is not diffused through it as in oblique or indirect poetry, like salt in the sea. Where the absorption of the material is complete, there is commonly embodiment of idea. The result is poetry at an intense pitch.

Frost is an emancipated traditionalist who does not, like Milton and Keats, make constant classical allusions or use personification. Nor does he invoke or address the spirit in the earth or air or sea like Wordsworth. If any references are made in his poems, they are consciously imported. He steals them, as he says, to new use, which is perfectly legitimate. A closer look shows no redundancies or needless repetitions in "Two Tramps." On the contrary there is insight and revelation but with enough exposition and explication to enable the reader to get the point. He is skilled in the use of antithesis in the fifth stanza:

> The water for which we may have to look
> In summertime with a witching-wand,
> In every wheelrut's now a brook,
> In every print of a hoof a pond.

Sharply apprehended glimpses of country life—tactual, auditive and visual—whet the sensibility; for example: "The sun was warm but the wind was chill"; a bluebird's song "so pitched as not to excite/ A single flower as yet to bloom"; and "It is snowing a flake." T. E. Hulme, who was always very much concerned about the romanticist's tendency to overdescribe by letting go and flying off into the infinite, would have approved of "Two Tramps." "They cannot see," Hulme would say of the romanticists, "that accurate description is a legitimate object of verse." And, "the great aim is accurate, precise and definite description." Stanzas three, four and five of "Two Tramps" can stand as examples of accurate, precise and definite description. These descriptions are as native to New England as broom sedge and worm fences are to Virginia.

Another resource of Frost as an artist is the use of imagination. By way of comparison, consider how Hardy in "The Dynasts" uses imagination in two ways. First, he uses it as a projective faculty by which to describe panoramically the scene at the time of the Napoleonic wars:

A bird's eye perspective is revealed of the peninsular tract of Portuguese territory lying between the shining pool of the Tagus on the east, and the white-frilled Atlantic lifting rhythmically on the west. . . . Innumerable human figures are busying themselves like cheese-mites . . . digging ditches, piling stones, felling trees. . . . Three reddish-grey streams of marching men loom out to the north. . . . These form the English army . . . looked down upon, their motion seems peristaltic and vermicular, like that of three caterpillars.

The second use of imagination is as common to Frost as it is to Hardy. It is the worm's-eye close-up as juxtaposed with the bird's-eye aerial view. While the armies of the Allies advance to the Battle of Waterloo, Hardy's imagination looks up at their passage from a position prone on the ground:

> The mole's tunnelled chambers are crushed by wheels,
> The lark's eggs scattered, their owners fled;
> And the hedgehog's household the sapper unseals.
>
> The snail draws in at the terrible tread,
> But in vain; he is crushed by the felloe-rim;
> The worm asks what can be overhead,
>
> And wriggles deep from a scene so grim,
> And guesses him safe; but he does not know
> What a foul red flood will be soaking him.

The effect of these two uses of imagination is interesting. The first is expansive and intellectual; the second is intimate, sympathetic and emotional. Frost's descriptive power in "Two Tramps" is of the second kind. Yet it is interesting to note that, in spite of his phrasing which leans more toward sensuous than intellectual usage, the emphasis is dominantly on the ideas. Here is a craftsmanlike use of the specific to reveal the abstract. The point in "Two Tramps" is a hardheaded one. The imagery by which it is revealed is genuinely sensuous:

> You'd think I never had felt before
> The weight of an ax-head poised aloft,
> The grip on earth of outspread feet.
> The life of muscles rocking soft
> And smooth and moist in vernal heat.

The poet can either release his emotion by telling us how he feels, which Frost does in "Two Tramps," by identifying but without labelling the emotion, or he can release it without either personal intrusion or commentary, a favorite objective (but not a common realization) of the Imagist poets. Thus, John Gould Fletcher in "Irradiations":

> Flickering of incessant rain
> On flashing pavements:
> Sudden scurry of umbrellas:
> Bending, recurved blossoms of the storm.
>
> The winds came clanging and clattering
> From long white highroads whipping in ribbons up summits:
> They strew upon the city gusty wafts of apple-blossom,
> And the rustling of innumerable translucent leaves.
>
> Uneven tinkling, the lazy rain
> Dripping from the eaves.

There are also two ways of realizing vigor in art: There is a force that comes from saying a thing so exactly the statement stands on its own. Or, a vigor that comes from elaboration and variation of a theme through deft, incisive repetition. When Frost says:

> But yield who will to their separation,
> My object in living is to unite
> My avocation and my vocation
> As my two eyes make one in sight.

he qualifies under the first category. "They knew they had but to stay their stay" does nicely for the latter. Each is effective as only a craftsman knows how to fetch it off.

Here we find no trace of archaisms like those that infect his first poems, words like *loth, wend, amain, frighted, abode, fain, wist, alway*. And although there are colloquialisms here, for example, "hit them hard," "spare to," and familiar contractions like "you're" and "you'd," no other backcountry words like "dunnow," "mebbe," or "boughten" are used. The cadence, too, is more accurate. Frost writes: "A wind comes off a frozen peak." In "Two Tramps" he communicates his inimitable sound of sense. "They judged me by their appropriate tool" or "and he half knew/ Winter was only playing possum," or "The lurking frost in the earth beneath." A thing freshly felt when naturally expressed belongs to its own time, and Frost's "sound of sense" is as much a part of the time in which we live as the prologue to *King Henry Fifth* was a part of the time to the initiated ears of those in the pit at the Globe, listening and relishing full-bodied Elizabethan language. When Frost writes:

> And one of them put me off my aim
> By hailing cheerily 'Hit them hard!'

this is plain Yankee speech to the ear. When it was suggested to an old Yankee hedge-trimmer that his work took a lot of bending over, he replied characteristically, "Oh, gee, more than a fellow'd think for." Another old-timer, after downing a piece of cherry pie, smacked his lips over the sugar, spices, cherries and pastry, and remarked by way of commendation, "You put the stuff to it." Frost's language is true to the man, the voice and the diction. "I don't want any words that are not my speech words," he says. "I don't want mere dictionary words." Neither does he use any. As for the voice, his personal inflection is different from the soft, slurred consonants and flat vowels of the Southerner or the Western burr and the Panhandle drawl. This quality in speech rhythm is as native to him as the rag is to a Dixieland jazz band. It is the earmark of his tonal inimitability, just as independence of viewpoint identifies his thinking. When he once acknowledged that "all there is to know is how to express yourself and knowing how to have something to say," he summed up his own achievement in "Two Tramps."

3. A Tragic Sense

"Home Burial," illustrative of a second theme—that of the tragic sense—in Frost's poetry, is a dramatic elegy. Its general theme is the tragedy implicit in the life of backcountry farm folk. I am here using "tragedy"—a very important descriptive term—in a loose sense. The form that Frost's tragic sense takes would be more accurately described as "pathetic" than "tragic." His poems in which "tragic sentiment" appears are not related to "a religious or philosophical background," to apply Allen Tate's words used in a different context. They are "pathetic tales" of the order of Wordsworth rather than of the order of Dante and Milton. The method in his pathetic tales of tragic sentiment is that of subjective drama which releases a character's state of mind without explanatory comment. The aim of drama in the theatre is activity. Frost's poetic dramas represent human states and reflections.

The source of this particular tragic sentiment is hardly environmental. It does not spring from the economics of submarginal farming. The unhappiness of people in a pre-tractor epoch is not measurable by the desires of a post-tractor era. If the income from working mountain alluvial is meagre, at least the overhead is negligible. Nor does it spring from the geography of isolated mountain terrain. There is no lack of human society in the intervales, and New England Yankees are not commonly so standoffish as is sometimes asserted.

I do not contend that a tragic situation cannot be intensified by environmental hazards—by remoteness, by lack of diversions, by inadequate conveniences. In "Home Burial" the core of the tragic situation is more fundamentally human and inward—a failure in intrafamilial communication. Just as the "dark" people in the "dark villages" of Sherwood Anderson's mid-American tales are aware of walls separating men, so these people north of Boston—a lonely housekeeper, a servant to "servants," an ineffectual hired man—cannot break down the wall of isolation separating one human being from another.

Yet the reason for their frustration is unlike the reason for the plight of the people in Anderson. The latter are tongue-tied and incoherent; their inadequacy is environmental and verbal. When they are articulate, their behavior is fantastic. The inadequacy in Frost's people is sometimes vocal as in his hired man and hill wife. But usually the dominant failure is in disconnection, as it were, in the flow of feelings. The circuit is cut, the flow interrupted, and repression, the chronic condition of their wounded spirits, seals them off from human intimacy and the possibility of regeneration and rehabilitation. Unable to share their inmost feelings, inwardly they slowly bleed to death.

The tragic sentiment flows from a plight or situation to which the people react according to whom and what and where they are. It is psychical rather than merely physical. And it takes several forms, has several effects. It may produce an inverted but bitter, stabbing resignation, as in "The Housekeeper." ("Who wants to hear your news, you—dreadful fool?") It may, on the contrary, result in a wistful suppression as in "A Servant to Servants"—("I'd *rather* you'd not go unless you must.") Or it may search the heart with the lonely repression of the hill wife whose husband is to learn the ultimate in finality. And it may stand reflected in the salutary impersonality of those left in the rueful "Out, Out—" where "they, since they/ Were not the one dead, turned to their affairs." In these culminating lines the tenuous tragic sentiment catches its poetic center like a filament of thread the needle's eye, and the tragic decisiveness is irrevocable.

In "Home Burial," where grief is the key to the situation, there is little action, but an impactive situation, which fulfills Chekhov's counsel to his brother Alexander. "The best thing of all is not to describe the emotional state of your characters," wrote Anton; "you ought to try to make it clear from their actions. . . . The center of gravity should be two: he and she. . . ." The young wife—the first exponent in the center of gravity—beside herself at the recent loss of her baby son, vents her inconsolable grief by attacking what seems to her the callousness of her husband—the second exponent—who has dug the child's grave in a nearby family burying lot where she could see him at work. These two talk out the disaffection and misunderstanding—the wife distraught and assertive; the husband, reserved and confounded. Temporarily he is obtuse. The poet does not take sides:

he presents; he is not proprietary. In the presentation we feel the tension shift in the scene where the husband, who is standing on the lower steps of the staircase looking up at his wife, ascends to where she looks out toward the burial plot. Meanwhile she descends the staircase, needling him with reproaches to which at first he replies with restraint. Dramatically the symbolic transposition of the husband and wife is excellently handled. It is a fact and it is a sign. The greater the art the more skillfully the symbolic is embodied. Later, in the *Masques,* although the ideas are dramatized the intellectual element will be more obvious than the human and poetic.

The psychological movement is more important in "Home Burial" than the muscular or the neural, but we have all three planes. What will inevitably exorcise the seemingly inconsolable grief of the afflicted wife is the husband's masculine reasonableness. He has heart, generosity and fearlessness of the fact—necessary resources in the day-to-day strain of human relationship. He also has common sense, and enough sensitivity to keep it from lapsing into matter-of-fact callousness. His common sense stanches his wife's grief and restores her reasonableness.

There is insight here. Amy, the wife, really wants to hug her grief. Grief-stricken she says, "The nearest friends can go/ With anyone to death, comes so far short/ They might as well not try to go at all." The unintrusive hand of the poet shows Amy's grief as an indulgence, magnified disproportionately. She is attempting to escape, her husband to face, reality. When it is inescapable, he believes a man should take what is coming to him without repining. His resolution counters her excited impulse; common sense effectively offsets agitation; the male the female; the cerebral light the moral dark. Even the interior of the house in which husband and wife stand is comparatively dark. Standing in the darkness of psychological conflict, they are isolated from the sunlit landscape toward which both look.

This domestic drama underscores a tragic awareness general in Frost's poetry. Tragic sentiment is not what he arrives at, it is what he starts from. There is also a leading statement—the affliction of inconsolable grief. As spectators to a tension between people really in love with each other, it is almost intolerable to see the wife keep open the wound that nature in time will close. The poet's sympathetic understanding—the dominant tone of the poem—restrains the reader from repudiating the bereft mother, and inherent justness keeps the poem exactly balanced between the emotional and the intellectual. Tenderness and affection are counterpoised by reasonableness and understanding.

Frost has written two kinds of drama. In the early poems there is the drama of social adjustment in human relationship. In the later poems there is drama of ideas. "Home Burial" is an example of the former; "The Lesson for Today," "Build Soil," and the two Biblical *Masques* represent the latter. There is satirical laughter, seriousness of intent and insight in all of these poems. In the domestic drama the virtue and defects of the poet as a dramatist are apparent. First, we see how capably Frost establishes the tension, how human relations are the source of the drama, and how in human beings it is the secret places of the heart that give rise to the situation. The dramatic edge is what is felt without being immediately said or shown. In his responsibility the dramatist must order the situation.

In form "Home Burial" is as carefully framed as "The little graveyard where my people are!/ So small the window frames the whole of it." The shock of compulsive feeling and the restraining form are carefully shown in the last incident where Amy opens the door by which she hopes to escape from her "insensitive" husband into the outside world. Once outside, her grief can be worn forevermore on her face so that sympathetic souls will draw near her in compassion. But she will not get far, for there is her determined husband who tells her, " 'Where do you mean to go? First tell me that./ I'll follow and bring you back by force. I *will!*—' " The appearance of someone coming along the road only heightens the drama, for pride of family is at stake. The outside world impinges upon this private intramural world of two people, and influences it by customs, rites and attitudes. Self-respecting families try not to make fools of themselves in public, no matter what happens at home.

Another important thing is what you hear while your ear listens: the idiomatic language of the phrasing, "I must be wonted to it"; the pitched inflections of the voice, " 'Don't, don't, don't, don't,' she cried"; or " 'Can't a man speak of his own child he's lost?' "; the deliberate rhythm " 'Tell me about it if it's something human./ Let me into your grief. I'm not so much/ Unlike other folks as your standing there/ Apart would make me out. Give me my chance.' ", and the audible accent, " 'I shall laugh the worst laugh I ever laughed./ I'm cursed. God, if I don't believe I'm cursed.' " Indeed—how can we deny it?—poetry sweats out of emotional tension like sap at the end of fresh-cut wood.

Nearly the most important thing technically in this poem is the dash and the accent. I recall hearing Frost say that two things he is proud of in "Mending Wall" are the "oh!" and the hyphen in "*old*-stone savage!" "It's a paleolithic savage," he cracks. This is the point—the real point—the correct reading of the poem so that we get all the subtleties, which the knack of the poet's art has put there. "The completeness of a person's education is looking on a passage called great writing," says Frost, "and thinking that he's not missing any tricks." So there is the "winnowing wind" in Keats's "Ode to Autumn," which Frost thinks people misread. The winnowing of course goes with wind—it's a kind of wind. "Trouble is they don't know how to read him [Keats]." The two dashes in "Home Burial" that carry more than their weight in suggestion are: "You'd think his memory might be satisfied—" (which leaves a lot unexplained, inexplicable), and " 'I'll follow and bring you back by force. I *will!*—' " (And we know that the husband's word is as good as his deed.) What Frost can do with a diminished thing—a dash, a pause, a syllable, an accent, would surprise even a Greek, let alone an ovenbird.

No doubt about it, he is lucky in discovering the variations in emotions through the sounds of words. Literally he has overheard his feelings, and like the Renaissance masters who learned to draw by painting, he has learned to hear by expressing himself. Of the Renaissance painters, John Ruskin wrote: "The brush was put into their hands when they were children, and they were forced to draw with that, until, if they used the pen or crayon, they used it either with the lightness of a brush or the decision of a graver. Michelangelo uses his pen like a chisel; but all of them seem to use it only when they are in the height of their power, and then for rapid notation of thought or for the study of models; but *never as a practice helping them to paint.*" This is applicable to Frost. He has had to discover how large a world of time and spirit the audible word encompasses. Inevitable it is that he should see that his art lay along the less-traveled road—the poet's way. His love of art is intense but not greater than his experience. He grew by it; it expanded the man. The technical and human insights compound each other.

One of his skills is to make the obvious sound different. He does it by the voice which is so intextured in the essential meaning that only by the variations in voice-tones do we understand the differences in emotional stress. "She let him look, sure that he wouldn't see,/ Blind creature; and awhile he didn't see./ But at last he murmured, 'Oh,' and again, 'Oh.'" He tunes language to the *human,* not the Yankee, voice. The tones in the poems are not the voices of people speaking in any particular region. They are the sounds of Frost's own vocal chords. "My sounds are not dialect; just accent," he explains.

In his development as an artist he has explored ways of adapting metrics to personal phrases, diction, speech-tones. The story of his progress is a story of the reactivation of metre by the speaking voice. He is apparently all ears for those poets in the great tradition of English verse whose ears are musical—the ears of the folk who give us the Ballads, the Scottish Dunbar, Shakespeare in the speaking as distinguished from the rhetorical passage, Chaucer in his *Tales,* and Milton in "Lycidas." It is personalizing of verse one hears in Frost's poetry. As you read the poems, you don't necessarily follow the groove of his voice in the sound-track, although it is undeniably there like under-sound. You inflect with your own voice-tone. You follow the sound of the voice—your own, as it were, just as originally Frost transcribed his voice-tones from words forming in his mind, initiated by a compelling emotion that sought and found the fusion of thought and feeling in expression.

What makes his poetry original is not the words by themselves. It is what these words are doing, which depends upon their place in the sentence; they are earmarked by rhythm and pitched to the tone of the speaking voice. By themselves they are ambiguous; in context they are alive. We must listen closely to them to hear them accurately, so that the originality does not escape. The *true* ear unerringly shapes the sounds in words to native uses. Because the words do not palpitate with anguish or pity, do not believe that they are without human emotion. They contain the grief, they do not exploit it. The emotion's in the tone (where it should always be felt), and not in the eye where it is commonly and mistakenly looked for in poetry. The anger of Milton's exhortatory "Avenge, O Lord, Thy slaughter'd saints" is in the tone as delight is in the tone of Donne's "Go and catch a falling star." Frost's strength does not consist in resembling Wordsworth in the skillful handling of technique. It is in his deviation from Wordsworth that his originality and his strength lie; for there is a temperate lucidity, which we find in "Birches" and "Home Burial," that by its disciplined effortlessness and inspired simplicity, reaches both extremes —the ideal pitch and the exactness of the naturalistic level. Only relaxed art can achieve this, even as in many sports events the great records come out of supremely relaxed efforts when the athlete is in "form." In "Home Burial" he shows the relaxed intensity of a man at the top of his skill.

There are booby traps in this theory, which Frost doesn't always escape. When poetic sentences skillfully imply more than is said, the provocative sentences start evocative ripples moving, and suggestibility is the result. But when the sentences fail to carry the potential charge, then they become monotonous. "Poetry atrophies," says Pound discerningly, "when it gets too far from music." And, in *The Backgrounds of Modern Poetry,* Professor Isaacs finds that one of the chief characteristics of modern poetry is taking speech "when it is the language of man in a state of excitement and making certain that that excitement lifts it above prose." He adds shrewdly, "There is a danger that the excitement may not be communicated." Poets of understatement like Frost must guard against the latter possibility.

In "Home Burial" there is also a problem in diction. In two successive lines the husband's phrasing would be better if it were less startlingly commonplace. One of his phrases is "You're a-mind to name" and the other is "'twixt those that love." I really wonder if anyone on a New England farm or elsewhere in the last hundred years has phrased his speech quite as quaintly as the husband does in these instances. These unnatural phrasings grate on my ear. And it must be remarked that these two, Amy and her husband, speak uncommonly well for the most part. They do not speak elliptically; they finish a thought. They are, moreover, intelligent, articulate, and they possess *sabiduria.* As a matter of fact, they speak, as the saying goes, in tongues.

Our awareness of this reduces the spontaneity of the presentation. It is a deliberate, not transcribed, speech. But it also shows that Frost's speech here is imaginative and not an attempt at dialect.

The highest merit of style is when we find it a medium through which something is said and not when it is a device by which things are shown. "Some words are to be called out for ornament and color . . . but they are better when they grow to our style," said wise old Ben Jonson, who, when he criticized Shakespeare stylistically, struck him at his most vulnerable point. Both "a-mind to" and " 'twixt" hardly seem to grow out of the husband's style of expressing himself. When Amy turns on her husband "such a *daunting* look" this grows to Frost's style, and we accept it. So, too, are the psychological shifts in expression impressive. "And her face changed from terrified to dull," and "She let him look, sure that he wouldn't see." These are revealing, just as the physical description is "right." "She, in her place, refused him any help/ With the least stiffening of her neck and silence." We can see this, and it is a stroke of genius that represents a fine thrust of power— one of the best, dramatically, in *Complete Poems*. The poet has given a complex emotional situation the distinction of simplicity.

4. World of Nature

"The land is always in my bones," says Frost, although it doesn't necessarily make him regional. He identifies the region; it doesn't identify him any more than it does Edwin Arlington Robinson. Frost is natively American less by a statement of patriotic intent than by being who and what he is—an emancipated traditionalist living in a certain geographical locality where for the most part the region and the people look, behave and talk as he represents them. His nativeness is a matter of being someone and having experiences. "Home Burial" reflects this kind of regionalism by a trans-regional poet. What matters in "Home Burial" is the human heart, a knowledge so intimate Frost makes us feel as Virgil does the "tears in things."

In "Spring Pools," representative of the nature theme in *Complete Poems,* beauty's the thing:

> These pools that, though in forests, still reflect
> The total sky, almost without defect,
> And like the flowers beside them, chill and shiver,
> Will like the flowers beside them soon be gone,
> And yet not out by any brook or river,
> But up by roots to bring dark foliage on.

The way "Spring Pools" begins recalls Thoreau's description of the purest poetry as "a true account of the actual." Poetry is a true account of the actual when the words are used not as symbols of things but to stand for objects themselves, as they do in this poem. The natural effect is breathing close. When the poet capitulates, the object takes over and the poem is either stock description (where the object dominates the poet) or rhetoric (where the poet inflates the object). Wordsworth makes us keenly aware that the poet is a human being with a difference. The poet learns to make things speak through him rather than he through them. This is what Paul Klee meant when he said, "Art does not render what is visible, but renders visible." To test a poem like "Spring Pools" you need to find out how soon you can forget the poet. Even once over lightly ought to convince a reader that in the first stanza Frost renders visible the flowers and the pools, the forest and the sky.

> The trees that have it in their pent-up buds
> To darken nature and be summer woods—
> Let them think twice before they use their powers
> To blot out and drink up and sweep away
> These flowery waters and these watery flowers
> From snow that melted only yesterday.

This final stanza is all one poetic sentence in which the charged, incantatory impulses of man are verbally contained. But the tone's the thing: the quiet but firm admonitory tone ("Let them think twice before they use their powers"). Here the eloquence is emotional, not rhetorical: a matter of feeling, not of language. In "Spring Pools" the resources of language release the energy in things and that's an end to't. It is a conscious self-discipline which compels his words to say exactly what he wants them to say without riding or forcing him off his intention. The poetic style is "strict and succinct," as Ben Jonson says, "where you can take away nothing without loss, and that loss to be manifest." "Spring Pools" is uncluttered. "The little more, and how much it is; the little less, and what worlds away!" The poem is its own excuse for being: an embodiment and an utterance, not a commentary.

A nature lyric like "Spring Pools" may appear to the casual eye as a low-altitude reconnaissance flight. Yet it would be a grave mistake to underrate it. The subject matter belies the significance both in the poem itself and in its relationship to the poet. It is actually a poem of memory and longing. For his fellow townspeople at Ripton (Vermont), he recalled the time and place where he wrote it—"sitting alone late at night in Ann Arbor, Michigan." And he added, "I'm used to thinking a lot about them (spring pools) in the spring. The pools I'm thinking of belong to this country."

Of all his poems "Spring Pools" is the purest nature poem. Evoking New England in springtime, when the melted snow is seen in pools with the wild flowers around them, it catches the season just before the buds on the trees appear. After these little pools soak into the soil, root pressure forces the sap up the tree bole through the cambium layer. Only a poet who knows the intimacies of nature from blowing to fading, who takes to the woods like a squirrel to a hickory knothole, will have given these spring pools a second glance. But they have, as we have pointed out, their own excuse for being. Nature is the great background; this is one of her multiple activities in the early spring.

So far as the observant poet is concerned what he sees here is both motion and color. There is no moral and no ulteriorities; only a quietly contemplative mood; a feeling of cherishability, so common to the poet; a gentle admonitory tone; and a strong desire to prolong the beauty represented by the transient spring pools. This is all and it suffices; for, among the nature lyrics, it is a beautiful, self-sustaining show bloom. In Emerson's words:

> Work of his hand
> He nor commends nor grieves:
> Pleads for itself the fact. . . .

5. A Strategic Retreat

"Directive" is a poem about retreat; it is not an escape poem. Nor are "A Lone Striker," "A Drumlin Woodchuck," or "Birches"—all of which belong to the same category—escapist poems. "Directive," in embodying one of Frost's principal themes, makes a very sharp point. It is not like Wordsworth's complaint that the world is too much with us, late and soon. It is a poem of robust counsel. "Back out of all this now too much for us"—the civilization of today cluttered and pre-occupied with detail—there is a brook, like a spring. If we can find this spring of simplicity, then we can "Drink and be whole again beyond confusion." Its prototype is Melville's "Lone Founts," not Wordsworth.

We must go back, leaving habitations and circumscribing township, back beyond a place spooked by former dwellers—the ghosted apparitions of time, symbols of the illusory intimate presence out of the past that haunt the present. You go back beyond an historical past into a geological one where nature was once the supporting plinth of man. "The ledges show lines ruled southeast northwest,/ The chisel work of an enormous Glacier/ That braced his feet against the Arctic Pole." You go back beyond the memory of man to the source of life itself—the brook that is the spring of springs. And if you desire, you can use the goblet to drink from it, the goblet a token of man's religious forms. Here, if you are the right one, you will find the goblet, for it is "Under a spell so the wrong ones can't find it,/ So can't get saved. . . ." Here to be lost is to be found, and the law for man takes precedence over the law for thing. Here you can get away from it all, but here you do not stay. There is nothing to interrupt your coming back again, to touch the common earth, like the heavenly propelled swinger of birches who finally reaches the earth where, as Walt Whitman says, "the press of my foot to the earth springs a hundred affections." You retreat; you do not escape. There is no dudgeon in your attitude, no aroused exhortatory prophetic indictment of the present. There is only a way to restoration and renewal for the humble and wise.

In form and spirit the poet does not, like a surveyor, set up an accurate route by transit and spirit level. This directive is more like an invitation to an enterprising venture, more like a personal Odyssey; a moral one, let it be said, which you go a-foot, the way you go most narratives. For "Directive" is a narrative poem, different from "Home Burial" and "Spring Pools," but like "The Bearer of Evil Tidings," "Love and a Question," "Two Tramps in Mud Time," "The Gift Outright," "Closed for Good," "Stopping by Woods," "Come In," "A Soldier." To Frost "the great thing is the story," and undoubtedly this is why he prefers *Walden* and *The Voyage of the Beagle* to other nature books. Each has a narrative angle. When he talks about compiling an anthology, the poems he thinks about are the shorter narrative ones, "yard-long" poems, like Christina Rossetti's "Goblin Market" and Sidney Lanier's "The Revenge of Hamish."

"Directive" not only shows Frost's knack at narrative, it also exhibits his sleight-of-art. When he describes the brook "cold as a spring as yet so near its source,/ Too lofty and original to rage," he skillfully exercises his conception of poetry as a renewal of words. He freshens language by taking words out of their ordinary usage and by reattaching them to their exact etymological meaning. The word pair "lofty" and "original" are as apposite as two dots of color in a Seurat landscape, and they are quite as individually juxtaposed. In metaphor he is fresh and original, especially in his use of the homely and familiar one of the cellar hole "Now slowly closing like a dent in dough." This homely metaphor is characteristic. He illustrates how one takes a thought and releases it through form. "Like a napkin," he says, "we fold the thought, squeeze it through the ring, and it expands once more." He says of finding one's style, that it is like a glass blower blowing into a tube, and shaping the glass with the mouth, so that form is pressure from within. He refers to the beauty of word and sentence that you get in Shakespeare, Milton and Keats, where every single line "pops like popcorn; turns white on you." And I've heard him say that "if a poem is a poem, it has direction the way a current combs the grasses all in one direction. The words comb the idea all one way."

What central idea does "Directive" liberate? It is contained in the symbol of the brook; for, although Frost is not primarily a naturalistic poet satisfied with the full force of an object's reality, as in "Spring Pools," where, indeed, the fact may be the sweetest dream that labor knows, nevertheless, his art combines an objective *and* a subjective reality. The objective reality is present in "Directive," and those who content themselves with it are cheated. As a matter of fact, Frost says of the "double-layer" poems, of which "Directive" is an example: "I don't care if you don't get the second layer. I like to stick in people's minds for a kind of catchiness." Yet Frost is not displeased with those who interpret the doubleness accurately. "If they are poetical about it and go the poem one better, I am pleased," he says approvingly.

Paralleling the objective reality in "Directive" there is a subjective one, but it is unlike the subjective reality of such a transcendental symbolist as Coleridge. Frost is a symbolist of the physical world of space and time. Coleridge was more concerned with the metaphysical. "In looking at objects in Nature while I am thinking, as at yonder moon dim-glimmering through the dewy window-pane," writes Coleridge in *Anima Poetae,* "I seem rather to be seeking, as it were *asking* for, a symbolical language for something within me that already and forever exists than observing anything new. Even when that latter is the case, yet still I have always an obscure feeling as if that new phenomenon were the dim awaking of a forgotten or hidden truth of my inner nature. It is still interesting as a word—a symbol. It is Logos the Creator, and the Evolver." One difference between Coleridge and Frost is that the latter doesn't try for a symbolical language to express what is already *inside.* His symbols originate in observation. What he looks at discerningly, he looks into, and the symbols he uses grow out of the observation as in "The Middleness of the Road" where universal blue is a symbol of absolute flight and local green is a symbol of absolute rest. In "Directive" the brook is as clearly a symbol of healing as the touch of the angel in the pool at Bethesda. It is suggestive that the spring or brook is a recurring image in "The Pasture," "A Brook in the City," "West-Running Brook," and *A Masque of Mercy,* as well as in "Directive."

The subjective Coleridgeian symbolism and the direct Frostian empirical symbolism suggest another angle of approach to the poem—

the angle of the reader. "We often hear people say that art and poetry are communication between the artist and his audience," says Frost. "I think a better and more accurate word is 'correspondence.' It isn't just saying *to* someone, as it is in communication. We have to feel that there is a similarity of feeling and ideas in the mind of a reader, and that our images will bring forth a response. That's what correspondence really is—bringing forth a response." Correspondence is what Frost elicits, but compare his correspondence with the transcendental correspondence of Swedenborg and Emerson. Swedenborgian correspondence is metaphysical, not empirical. In *Heaven and Its Wonders and Hell,* Swedenborg writes: "The whole natural world corresponds to the spiritual world, and not merely the natural world in general, but also every particular of it; and as a consequence everything in the natural world that springs from the spiritual world is called a correspondent. It must be understood that the natural world springs from and has permanent existence from the spiritual world, precisely like an effect from its effecting cause." In both Emerson and Melville there are comparable statements. "Every natural fact is a symbol of some spiritual fact," asserts Emerson in *Nature,* and in *Moby Dick* Melville exclaims: "O Nature, and O Soul of man! how far beyond all utterances are your linked analogies! not the smallest atom stirs or lives on matter, but has its cunning duplicate in mind." Frost's "correspondence" is at once more general and more particular than transcendental correspondence. "Sitting by a Bush in Broad Sunlight" suggests Frost's awareness of a spiritual force. The particular phenomena of nature can elicit a response quite as readily as awareness of spirit, and not necessarily in any sense of parallelism such as the transcendentalists suggest. Frost's correspondence includes the woodchuck as woodchuck. He keeps distinctions unblurred which is the point of "A Rose Family" ("The rose is a rose,/ And was always a rose."), and this separates him from the transcendentalists like Emerson for whom Love is heat on the plane of Understanding and supernal Love on the plane of Reason.

Although the brook in "Directive" does have a dual reality, as we have shown, there is no dualism in "Spring Pools." We can experience empathically a correspondence with either the brook—"your destination and your destiny's"—or with "these flowery waters and these watery flowers/ From snow that melted only yesterday." Those who in approaching literature stop with recognition of objects or incidents which have a place in their immediate experience have really never discovered the vivid response of correspondence.

6. Fatefulness

An effective representative of the theme of fatefulness is the sonnet "Once by the Pacific." Because it was written, Frost notes, "forty years ago, before the two World Wars," he anticipated these holocausts. He says wittily that "poems are not remembered in tranquility; they are anticipated in tranquility." Actually, he explains, he "fumbled" with it when he was in college, dropped it, and later when he remembered "a line or two," finished the poem:

> The shattered water made a misty din.
> Great waves looked over others coming in,
> And thought of doing something to the shore
> That water never did to land before.
> The clouds were low and hairy in the skies,
> Like locks blown forward in the gleam of eyes.
> You could not tell, and yet it looked as if
> The shore was lucky in being backed by cliff,
> The cliff in being backed by continent;
> It looked as if a night of dark intent
> Was coming, and not only a night, an age.
> Someone had better be prepared for rage.
> There would be more than ocean-water broken
> Before God's last *Put out the Light* was spoken.

"I must lay aside the pleasant patter I have built up for years and seek the brutality, the ill-breeding, the barbarism of truth," says Yeats. His rather self-conscious girding of the loins sounds tardy. Frost seems not only to have been aware of the barbarism of truth at an earlier age; he has written always with it in mind, and that is why there is such a peculiar force in "Home Burial" and "The Self-Seeker" and "The Housekeeper"—grim little dramas exactly set before us. For there is a "barbarism" in the general fatefulness of man as well as specifically in grubby human relations in the "booble-alleys" of London or the New York Bowery.

At first reading "Once by the Pacific" seems to represent a trial by the elements. This reading is re-enforced by the "night of dark intent" as though some unequivocal sinister force was in action. Then the mood is extended temporally into "an age." Before the gloom enshrouds us there is an urgent feeling we must batten down our hatches for an all-out storm. "Someone had better be prepared for rage." And over all, in time and space, the ominous feeling intensifies in the last two powerfully evocative sentences:

> There would be more than ocean-water broken
> Before God's last *Put out the Light* was spoken.

The trial, we infer, will be enduring but not unendurable. A lot will happen to us—a lifetime, an age, man's duration on earth, perhaps, before the light will be quenched.

The tone of this sombre, Lucretian, brilliantly compact poem is no less fateful for being quiet in that terribly quiet way of Grant in the *Memoirs* when he writes of violence in battles, as at Vicksburg or Shiloh or Donelson, where as you read a thin stream of human blood seems to run off the page. No blood is yet spilled in "Once by the Pacific," but how prophetic the poem written before World War I has been! Already we have been through a second and are presently involved in a third world-wide struggle.

Frost's vision of reality is not in the least like Hardy's. Men are not plagued by such bitter circumstances that they are no match for the opposition. They do not endure supinely or indifferently or inadequately the circumstances that beset them. They are well-equipped fighters in a tough struggle. The tone and spirit are different in Hardy and Frost because there is a different situation. To the latter mankind is not entangled in a deterministic snare from which they find no possible extrication. His vision irradiates man's advantages. Crass casualty does not always obstruct the sun and rain; and dicing time doesn't "invariably" for gladness cast a moan. His tone is hopeful; his spirit is sanguine. Will, resourcefulness and ingenuity, rather than foreboding, resignation and endurance, are the keywords in his vision. He is not by any stretch of the imagination a poet of consolation.

Neither is he an optimist who ignores pain and evil in favor of an Emersonian "Benevolent Tendency." He is a cautious meliorist who believes in the exploration of possibilities. His protagonist, man, has ideas that he hasn't yet "tried." No matter how badly things have gone, Frost thinks there is a fractional advantage on man's side. The odds he quotes in favor of man's winning through are narrow—fifty and one tenth to forty-nine and nine tenths. A tight squeak, surely! In Emerson's phrase, of which Frost would presumably approve, man "antagonizes on": conflict and struggle and tension are in the order of things. Frost takes his motto from Thomas Gray's "Ode on the Death of a Favourite Cat": "And be with caution bold."

The poet looks elsewhere for help than to the impersonal forces of nature. Frost says:

> We may as well go patiently on with our life,
> And look elsewhere than to stars and moon and sun
> For the shocks and changes we need to keep us sane.

In an early poem—"Stars"—he makes a statement which no later poem contradicts. Accurately, he alters his first reaction upon seeing the stars—"As if with keenness for our fate"—to the realization of their impersonality. Then they are in the great outer universe

> . . . with neither love nor hate,
> Those stars like some snow-white
> Minerva's snow-white marble eyes
> Without the gift of sight.

Impersonal though the universe may be, man is no more hapless now than he has ever been. Once, when discussing Tolstoi's deterministic theory of history in *War and Peace,* he said, "It's all out of my hands; I just use my brains." He implies, of course, that he is aware of how much we are at the mercy of forces beyond our ken. He knows the only credit we deserve is for what we do with our God-given intelligence in the face of the inevitable. He has always been interested in what Robinson Crusoe symbolizes—the resourceful man on his own— "how the limited can make snug in the limitless."

A sense of history has made Frost aware that Fate is neither for nor against us, and there is good cause to think that his kind of Fate works through us, where Hardy overemphasizes an unwitting Fate which is above and external. While Hardy dips the beam toward negativism (and this in spite of his belief that he was an "evolutionary meliorist"), Emerson tips it to the other extreme. By personalizing a Benevolent Tendency, Emerson seeks to annul the actions of an untoward Fate. Frost takes a middle position. He is a rational meliorist letting "what will be, be." He seems to say, "It's a tough go, but when man has his wits about him, it need be neither dull nor bitter." He likes to see evidence of energy, enterprise, ingenuity, initiative and especially of courage and action. Poems like "On a Tree Fallen Across a Road," "One Step Backward Taken," "Riders," and "Sand Dunes" point up his belief in human resourcefulness.

Fatefulness—the inevitable water piled on water breaking against a shore lucky to have a continent in back of it—is the dash of bitters in his poetry. But the master image in *Complete Poems* is light whose counterimage of dark dominates sombre poems like "Acquainted with the Night," "Into My Own," "The Thatch," "Bereft" and "Design." The movement is from dark to varying intensities and kinds of light: the welcoming warmth of the sun in "Happiness Makes Up in Height," the subtle transforming light of the moon in "The Freedom of the Moon," the aspiratory pull of the stars in "Choose Something Like a Star," and the beauty of the starlighted night in "The Literate Farmer and the Planet Venus." There are also degrees of intensity in *Complete Poems:* for we can readily pass from the clarity and geniality of common light in "Atmosphere" to the luminous effect of light through falling snow in "Afterflakes," and to radiance in "The Master Speed." Like Goethe and Tolstoi, like Emerson, Thoreau and Whitman, Frost is one of "the sons of light;" not, like Nietzsche and Dostoevski, Baudelaire and Poe, one of "the intimates of Hell." Frost, the realist, takes a steady look at things without succumbing to resignation and despair. He does not moan, "I, a stranger and afraid/ In a world I never made." He takes the world as he sees it, accepting and rejecting, exercising selective judgment and revising wherever he has to.

It is interesting to compare Frost with Housman and Wordsworth. Housman is disenchanted with life as it must be lived—"The troubles of our proud and angry dust/ Are from eternity, and shall not fail."

Wordsworth is joyously responsive to life—"O Joy! that in our embers/ Is something that doth live,/ That nature yet remembers/ What was so fugitive!" Frost's attitude is neither one of joyous participation, nor yet one of *tedium vitae*. He doesn't ask for any special immunity; he will take life as it comes, with dry-eyed restraint. "But the strong are saying nothing until they see," he knows. While Housman conveys a sense of irrepressible melancholy, Wordsworth reassures us with an even-tempered serenity. In Frost, for whom the savour of life is bitter-sweet, there is shrewd reasonableness and deliberation. He is interested in everything that possibly could happen. There will yet be time "before God's last *Put out the Light*"! The menacing storm only intensifies the foreboding without daunting him. He regards unblinkingly its inimical threat. Wave after wave, feral nature beats upon the land and works into the human spirit, prophetically foreshadowing not only a natural but a human capacity for destruction.

7. Self-Trust

The dominant theme in Frost's poetry is affirmation. Some aspect of this theme is in all of the poems which we have selected. There is nothing in the poet's temperament or attitude to belie it. Again and again, in spite of hell and high water, he has considered this the best time in which to be living. When the situation is comparatively free of care, his affirmation responds gaily to the great over dog (in "Canis Major"). There is no backdown in the man; there is no halfheartedness in the poetry. The salient thing in his philosophy is the belief that he is equal to anything that can happen to him. His trust is positive and rugged, and resistant as unmossed rock. In the light of tragic reality such trust represents the reaffirmation of man's hope.

Since he is a verifiable realist, his "vision" is reality; his reality isn't "vision," as it seems to be in his fellow New England poet Edwin Arlington Robinson. He is not lured by any Light or Word or Gleam or Vision. The tentative Robinson *feels* the "coming glory of the light"; the sanguine Frost *chooses* "something like a star," to stay his mind on and "be staid." A romantic writer dreams about possibilities and the way it seems or the way it might be. Frost, on the other hand, doesn't write about anything that can't be verified in fact. To him the way it *is* is a sufficiently important discovery. Since he sees the universal in the heart of the specific he focuses on the specific imagery of a material, visible world.

"Willful Homing," representative of the theme of trust, reflects Frost's belief in the invincibility of single-mindedness. More dramatic than meditative, it differs from "Once by the Pacific," which was more meditative than dramatic:

> It is getting dark and time he drew to a house,
> But the blizzard blinds him to any house ahead.
> The storm gets down his neck in an icy souse
> That sucks his breath like a wicked cat in bed.
>
> The snow blows on him and off him, exerting force
> Downward to make him sit astride a drift,
> Imprint a saddle and calmly consider a course.
> He peers out shrewdly into the thick and swift.
>
> Since he means to come to a door he will come to a door,
> Although so compromised of aim and rate
> He may fumble wide of the knob a yard or more,
> And to those concerned he may seem a little late.

The tone of affirmation, just as in "Birches" and "Directive," is a suggestion, not a command, and it is caught not on a rising cadence but on a falling one, like the song of a bird drifting earthward. It is never plaintive, never a note of self-pity.

The theme of "Willful Homing" clarifies the purposeful, though delayed, progress of a man's journey. The protagonist, like Odysseus, is up to his challenge. He knows what he is in for, and, like a blue-tick hound on a cold spoor in dry terrain, he stops to look over the situation. Shrewdly, he "peers out" into the storm like any man, or perhaps like everyman today in the twentieth century beset by a common befatedness. This man has made up his mind that he is going to get home, and although put off his time schedule and directionally deflected, he intends to make it. Obviously, the implication in this poem is general. The poet means that mankind, which has a destiny to fulfill, will, under its own power, get wherever it intends to get. The poet's attitude is sanguine. His tone is quiet. His imagery is familiar (*e.g.,* imprinting a saddle on the snow drift); the language is simple and colloquial (*e.g.,* souse and fumble). And the presentation is direct; the focus in the poem never wavers from the struggling man. The verse technique is deceptively simple, almost casual. Such is the poet's skill. The feeling communicated is one of enkindling courage, for, as the poem implies, he who is determined he is going somewhere is going to get somewhere.

The important thing in "Willful Homing" is that you are *in* the storm, and you've got to get out; you're expected elsewhere. There are those who are concerned, and, as in "Stopping by Woods," you feel a sense of duty and responsibility, not only to yourself but to others. One must act in one's own behalf to survive. Human dignity, courage and assertion of will are at stake—personally *and* socially. It is interesting that no bewilderment, fear, or indignation of man at his plight is reflected. When you are befated, you are befated. But this is the occasion of a man's strength, whether he is the homing man or the poet wrestling with his form. The skill of the latter is great as it shows in the play of the words, each one of which slips into place like stones in a wall. Great, too, is the protagonist's courage, for he shows the confidence of resolution which is greater than the confidence of hope.

8. Yankee Comedy

Scratch Frost and you touch a rascal. "When I talk somewhere," he says, "I like to be rascally. That's what stimulates me." There is no doubt about it, the comedy of human relations, historical or extra-historical, has been a constant source of amusement to him. I suspect that few people have ever regarded the Book of Job as a springboard for laughter. In his own rascally way Frost has. And it's the Jobian in him that laughs longest—the nonconformist Jobian. For *A Masque of Reason,* a serio-comic drama, is one of the most angular of Frost's poems. It is compact of parallels, ambiguities, ironies, paradoxes, antitheses, symbols, intrinsic and implied. The first parallel is between the poet and Job, the nonconformist, who in both heart and mind challenges the established doctrines in Jewish orthodoxy. The poet, too, is a nonconformist Yankee squaring away at traditional tenets. First of all, the poet called the Masque *"a New England Bibilical"* [my italics]. Indeed, Frost in writing about the Old Testament is writing about the book which influenced the development of early New England more than any other.

Paradoxically the poet, who is nonsectarian and not a churchgoer, turns to the Bible for his material. But he knows what's going on inside the churches, in religion. Once, on driving by a Congregational Church in a small New England town, he looked toward the fine, white-steepled building, and said significantly, "I don't go to church, but I look in the window." What he sees and thinks about religion is a caution. The bells he hears do not ring him into service. Sectarianism is hardly the concern of a man whose God is the framework of the Universe. When on the subject of religion he pantomimes almost violently an eggbeater whirling as it beats up eggs, and imitates the froth spurting as the beater whirls. "Religion's the froth," he exclaims with a kind of passionate assertion. And he reiterates, "All froth!" Again, on another occasion, he contended that philosophy came into the world to suppress religion so science would have a chance. Here we have tripped pretty glibly from the parallel of the righteous man Job, a native of the land called Uz, and that rascally man Frost, a native of the land of Ripton, to the paradox of the latter day, nonconformist New Englander writing a masque of reason, not faith. Moreover, we recall Frost's belief that religion's antithesis, science, won the upper hand because of philosophy's discomforting anti-pietistic arguments. In *A Masque* itself we shall see the ambiguities, ironies and symbols, and humor as the crux of the situation.

In *A Masque of Reason* the eternal politics of the Bible are treated as cavalierly as Frost would himself prefer to have the *Masque* read. It is a comic supplement to one of the great tragic books of the Old Testament. The essence of Frost's humor is, as we have previously noted, a sense of justice which counterbalances pity and restrains it from sentimentality. When it comes to treating religious subjects, Frost begins to kick up his heels. Frost only affects to be very tough. A rough-and-ready justice better characterizes his attitude. In *A Masque* our first impression of God is that He is a teaser, with a broad sense of humor. The author of the Biblical Job had conceived of God greatly, as a majestic and exalted Being—"He beholdeth all high *things; he is* a king over all the children of pride"; with the omniscient view—"God thundereth marvellously with his voice; great things doeth he, which we cannot comprehend"; and the power to search the heart in its secret places—"I know that thou canst do every*thing,* and *that* no thought can be withholden from thee." Nor had He been too busy to be concerned with all of Job's afflictions and remonstrances. "Then the Lord answered Job out of the whirlwind." He was serious and grave, if not solemn. "Wilt thou also disannul my judgment? wilt thou condemn me, that thou mayest be righteous?" Frost's God is an irritating one. He prods and mocks Job. He speaks in equivocal statements and the dark places still remain sealed, the human mind untouched by rays of light. He explains very tardily the practical joke He has pulled on patient Job. Satan, who appears at the end, performs like a state department sub-chief of protocol. Thyatira, Job's wife, is not so shrewish as bright. Frost's *Masque* is on first glance composed of an anthropomorphic *dramatis personae* in which all four actors have bit parts. The poet is the protagonist and Job is a sorely beset man, like a refugee from a universal concentration camp, trying to argue his case before an appallingly dogmatic and whimsical overlord. This is, I say, the first impression.

Let us see how this impression is encouraged. First, as to time, we see that the meeting of God with Job and his wife takes place about a thousand years after Job's trial by affliction. God enters uniquely; *deus ex arbre.* Job is my Patient (an unsubtle pun). At first God behaves like a schoolmaster who has chastened one of his erring pupils this side of mortality, and who, in his self-righteousness, casually mentions it when he next inadvertently meets his victim. Job, an honest and courageous victim, is a fighter. The memory of the fiery and protracted ordeal by which he was annealed is still fresh in his mind. His amiability rises above God's condescending wisecracks. He is like a man who has run and won a race between perpetual anxiety and deferred serenity. But he still has questions to ask, and he is no longer plagued by those awful God-inflicted torments. Job is quick-witted, like his wife, beside whom God appears at first a bit sluggish and obtuse. Perhaps God is embarrassed by the thought of tormenting one of his most deserving. This would be a generous way of interpreting the situation. Belatedly and apologetically God thanks Job for being such a splendid object lesson:

> I've had you on my mind a thousand years
> To thank you someday for the way you helped me
> Establish once for all the principle
> There's no connection man can reason out
> Between his just deserts and what he gets.
> Virtue may fail and wickedness succeed.
> 'Twas a great demonstration we put on.
> I should have spoken sooner had I found
> The word I wanted.

This statement must have impressed Job subconsciously as a pretty flimsy piece of divine subterfuge.

When Job's wife, Thyatira, is introduced to God by Job, she says, "I'd know You by Blake's picture anywhere." To which Frost's very unsolemn, undignified, wisecracking God replies, "The best, I'm told, I ever have had taken." He is a God of limits. He is not only apologetic; He not only cracks shallow, stale jokes; He is not omniscient. He can't answer Thyatira's question why the witch of Endor was burned for witchcraft. "That is not/ Of record in my Note Book," he replies weakly. When Thyatira persists, God puts her off dogmatically, the way all searching inquiries are put off by fiat. He answers flatly:

> She wants to know why there is still injustice.
> I answer flatly: That's the way it is.

And what a disingenuous insinuation He makes, as though to stop Thyatira's mouth with a wisecrack!

> JOB: "Oh, Lord, let's not go *back* to anything."
> GOD: "Because your wife's past won't bear looking into?"

But Thyatira comes right back at God when she says, among other good things:

> All You can seem to do is lose Your temper
> When reason-hungry mortals ask for reasons.
> Of course, in the abstract high singular
> There isn't any universal reason;
> And no one but a man would think there was.
> You don't catch women trying to be Plato.
> Still there must be lots of unsystematic
> Stray scraps of palliative reason
> It wouldn't hurt You to vouchsafe the faithful.
> You thought it was agreed You needn't give them.
> You thought to suit Yourself. I've not agreed
> To anything with anyone.

The patient, sympathetic, understanding Job calms his wife, saying, "God needs time just as much as you or I/ To get things done." Job literally takes the words right out of God's mouth—a very understanding man, this Job; a man who is righteous and alert.

God may be the God of Israel to the orthodox Jewish worshippers, or the God of the Universe, to the author Job. To Frost, He is no *Deus absconditus,* but a God with a human sensibility. Of Thyatira, He says, a little reminiscent of Jove to Leda, "She's beautiful." God is also not ungenerous. Of Job's ordeal and the truth it established, God admits, "We groped it out together." Of science, He is less generous:

> My forte is truth,
> Or metaphysics, long the world's reproach
> For standing still in one place true forever;
> While science goes self-superseding on.

It is God's claim that together He and Job . . .

> Found out the discipline man needed most
> Was to learn his submission to unreason.

When Job asks why the object lesson had to be at his expense, God gives a very reasonable explanation:

> It had to be at somebody's expense.
> Society can never think things out:
> It has to see them acted out by actors,
> Devoted actors at a sacrifice—
> The ablest actors I can lay my hands on.
> Is that your answer?

Aware that God is a shrewd guiding force, and perhaps a rational one, Job persists. He is as robust and credible as Milton's Satan. He is curious but this side of inquisitiveness. He is tactful and becomingly humble and self-respecting, deferential and wise. His infectious amiability warms up God's cordiality; for out of Job's inquiry comes God's sagacious, if ingenious, explanation of the trial by torment. God's great respect for one man—for this native of the land of Uz—is as much as to say He had found a common denominator of what might be not a world full of temporizers who serve Him by tremulous ecstasy, or beef-and-brandy skeptics, or abject gleaners of the crumbs of transcendent charity, but a world of virile, intellectually honest Jobs:

GOD: Job, you must understand my provocation.
　　The tempter comes to me and I am tempted.
　　I'd had about enough of his derision
　　Of what I valued most in human nature.
　　He thinks he's smart. He thinks he can convince me
　　It is no different with my followers
　　From what it is with his. Both serve for pay.

　　　　　　He could count on no one:
　　That was his look out. I could count on you.
　　I wanted him forced to acknowledge so much.
　　I gave you over to him, but with safeguards.

The fact is Job's ordeal was a rather presumptuous act upon God's part to restore a sadly depressed prestige. "It was just God showing off to prove to Satan He could count on Job." This is the point of the *Masque,* whose message is the necessity of man to learn like Job his submission to unreason. The whole thing is a comedy—a New England comedy. Job's wife is witty, animated, articulate, intelligent and feline. Satan, the antithesis of God, is a natty, sharp-tongued antagonist of God's taunts:

GOD: Don't *you* twit. He's unhappy. Church neglect
　　And figurative use have pretty well
　　Reduced him to a shadow of himself.

Satan's presence is ambiguous; he acts like a hornet with its stinger drawn. Certainly his effect upon God or Job is about dustweight;

hardly palpable. He is like a poltergeist whom God evokes as by thaumaturgy, and whom He taunts with mocking jibes.

The tone in *A Masque of Reason* may appear to the reverential as of too great levity. And the arguments may appear to the tough-minded as too much like clicking the trigger with the safety on. They are invented rather than inspired. Yet, no one can gainsay the wit that is here —a wit that is in the insight which the words release. For example:

> Get down into things
> It will be found there's no more given there
> Than on the surface.

or,

> Disinterestedness never did exist.
> And if it did, it wouldn't be a virtue.

The folksiness of the *Masque* will probably alienate or mystify the orthodox. The gusty bonhomie and occasional harlequin blandishment will infect others with a sense of the comedic. The poet does pay God a noble compliment; he conceives of Him as a wit. This is just where Frost offends many readers. He handles, it seems to them, sacred subjects with a secular touch. His arch-human God is given to wry human prankishness and pleasantries. *He* lacks dignity; *He* is too unlawful for words. And those who, perhaps erroneously, consider a sense of humor as a human rather than a divine endowment, are shocked. But then aren't all divine traits—justice, love, mercy, pity, omniscience, omnipotence—attributions conceived in and ascribed by a human intellect? Man speaks for God since God is not in a *human* position to speak for Himself.

On the positive side, Frost's streak of artful drollery, unsolemn like the English, or carefree like the Latins, reduces the wit in some of contemporary poetry to neither a self-conscious whimsy as in E. E. Cummings, nor a precious rhetoric as in Wallace Stevens. It is at once ebullient, risqué, philosophic, spontaneous and corny. It depends upon the occasion; it flows out of euphoria. It is a letting go, with as much surprise to oneself as to the next fellow. As much as if to say, "Well, now, I never!" Too frequently Frost is deliberate. Some of the broader wisecracks are labored; hauled up, as it were.

The real thing here is the poetry—the rapture of the word—that is not rhetorical. It is the rapture of exactness. Frost's daemon is the performance in language worthy of man's experience—each part, episode, event, sentence, word, like an arc, suggests a greater whole. I think this is the daemon the poet most cherishes. It is the essence of his originality, which consists in knowing when he is original, a virtue not commonly practised by contemporary footnote poets. Had he imitated himself, there would be manner, not matter.

In the dialogues, monologues and masques as well as in the lyrics, Frost focuses on individual consciousness. In the former, the focus is on the characters; in the latter, it is on himself. In his attitude toward the people he writes about, he is usually sympathetic. When he laughs, as he often does, the laughter is not commonly mocking or scornful but teasing. The laughter is certainly not cold, contemptuous, or harsh.

Frost isn't superficial or facile. The superficial man does not explain; he explains away. Frost does not explain away, even if he does fail to explain with utmost satisfaction. The point is, he isn't solving anything. He is showing us something. He gives us a dramatic re-enactment of our epoch's perennial problem: the inability to reconcile human affliction with heavenly knowledge. Rather than start with Mary and Warren ("The Death of the Hired Man"), he transforms them into Job and Thyatira, and makes Job see again that God is not answerable to man for his afflictions. The experience of God is universal; that of man is particular. The plane of God's omniscience does not intercept, it exists higher than the human plane of man's knowledge.

I have noticed that Frost never exposes to ridicule those who have worked hard or struggled enduringly. He goes along with them, serving their needs, supporting their initiative and courage, defending their hopes against all the formidable opposition of chance and circumstance. This is probably why in A Masque, Job, the unbeaten inquirer, comes off so well. In the eyes of the humanistic Frost, he is a symbol of the heroic; one of the great symbols of our time. As Dr. Victor Reichert, Rabbi of the Rockdale Avenue Temple in Cincinnati, says, "Frost's God is a mystic presence," and his attitude toward that mystic presence is one "of bold humility." The viewpoints of Job in A Masque of Reason and his latter-day poetic biographer are interchangeable.

The center of a man's poetry may be what irritates him as in Housman; in what fascinates as in Walt Whitman; in what scares as in Emily Dickinson; in what inflames as in Archibald MacLeish. The center of Frost's is partly in what amuses him. He raises amusement in serio-comic poetry to the level of philosophic detachment. The purpose is serious, the manner is light. If the suspect situation or foible is what Frost is serious about, there is no denying his ability to pass Arnold's rigorous test of "high seriousness" as a condition of poetic excellence. High seriousness that is applied only as a test for tragedy would be a very incomplete one. Musingly, at one extreme, Frost contemplates calmly the soundless vortex of infinite darkness; and, at the other extreme, he writes with amusement of Brown's famous descent by gravitational pressure. Because he possesses a tragic sense, he is able to laugh. He has what Keats said Shakespeare possessed—"Negative Capability." In the world of Shakepeare's imagination, which was one of illusion and complete in itself, the dramatist could enjoy the suspension of doubts, uncertainties and mysteries because only his art, not his philosophy, was at stake. He was indeed *master* of the revels. Frost also could pivot nicely on the strange turns of negative capability. Who among the poets in our time has taken such pleasure in weighing uncertainties, stalking doubts, testing mysteries "without any irritable reaching after fact and reason?"

The gift of humor is a great one—one of the greatest I think—the wonderful sense that enables us to laugh and be laughed at this side of malicious derision. In Frost it is sly and droll, a combination that pairs admirably with the detached point of view of a negative capabilitist. Detachment helps to clarify Frost's tone of bi-partisanship in "To a Thinker," "The Bear," "Mending Wall" (in fairness he refers twice to the dominant viewpoints), "The Egg and the Machine," and "The Middleness of the Road." "To a Thinker" and "The Bear" are characteristic of intellectual detachment. He is laughing slyly at the extremist who shifts from left to right without establishing a point of balance. His viewpoint is not only detached, it is also fearless. His unintimidated laughter blows dust in the eyes of scholarly pretense, unwinds a coil of satire with a noose at the end to catch all hasty generalizations, and sets a subtle hairspring trap of irony at the burrow-mouth of all entrenched prejudices. Consider, in *Steeple Bush,* how his astringent wit scores ineffectual prophets of disaster ("The Broken

Drought"), the pretenses of power politics ("U.S. 1946 King's X"), the arrogance of science ("Why Wait for Science"), the well-intentioned but dim-witted social planners ("The Planners"), vapid theorists ("Etherealizing"), and myopic internationalists ("An Importer").

His humor is often just plain fun as in "the conundrum" poems like "Waspish." "There's some of the devil in me," Frost once said to one of the more promising younger poets. For sure! The heart of *Huckleberry Finn* is a moral conviction that the human being has a natural right to personal freedom. The essence of *Moby Dick* is a speculation on the identity and purpose of the ultimate force at the core of the universe. The center of *The Scarlet Letter* is a psychological insight into the effect of guilt upon conscience. In Frost the essence of his humor is the thoughtful laughter of the independent man at the foolish-wise, bitter-sweet, strong-weak idiosyncrasies of *homme moyen sensuel*—the tangy laughter of a humanistic perfectionist in whose soul the iron has bitten. And, moreover, it is, as we have seen, philosophic; it is concerned with the *implications* in things.

DIMENSIONS IN NATURE, SOCIETY, SCIENCE AND RELIGION

> But it is the height of poetry, the height of all thinking, the height of all poetic thinking, that attempt to say matter in terms of spirit and spirit in terms of matter.
>
> ROBERT FROST

1. Versed in Country things

Man may be in the foreground, but the drama of man's life is acted out for us against a tremendous background of natural happenings: a background that preceded man and will outlast him; and this background profoundly affects our imagination, and hence our art. We moderns are in love with the background. Our art is a landscape art.

JANE E. HARRISON: Ancient Art and Ritual

In "Dimensions in Nature, Society, Science and Religion," Frost's ideas about nature, men and God will be discussed. The first section—"Versed in Country Things"—focuses on nature. But whether it is bird, animal, fish, plant or flower about which he writes, man is never relegated to a naturalistic plane.

Upper New England is the time-bound world of Frost's poetry: partly elemental and geological, partly historical and psychological. The first time-sense that crops up in his poetry is the one the geologist reads in the rock scorings and strata of mountain ranges. These mountains, which appear ready to stand from everlasting to everlasting, are the glacier-formed early Paleozoic Green Mountain range, and the comparatively youthful post-Paleozoic White Mountain range whose spine stiffens wedge-shaped New Hampshire. "The ledges show lines ruled southeast northwest,/ The chisel work of an enormous Glacier/ That braced his feet against the Arctic Pole." Geologically inclined Frost refers knowingly to a cliff's talus and trilobites in rock specimens, to drumlins and geodes.

The second time-sense represents the effect of man on his environment and contrariwise, the effect of environment upon man. In Frost's dramatic monologues and dialogues we glimpse the alterations in customs, ways of life, habits. The country we say changes with the "times," but what makes it change is the subtle response of man to technological development. So, instead of hand cradles and kerosene lanterns, there

are now mechanical harvesters and electricity. The feel of the pre-ma-
chine age farmer is in "The Code" and "In the Home Stretch," in
"Blueberries" and "From Plane to Plane."

Thoreau said that when some men spoke of Walden, he saw only
"a shallow, dull-colored body of water without reflections or peculiar
color," but when his friend George Minott, the poetical Concord
farmer, referred to it, he saw "the green water and reflected hills at
once, for he *has been* there." Frost's references to local history—Fran-
coniana or Derryana or Riptoniana—are indigenous, for he knows
these things; he has seen and felt them.

He calls the intimate, unusual experience in nature a "favor." One
he captured in "Dust of Snow," and another, in an English setting, is
"Iris by Night." A further favor goes back to the Franconia days, when,
as he sat by a farmhouse window looking at a brilliant sunset, suddenly
an owl appeared, banked against the window and dropped away. Briefly
he glimpsed the owl's wing-quills and the downy breast feathers. And
again, while stopping at Bailey's Falls on the east side of the Middlebury Gap in the Green Mountains, as he peered into a shallow cave,
the interior was incredibly bright as if the floor of the cave were laid
with gold. It was a *lusus naturae* caused by intense light falling over his
shoulders and illumining a green-gold moss which carpeted the cave,
and which he later identified as phantom-gold moss. "And what I
would not part with I have kept."

Favors like these—the owl banking in the sunset sky, the crow
shaking snow from a laden branch, the phantom-gold carpet in the
cave, or whorled pogonias found at the edge of a cutting—make him feel
"prosperous." As cherishable moments, their meaning consists in what
they suggest to a poet's receptive mood. The scientific naturalist adds
freshly discovered plants to manuals and herbals; Frost transmutes
nature favors into poetry. Of his pleasure in flower or orchard or flighting bird, he says in "A Prayer in Spring":

> For this is love and nothing else is love,
> The which it is reserved for God above
> To sanctify to what far ends He will,
> But which it only needs that we fulfill.

II

"However it is in some other world," says Frost, "I know that this is the way of ours." His world is identical with John Muir's home address, "Earth-Planet, Universe." But, of course, there are worlds within worlds, and surely we would not press the poet on an intimate knowledge of United States Steel or State Street finance. It is the world of country things in which he is well versed, and only by reading his poetry closely do we see how accurate is his knowledge.

Country things mean, first of all, the natural background, and our relationship to natural phenomena may be familiar without being intimate. While we walk along a woodland path there may be a dozen rattlesnake plantains in flower by a fallen fir, but unless we look closely we will not see them. Thoreau reminds us that, where there is no intention of the eye, man sees little. Similarly with the ear. A couple of nature's picked voices like the hermit thrush and the veery may be singing, yet without an intention of the ear, they will not be distinguished from each other nor from the simple eloquence of other articulate woodland things. To be in *rapport* with the world of nature requires an unself-conscious awareness. Country-bred poets like Wordsworth and Whitman, Burns and Bryant, Hardy and Frost, are endemic not by birth in rural regions, but by unself-consciously absorbing and communicating native sights and sounds.

Frost had a farmer's unself-conscious eye before he had a naturalist's. He is like William Ellis, an English farmer of Little Gaddesden, a humble writer on sheep, of whom Edmund Blunden once wrote: "When he takes up a handful of soil, his speech answers the weight, colour, and touch of it." This quality of unself-conscious earthiness, whether in speech or attitude, in sound or image, is perceptible not in any particular one of Frost's poems, but pervasively; and nothing short of *Complete Poems* gives its full effect. Yet any one of many poems shows something of the quality. The poet writes of an oak clinging tenaciously to leaves the early frost has nipped and the northwind lashed. Falling only after a severe flailing, the winter walker finds some on the crinkling snow-surface in late February and mid-March; the others hold on. He writes from perceptive observation in "Reluctance":

> The leaves are all dead on the ground,
>> Save those that the oak is keeping
> To ravel them one by one
>> And let them go scraping and creeping
> Out over the crusted snow,
>> When others are sleeping.

If the first test of a poet versed in country things is unself-conscious awareness, the second test is accurate identification. As an illustration that Frost's senses report accurately, the blueberries in Patterson's pasture are honest-to-goodness blueberries whose true color is "ebony." "The blue's but a mist from the breath of the wind,/ A tarnish that goes at a touch of the hand." What he sees is truly observed, like the water flower called the floating heart, "with small leaf like a heart,/ And at the *sinus* under water a fist/ Of little fingers all kept down but one,/ And that thrust up to blossom in the sun." His identification of sound is also accurate. He hears "the Hyla breed/ That shouted in the mist a month ago,/ Like ghost of sleigh-bells in a ghost of snow." His analogy of the peepers and the bells does double duty. It unites a definite season with a particular sound. The "Hyla breed" does sound like shouting when you stand up close, and yet it is strange, too, how muted the sound is a field away. "Like ghost of sleigh-bells" is "true." He is just as accurate when he refers to "Musk/ From hidden grape-vine springs," or remarks with Keatsian sensitivity how "the petal of the rose/ It was that stung." One has to be only slightly versed in country things to notice such accuracy. Examples are plentiful in the *Complete Poems:* the lupine "living on sand and drouth"; the birch "though once they are bowed/ So low for long, they never right themselves"; the ovenbird "Loud, a mid-summer and a mid-wood bird"; night-hawks "each circling each with vague unearthly cry"; the buds of the purple-fringed orchid "that were pale as a ghost"; and "the leafless bloom of a plum is fresh and white"; turtle eggs are "Torpedo-like, with shell of gritty leather"; and he sees the woodpile where "Clematis/ Had wound strings round and round it like a bundle."

We find originality in expression among writers more frequently than originality in observation. Yet originality in observation is also what it takes to be well versed in country things. Once while reading his poems, Frost called attention to details which the average reader might not have observed in immediate experience. In "A Young Birch," he says, "The birch begins to crack its outer sheath/ Of baby green and show the white beneath,/ As whosoever likes the young and slight/ May well have noticed." "There is only one kind of birch that has white inner bark," he says. "Not many people would know this unless they looked carefully." He had in mind, he once told me, not the White Mountain birch, but the common birch. And he said, "I'd rather be right than wrong in such things." So he verified his observation by looking at birch copses in southern New England, to see if birches always do bend to left and right, as he said they did in "Birches." This is not only looking close; it is seeing, as Thoreau remarks, "What is to be seen." This example of his originality in observation confirms the third basic test in being well versed in country things.

An interesting sidelight in his observation of natural phenomena occurs in "The White-Tailed Hornet." Here he seems to be not only a natural observer but a critical one, satirically examining natural instinct. When, one day in his kitchen doorway, he sees a white-tailed hornet, apparently mistaking a nailhead and a huckleberry for its common prey the housefly, he wonders if human beings haven't paid too generously a compliment to the infallibility of instinct in insects. "Won't this whole instinct matter bear revision?" he asks. With this inquiry he takes off on a conjectural flight. Haven't we knuckled under to the lower creatures, he is suggesting, and in our attribution made them more worshipful, humorous, or conscientious than they have a right to appear? But, we query, just how serious is the poet? One risks misinterpreting his intent when the discussion of such a poem becomes solemn. Yet the poet does not appear to have tongue in cheek.

Accurate as he may be in observing a particular white-tailed hornet, insect reasoning power still comes off well this side of fallibility under the close scrutiny of such distinguished naturalists as Thomas Belt and Henry W. Bates. One can do worse than institute some "downward comparisons" by looking into *The Naturalist in Nicaragua* (1874), where Belt tells how he once saw a wide column of *Ecitons* (whom he places at the top of the *Articulata* in intelligence, and above wasps and bees and other *Hymenoptera*) cross a watercourse, along a small branch "not thicker than a goose quill," by widening the natural bridge to three times its width. A number of ants were clinging to it and to each other on each side, "over which the column passed three or four deep." "Except for this expedient," comments Belt, "they would have had to pass over in single file, and treble the time would have been consumed."

On another occasion, he noticed that the leaf-cutting ants (*Oecodoma*) which, in order to get to the trees for their food, had to pass over the rails of a mine tramway lost many of their followers when the passing trams crushed them. So they tunnelled underneath each rail, and when their tunnels were stopped up with stones, they did not venture again over the rails but set about making fresh tunnels underneath the rails. "Apparently," as Belt thought, "an order had gone forth, or a general understanding been come to, that the rails were not to be crossed." And in *The Naturalist on the Amazon* (1863), Bates tells how a small pale green sand wasp (*Bembex Ciliata*) in the Santarem would take a few turns in the air around its freshly excavated sand burrow to mark its position, and then it would dart into the forest after flies. On its return it would go directly to the burrow with the fly which it had caught, deposit it in the burrow and lay an egg on the body of the fly benumbed by a sting. This fly is to serve as food for the grub. Finally, the wasp seals the entrance to protect the grub. To Belt the activity of the Bembex, which Bates observed, was neither mysterious nor unintelligible. It was a mental process which differed from man's "only by its unerring certainty." And here, of course, the English naturalist and the American poet look away from each other; the former, a scientific naturalist, looks down, and the latter, "dangerously skeptic," looks a little up.

III

Frost disclaims being a regionalist, although it is not by chance that he finds himself living among plain, solid, nasalized Yankees, rooted in a region. Yet he is not a rural spokesman. Yankees are no smarter or more cussed than cotton choppers in Texas or orchardists in the Wenatchee Valley, and the tradition of the sharp Yankee trader like David Harum has run its course and petered out. Aspects of the New England Yankees are in his poems—especially in the longer ones. The present generation bears as much resemblance to David Harum or, by extension, to Simon Suggs, as it bears to Indian prototypes noted for sharp practices like the Unktomi of the Sioux, or the Old Man of the

Blackfoot. I find little tight-lipped terseness or emotional austerity in Frost's account of them. Instead, they have a neighborly love of talk, a notable lack of natural cunning, and, on occasion, let go in neurotic outbursts. This is the impression communicated in "In the Home Stretch," "Home Burial," "The Self-Seeker," "Snow," "The House-keeper." But when these people have their backs to the wall they can endure what has to be endured. Their environment makes them good at this.

Among themselves these Yankees are as garrulous as the witch of Coös, the relict of Toffile Lajway. Hill folk make good storytellers. The isolation and the leisurely pace of rural existence stir the imagination. When hill folk come into a crossroads store from up in the pass, it is too long a trip not to while away a little time in visiting over the cracker barrels. Old Indians, it is said, made a competition of yarning. Sitting by the tipi fire, they would, at the end of each long yarn, invite a better one. "Tie one to that!" they would challenge. Frost ties one in "Paul's Wife" and another in "Two Witches." Toffile's relict and the pauper witch of Grafton belong to the same tradition as the Negro conjure doctor who prepares his charms or "lucky bones" out of crayfish. All the conjure the witches of Coös country possess is hearsay power and circumstantial evidence to defend their "kiting" and encounters with skeletons. Although the witch of Coös uses no "madstones," she casts an effective spell and refers casually to her power to summon spirits. She has for evidence of a sharp encounter with a skeleton of her victim, the "imaginary" finger-pieces of the hand which, she says, she struck off when he came toward her. She inquires of her son, also a "believer": "Where did I see one of those pieces lately?/ Hand me my button-box—it must be there."

These "two old-believers"—mother and son—in "The Witch of Coös," says Frost, are "of the vintage that followed the war between the states. You always see lots of them after wars," hoping, one suspects, to establish communication with "the dear departed." Another witch, Arthur Amy's wife, the pauper witch of Grafton, is presumably of a similar vintage. A mocker, she takes herself less seriously than Toffile's widow. But her conjure is just as notional as that of Southern "believers." While some Negroes in the South bury under the back door-step, in anticipation of a successful year, the first boll of cotton that appears, the pauper witch of Grafton prevails on her accommodating husband to make a cast to gather conjure for her:

> Up where the trees grow short, the mosses tall,
> I made him gather me wet snow berries
> On slippery rocks beside a waterfall.
> I made him do it for me in the dark.
> And he liked everything I made him do.

Embedded atavistically in hill folk is a layer of superstition. Uncover this layer, and one bares curious beliefs: some salty and savored; others fantastic and whimsical. In the Arkansas "hollers" they lay shingles at the proper time of the moon to keep them from warping. Good Friday is the best time, they think, to plant a garden. Shake a tablecloth after sundown and you invite bad luck. (It is also a sign of slack housekeeping!) Cotton in the sugar bowl will bring good luck; in the pocket it keeps money away. When men live their lives close to rivers and cotton patches, their beliefs are inextricably intertwined with the inscrutable forces that determine their lives: a drought, a blight of insects, the local market for the crops they raise, the river itself.

One versed in country things will find different ways in which they are expressed in Frost's poetry. First, there are the saws which he quotes casually: "A little dust thrown in the eyes,/ Keeps a man from growing wise." "We all must eat our peck of gold." "It's knowing what to do with things that counts." Secondly, there are wise thoughts: "Good fences make good neighbors." "What we live by we die by."

In Frost's poetry one hears a good deal about the farm, orchard and sawmill, less about the smith with his hammer, the cooper with his maul, or the farmer with a bull-tongue plow. While the farmer worries about the seasonal ritual of sugaring off, plowing, planting, mowing, haying, harvesting and getting up the winter's wood supply, and the daily ritual of milking, his wife is occupied with churning, baking, washing, and in season, pickling and canning. In the spare time there are stumps to grub out, wood to chop and split, manure to haul, wall to lay, strawberry beds to weed and gardens to make. The intimacies of a farmer's life are his chopping block, tool shed, tote-road and weather vane. This is how it is north of Boston, on the ridgelands and in the valley bottoms.

Frost's tradition is turn-of-the-century rural. The cooper shops and tanneries are closed, and the farmer who first used a turning plow for spring breaking and then a light cultivator for cleaning corn middles now does his farming with a heavy-lugged tractor. Neither is there any reference to housewives who weave linen from the lint of wild nettles. Housewives occasionally spin and weave, but not with primitive materials. The rhythm of the seasonal ritual is the same for both the early and late nineteenth-century rural folk. Only the tempo is changed.

We read in the poems the cycle of the seasonal ritual. We glimpse the sugar bush where "the maples/ Stood uniform in buckets, and the steam/ Of sap and snow rolled off the sugar house." This is early spring and the tasks that follow sugaring off are cleaning the pasture spring and mending wall. After the plowing we put in the seed, and a little later, we stop to watch where "the sturdy seedling with arched body comes/ Shouldering its way and shedding the earth crumbs." Now it is time to bush the peas and whet the scythe before the first mowing in June.

They say that what one hears in *The Pickwick Papers* is the sound of coach-horns. In *Complete Poems* it is the sound of the mower's scythe "whispering to the ground," a sound that is part of the year's ritual in the grassy places of the world. In August, all hands turn to pick blueberries; in September, everyone is busy in the apple orchard until a man's sleep is troubled by fatigue. ("For I have had too much/ Of apple-picking: I am overtired/ Of the great harvest I myself desired.") In midautumn, the leaves are raked up ("I may load and unload/ Again and again/ Till I fill the whole shed,/ And what have I then?") And, in November, the buzz saw snarls and rattles in the yard while "stove-length sticks of wood" are cut for the winter fires. In December, the young fir balsams go for the Christian trade—"The trial by market everything must come to." Then country people burrow in their "strategic retreats" for the long winter, reconciled, perhaps, to the fact that "You can't get too much winter in the winter." The whiplash northwinds bite, and the rabbits girdle the tender bark on wild apple trees in some "Winter Eden." In spring the thawing wind will "Bring the singer, bring the nester;/ Give the buried flower a dream;/ Make the settled snow-bank steam;/ Find the brown beneath the white." The seasons have again come full circle.

One has to be versed in country things to see, as Frost has, the imperceptible changes. "Each season," says Thoreau, "is but an infinitesimal point. It no sooner comes than it is gone. It has no duration." He adds, "It simply gives a tone and hue to my thought." "The Oven Bird" identifies the passing of a season quite as definitely as "The Onset" marks the advent of a new one. ("Always the same, when on a fated night/ At last the gathered snow lets down as white/ As may be in dark woods, and with a song/ It shall not make again all winter long/ Of hissing on the yet uncovered ground.") The faint syllabic whisper of the season's first wind-blown snow in the dry, tough, frozen grasses is a characteristic sound in this country. There is the moment in spring familiar to every country dweller when winter breaks. It is the time— the infinitesimal point, as it were—when the sun on the hillside lets go "Ten million silver lizards out of snow."

Seasons are sharply distinguishable in New England: dawdling springs, erratic summers, gaudy falls and implacable winters. These differences are more felt than remarked upon in Frost's poetry where evocation is creation. Like all good describers, he lets you see and feel without multiple detail. What you feel is blowing rain, and the loneliness of life in a small, shabby backcountry village, snug in a mountain pocket. What you see is the season folded in a flower and the weather in a tanned leaf clinging fast to its branch from one season to the next, and the narrow well-beaten woodchuck runways in upland pastures. Or you hear the hum of insects above the breathing quietness of a still summer's night, and the sound of the first snow skirring in the stubble, or boulders in a flooded streambed bumping their heads together dully. It always seems remarkable that without so much as mentioning it Frost is able to communicate the haunting sweet-sadness in the hermit thrush's note at evening, heard in darkening wood aisles. "Far in the pillared dark/ Thrush music went—/ Almost like a call to come in/ To the dark and lament." The sound is communicated, not by descriptive identification of the bird's note but by the feeling evoked. Evocation, we repeat, is creation, and incantation such as this is the effect of creation. A mountain forest is like an amplifying shell for one hermit thrush, increasing its musical resonance into cool, sweet, variable, well-defined and always haunting notes.

The need of being versed in country things also extends to the

vocations of the people and what they measure a man's skill by. Out on
the Oregon Trail, Parkman thought the only necessaries were a horse,
a rifle and a knife. A man was measured by how he handled those three
necessaries. Those who fish along the muddy runs and creeks in the
Midwest and South are measured by the string of crappies or cats, blue-
gills or carp they bring home. In the Kentucky mountains a man's skill
is in his quickness with the trigger of the squirrel rifle at thirty paces.
In the Arkansas country a man is measured by the way he handles a
gun or "reads signs" along the creek banks or finds stray mules. North
of Boston you are measured on a farm by the way you handle a plow or
a tractor, a cow or an ax. The code is briefer than the shorter catechism.
"The hand that knows his business won't be told/ To work better or
faster—those two things." The man who builds a load of hay isn't to
be interfered with, but if he fails to stack it well, he will have a sharp
critic. For every man is your peer on a farm. Similarly in the lumber
camps. While splitting "good blocks of beech" in the yard, the poet
knows the lumberjack can and will judge him first as an ax-man. "Except as a fellow handled an ax,/ They had no way of knowing a fool."
So with an air of marked respect Frost listens to Baptiste assert the
superiority of hickory for ax-helves—"good hick'ry what's grow
crooked./ De second growt' I cut myself—tough, tough!" Ash, they say,
for hammer handles because it cracks before it breaks, but hickory for
ax handles, although it usually breaks without warning. And black
gum for plowshares and walunt for gunstocks! One has to be versed in
country things to know what Baptiste prefers and why.

IV

There is in Frost's attitude toward nature an enkindling humor
that identifies his viewpoint and modifies the impersonality which he
recognizes in nature's forces. He does not show a solemn face; he is on
good terms with nature; he does not blame it as an oppressor of mankind. Like Thoreau, he feels no estrangement from the inalienable
earth. "The way of understanding," he says, "is partly mirth." A writer
might borrow a good many things from his forerunners, but not a sense
of humor, and never a particular articulation of it. Drollery is becoming
to, even as it identifies, his world of nature where grasshoppers are
waggish and cows sometimes get a jag on in apple time.

His nature poems are not revelations. He is on the side of the exact observers. In lieu of mystical vibrations, there are strong sensory responses in his poems. The choice between German transcendentalism and Greek clarity would not be difficult to him. His vitality is too earthy to be attracted by mysticism. The challenge he accepts is to represent natural phenomena in the hard, clear light of the common day—a sufficient test, it is true, for all the refinements of any art. Like all who ballast their art with fact, he is, as already identified, a verifiable realist. His insights are invariably rational, and what he succeeds in doing is what every writer has to do—establish his own reality. Consequently, his world of reality is not a transcription of a thing directly observed, such as we see in Thomas Sheeler's paintings; it is an imaginative transmutation.

The center of focus in his world of reality is always mankind in spite of searching glimpses of metaphysical meanings in nature. In "Desert Places" what concerns the poet is a psychological situation involving man's relationship to the immediate world in which he finds himself. A similar human relationship motivates other nature lyrics like "Tree at My Window" or "Sand Dunes." "Spring Pools" is the exception which only proves the rule. He never stresses, like Coleridge, the detachment of man from nature. "O Lady! we receive but what we give/ And in our life alone does nature live." Nor does he, like Matthew Arnold, seek to exalt man by deprecating nature. "Know, man hath all which Nature hath, but more . . ./ Man must begin, know this, where Nature ends;/ Nature and man can never be fast friends." It is not by chance that Frost's epigraph to "Lucretius versus the Lake Poets" is from Landor. "Nature I loved; and next to Nature, Art" may be taken as a scale in his hierarchy. He may place man at the top but it is not because, like the overwrought Arnold, he thinks man and nature cannot be fast friends. Nor is it because, like the dejected Coleridge, he believes that only in our life does nature live.

Since the contest between man and nature is not a grim one in New England, only rarely, as in the extra-New England poem "Once by the Pacific," is there the appearance of a menacing sentience which Hardy and Melville felt. North of Boston nature is not usually regarded as an "untameable Ishmaelitish thing." Nature is a positive force, and when, in "The Last Mowing," the meadow is left unmowed, and when, in

"The Birthplace," the mountain farm is abandoned, flowers and woods seed in rapidly and nature reclaims its own. But this is all pretty tame in view of the potential wrath of wind and water.

Frost's relationship to the traditional attitudes toward nature in poetry is interesting. A seventeenth-century English poet like Vaughan makes us aware, although not for the first time in the history of poetry, of the spiritual aspects of nature. The serenity of an ineffable moonlit night moves him. "I saw," he says, "Eternity the other night,/ Like a great Ring of pure and endless light,/ All calm, as it was bright." An eighteenth-century poet, like Collins, expands our range to include the physical aspects in the natural world when at evening he is sensitively aware:

> Now air is hush'd, save when the weak-eyed bat
> With short, shrill shriek, flits by on leathern wing;
>   Or when the beetle winds
>   His small but sullen horn,
> As oft he rises 'midst the twilight path. . . .

John Clare joyously proclaims that song's eternity is in nature:

> Melodies of earth and sky,
> Here they be.

The early nineteenth-century romantic poet, like Wordsworth, in his awareness of a presence that disturbs him with joy of elevated thoughts, increases our range of perception by touching chords of natural piety. He feels:

>   . . . a sense sublime
> Of something far more deeply interfused,
> Whose dwelling is the light of setting suns,
> And the round ocean and the living air,
> And the blue sky, and in the mind of man:
> A motion and a spirit, that impells
> All thinking things, all objects of all thought,
> And rolls through all things.

In the history of verse it is invalid to claim that Frost has expanded the range of man's perceptions in any of these three ways. Yet he has succeeded in intensifying each one of these—the spiritual, the physical and the metaphysical. On one level "Good-by and Keep Cold" may be a parable about education. On another level, it suggests that the trees man has domesticated in his apple orchard are, like himself, inseparable parts of an organic natural universe, and, in consequence, there is a limit to what man can do in protecting them after they have been planted and nurtured. The implication is not that the forces of nature are arrayed in opposition to man, but that he has learned to trust in ultimates beyond himself. Half playfully, the poet says, "Something has to be left to God." The sentence could carry an intonation of rebuke *if* man thinks he controls all. This is the core of what Frost contributes to our range of perception—a no less vivid apprehension of the spiritual for its temperateness than the lines from Vaughan. The intensification of man's range of perception at the physical level (as in "Birches") is a commonplace in this poet. At the metaphysical level, he is aware of the vast outer world of stars and galaxies (as in "The Star-Splitter") and of the inner world of man (as in "The Bear") without tipping the balance!

It is precisely in such equilibration that Frost's most idiosyncratic quality as man *and* poet is apparent: the quality of temperate lucidity —as of things seen or moods realized. He is a temperate man and the poems reflect temperateness. Neither, at one extreme, do his poems show any astonishment; nor, at the other, is there dismissal, although most certainly there is vigorous satire. The poetry also reflects clear-eyed, not hard-eyed, lucidity. It has to do with grief not grievances. What the poet feels is warm with emotion. What he sees lights up with meaning. His poetry avoids the solemnity of Bryant and the indefatigable prolixity of Wordsworth. He possesses the enabling grace of Yankee humor and uncommon good sense. No less than Bryant he realizes the stakes are mortal but he *plays* for them, he doesn't agonize over them.

Frost's significance as a nature poet consists not only in the attribution of intrinsic value to spring pools or mowing fields, to dark woods or winterbound orchard, but also in his ability to communicate these values to the common consciousness. The reality is his intimate association with nature and man, but the truth is what he makes of this association in his art without depending upon extrinsic accessories, like the "spirits" of nature in Milton, or mythological associations in

Spenser, or Keatsian personifications. He is noticeably free of deriva-
tions from traditional nature poets. With the exception of the Theoc-
ritan *dramatis personae* in "Build Soil," there are no hedgerows and
coppices, wood-gods and tabors.

Complete Poems is warm with the images of intense beauty nature
makes in the mind of a sensibilitist. There is a perceptible pulse in
everything he writes which makes his grammar of nature bear a little
toward the verb. It is precisely these active images with the voice-tones
identifying them, and the truth to fact which they represent, that makes
Frost's nature poetry a contribution to literature. His fundamental
knowledge is gleaned from so rich a natural background readers of
Complete Poems find their awareness of the world of nature sharpened
and intensified.

Nature is the medium by which the human spirit extends its
growth, the soil in which it develops. Realizing this fact, Frost has
not substituted the meanings of art for the meanings of nature, but
found in nature the direct sources which his art has ordered and clari-
fied. This is the significance of his poetic effort: a cultivation (rather
than as in Thoreau a naturalization) of the human spirit in the world
of nature.

2. Realmist

The loggerhead turtle lays its eggs on a sandy shore, and when the young
ones are hatched out they dig their way to the surface and make for the sea. . . .
[They] have an inborn bias to make for the more illumined horizon. . . . Com-
paring great things with little, we may liken man to loggerheads; he has, on the
whole, a bias for making toward the more illumined horizon.

SIR J. ARTHUR THOMSON: *The New World of Science*

Evidences of Frost's topical interest in social, economic and political
issues appear early—*New Hampshire* is a prime example—and increase
sharply in the later poetry. "Departmental" forthrightly criticizes
regimentation, and "To a Thinker" governmental extremes. "The Bear"

twits our unbalanced enthusiasms in any direction, and "A Lone Striker" renounces machine service for free wheeling on nature's open roads. "The Lesson for Today" compares medieval and modern shades of historical darkness, and decides that men have tried "to grasp with too much social fact/ Too large a situation." "A Case for Jefferson" taunts reformers who are "Freudian Viennese by night," and by day "Marxian Muscovite." Overtones of Frost's topical reactions in an epoch of stainless steel, plastics and astrophysics, of New Deals, Fair Deals and T.V.A.'s, of isolationism and internationalism, of death by war and death by automobiles are heard in "Haec Fabula Docet," "The Planners," "U.S. 1946 King's X," "Bursting Rapture," "A Considerable Speck," "To a Young Wretch," "A Roadside Stand."

Although Frost does express "opinionations," he does not pose as a prophet of industrial indices or an analyst of *Realpolitik*. A close examination of "Build Soil" will confirm that he is a "realmist." In the light of social planning during Presdent Roosevelt's administration of the New Deal, Frost's solution of the basic problem of the under-privileged minorities is no more specific than Emerson's solution of the slavery issue in the "Ode, Inscribed to W. H. Channing." Emerson would liberate the imprisoned thoughts in himself; Frost bids us to "a one-man revolution" because "we're too unseparate out among each other" and "inside in is where we've got to get." There is nothing peculiarly atypical or modish in this reaction. Like Emerson, he is a prober into the nature of things and, as becomes a philosophic poet, detached from but not elevated above the concerns of his time. "But these are universals, not confined/ To any one time, place, or human kind," he says in "The Lesson for Today." Because his vision is an actualist's, not a dreamer's, ideal relationships in utopian spheres of social behavior only invite his mockery. "The opposite of civilization," he thinks, "is utopia," and we know by the way he says it that he nourishes the limited expectations of the former rather than the vast improbabilities of the latter. He derides unsparingly and equally the socialistic anthill and the utopian Palace of Crystal. "I own I never really warmed/ To the reformers or reformed."

An independent middle-of-the-roader, he says humorously, "I never dared be radical when young/ For fear it would make me conservative when old." In "Build Soil" he reminds us that he was

"brought up/ A state-rights free-trade Democrat," but he has not remained one. Manoeuvring himself so he can be free to try new ideas, his resourcefulness is intellectual and spiritual; the deeper commitment is to his art. His reactions to politics and social planning are conditioned by his fundamental caution and reserve. He is assertive, it is true, rather than tentative, but he is cautious, too, and a master at retreat, a tactic by which notable victories have been won in and out of military campaigns. A careful listener, when he reports anything his admission is, out of *Hamlet,* "So I have heard and do in part believe it." Sagaciously, he would not abandon a belief because "it ceases to be true." "Cling to it long enough, and not a doubt/ It will turn true again, for so it goes." As a weigher and considerer, he argues disinterestedly from an independent viewpoint. Once while discussing the Negro question, he said characteristically, "I am neither for nor against [the Negro]."

Basic in his attitude is his doctrine of counter-wisdom. An expansive imagination matches opposites. "All truth," he says, "is dialogue." He acknowledges the existence of two sides, has a conviction about the comparative importance of each, and a reasonable skepticism of the person who cannot recognize clearly the difference between these sides when they appear in varying disguises and masquerades. Those seduced in our time by the so-called "higher treason" represent to him not a failure in sentiment but a falure in intellect. Unfooled by fashionable allegiances and ingrown alliances, he suspends judgment until he is sure of his ground. "I have a mind myself, and recognize mind," he says, "when I meet with it in any guise." He is more interested in becoming acquainted with the world than in attempting to change it. This is the drift of his poetry—toward understanding rather than reform.

Any sociologist or economist bent on discovering something specific in Frost's poetry about the hygiene of backcountry people, or the problems of the poor farmer on submarginal land, or the operation of social security among the New Hampshire mill workers must be immediately disabused in his intent. But if he is looking for the larger issue, he will not be disappointed.

One of the central issues is the conflict within the individual between his conscience and his natural self, a conflict Mark Twain dramatized in *Huckleberry Finn*. It is a personal issue which involves all the others, for at all points we impinge on the outside world:

> The world's one globe, human society
> Another softer globe that slightly flattened
> Rests on the world, and clinging slowly rolls.

Wars, he says, are "but politics/ Transformed from chronic to acute and bloody." If wars are evil, and indubitably they are, the reason for them is not outside but inside the human heart. And it is there we will possibly find the cure:

> But inside in is where we've got to get
> My friends all know I'm interpersonal.
> But long before I'm interpersonal
> Away 'way down inside I'm personal.

Tityrus suggests that "Bounds should be set/ To ingenuity for being so cruel/ In bringing changes unheralded on the unready." Human progress comes from self-discovery and self-conquest. In "Build Soil" he recommends, if Tityrus is the poet's alter ego, to get "inside in."

> Build Soil. Turn the farm in upon itself
> Until it can contain itself no more,
> But sweating-full, drips wine and oil a little.
> I will go to my run-out social mind
> And be as unsocial with it as I can.
> The thought I have, and my first impulse is
> To take to market—I will turn it under.
> The thought from that thought—I will turn it under
> And so on to the limit of my nature.
> We are too much out, and if we won't draw in
> We shall be driven in. . . .

A second issue equally formidable is the conflict between the individual and social forces. This issue has two aspects: the relationship of the individual to his fellow man, and the relationship of the individual to the state. Frost advocates a responsible human freedom to oppose authoritarianism, whether of state, party, creed or person. And he is just as firmly opposed to regimentation as he is to standardization, or mechanization and uniformity. Three reactions compound his viewpoint:

Pressed into service means pressed out of shape.
                                    "The Self-Seeker"

He never would assume that he'd
Be any institution's need.
                                    "A Lone Striker"

I have none of the tenderer-than-thou
Collectivistic regimenting love
With which the modern world is being swept.
                                    "A Considerable Speck"

What has he to offer us here? Does he see man as beset by the institutions of society, the product of man's own endeavors? If he does, is the corrective within the power of man? Does he believe that, if man created these conditions, he can change either his environment or the institutions, and in changing them legislate virtue? Or, does he think the only possibility is to alter human nature?

Frost believes in private initiative and no coddling; he applauds energy when it is directed to human ends; he accepts the products of technology when they advance self-growth. He knows "hunger is not debatable," and that freedom from fear is earned not given. In 1936 he contended that the New Deal administration was doing a little good too hastily. It hadn't properly sized up the situation—the needs of the people and its capacity to satisfy them. It was too much "presto chango." The result would be ameliorative but not curative. Good ideas were Old Age Pensions and Unemployment Insurance. Then he suggested a stimulating idea: that since justice was the basis of government, socialism would never replace existing forms of government. "Socialism," he contended, "is only an ingredient of government." "Build Soil—A political pastoral" compresses this idea:

               For socialism is
        An element in any government.
        There's no such thing as socialism pure—
        Except as an abstraction of the mind.
        There's only democratic socialism
        Monarchic socialism—oligarchic,
        The last being what they seem to have in Russia.
        You often get it most in monarchy,
        Least in democracy.

There is, as he states it, either *patria* or *matria,* and socialism is more mothering than it is fathering. "In socialism we are all treated by our mother, not by our father who is sterner stuff." The problem today— post-World War II—is "how to crowd and still be kind," and he says, "When there's distress there's a tendency to snuggle up. And we can stand that only a short time, then we become irritated."

By logical extension, he opposes fascistic *Realpolitik* because a dictator in wielding power tyrannically violates the sanctity of human justice. In the democratic pantheon of American heroes, he lauds Washington as a truly great man, we recall, because he refused dictatorship. Benevolent despots are rare, indeed. Strictly speaking, the Greek tyrant, like Peisistratus, was not a dictator. The power vested in one man stood for the rights of the many against the few. Yet political progress, Frost thinks, is not linear but cyclical. The cycle starts with an absolute monarchy, passes to a limited monarchy, then to democracy, and finally to the mob, and from the mob to the herogod, from which point it starts to rotate again. A relaxation of governmental will leads inevitably to a tyranny of individual wills and the encroachment of one will—presumably the stronger—upon another. Since the basis of government is justice and the basis of justice is law, there must be an attempt to balance the will of the many who are governed by the will of the few who govern. The inscription on the Supreme Court building at Washington reads: "Equal justice for all under law." When rulers rule lawfully, justice prevails and good government results. When justice grows too severe, the ingredient of socialism with its virtue of mercy should be applied. As a form of government, socialism would lead to the decline in justice when mercy is exalted above it. So, he thinks, the nub of democracy should be "power divided against itself," illustrated in our government by the legislative body which checks the executive while the judiciary balances them both. He refers to Pericles's great oration in Thucydides's *History* as a dramatic touchstone. "It's [democracy] all there," he says; "it hasn't changed any." A sound democrat, by his own definition of democrat, is "an equalitarian"—"like Oliver Cromwell." The test of a democrat is "if you have never said anything snobbish against trial by jury." What he likes to see is that kind of freedom where there is an adventure of ideas in the actions of men. It must be an adventure where the initiative and the enterprise and the power are not exploited but controlled for the general welfare. In *A Masque of Mercy,* Keeper recommends, "Live and let live, believe and let believe."

A third central issue in our time is the relationship of the individual to the universe, a relationship which will be more fully discussed in the following section. The advances in the biological sciences have either made man feel dwarfed by the basic facts of existence, or, at the opposite extreme, they have made him assume arrogantly that he is the overlord of his own destiny, and that he exists to satisfy his own desires without respect to anyone else. Reflecting on the latter viewpoint, C. E. M. Joad writes, "The gods take their revenge against man's impatience. He is cast down and through suffering made to realize his true nature. In the chaos and confusion he recognizes the need for a higher reality than his own." Although Frost doesn't pass judgment on his age, "The Lesson for Today" indicates that he sees the issue clearly enough. He proffers common sense. "Seek converse common cause and brotherhood," he says, "with poets who could calmly take the fate/ Of being born at once too early and late." Who would they be? Certainly one of them would be Lucretius. He also says, "You would not think you knew enough to judge/ The age when full upon you. That's my point." Indeed, it is very much *his* point.

II

How does Frost react to the universe as science presents it to us? A finite universe, governed by the laws of Riemann's geometry, its energy continues to assume a less available form in the passage of time. Shadowy, wave-like, particle-like electrons are the ultimate material constituents, familiar but elusive. Their behavior can be studied, but their substance cannot be pictured. We can deal with these electrons only by mathematical symbols. Not alone "an age of anxiety," it is also an age of abstraction, of electrons. Science which has exorcised so many superstitions during the last couple of centuries seems now to have spooked the universe with its own hypothetical magic of mathematical formulae like Einstein's formula: $E = MC^2$ or Energy equals Mass times the velocity of light squared.

If it seems to be an unfriendly universe, our theoretical scientists, like Schrödinger and Jeans, Max Planck and Eddington, Millikan and Einstein, are hardly to blame. They tell us what they have discovered. To Bertrand Russell and in historical summaries like Carl Becker's *The Heavenly City* the universe appears unfriendly. First, Russell says:

That man is the product of causes which had no prevision of the end they were achieving; that his origin, his growth, his hopes and fears, his loves and beliefs, are but the outcome of accidental collocations of atoms; that no fire, no heroism, no intensity of thought and feeling, can preserve an individual life beyond the grave; that all the labours of the ages, all the devotion, all the inspiration, all the noon-day brightness of human genius, are destined to extinction in the vast death of the solar system, and that the whole temple of Man's achievement must inevitably be buried beneath the debris of a universe in ruins—all these things, if not quite beyond dispute, are yet so nearly certain, that no philosophy which rejects them can hope to stand.

Now Becker:

What is man that the electron should be mindful of him! Man is but a foundling in the cosmos, abandoned by the forces that created him. Unparented, unassisted and undirected by omniscient or benevolent authority, he must fend for himself, and with the aid of his own limited intelligence find his way about in an indifferent universe.

In view of this alien universe, how does poetry serve man's needs? The basis of science is observation, experiment and the recording of data. Its "point of drive" is disinterested curiosity. Its aim is to find out the fundamental principles, or natural laws, or uniformities underlying the whole. Science advances, as Jeans says, "by providing a succession of approximations to truth, each more accurate than the last, but each capable of endless degrees of higher accuracy." On the other hand, poetry is a matter of passion *and* thought; it arouses our imagination and in making us feel and think, it influences our attitude toward life. Ezra Pound refers to the function of literature as *"nutrition of impulse,"* by which he means a force that eases the mind of strain and feeds it and incites us to continue living. Frost says poetry is "words that have become deeds." Words become deeds and nutritive to impulse when the feeling rises to passion as in Shelley's "The Mask of Anarchy":

> Rise like Lions after slumber
> In unvanquishable number,
> Shake your chains to earth like dew
> Which in sleep had fallen on you—
> Ye are many—they are few.

Or, as in Milton's cry of vengeance for the Protestants slaughtered in the valleys of the Vaudois by the French soldiers who fled from Cromwell:

> Avenge, O Lord, thy slaughter'd Saints, whose bones
> Lie scattered on the Alpine mountains cold;
> Ev'n then who kept thy truth so pure of old,
> When all our Fathers worship't Stocks and Stones,
> Forget not: . . . .

It is the purpose of poetry to whet our sensibilities and make us more alive by intensifying our feelings. It can invigorate our whole consciousness and quicken intellectual and aesthetic values by the perception of beauty. Ethical values originate when poetry arouses us to actions. Shelley is wise when he says "the great instrument of moral good is the imagination and poetry administers to the effect (*i.e.,* moral good) by acting upon the cause (*i.e.,* the imagination)."

Science is not concerned with how we feel. Nor does it contribute quite as directly as poetry does to the sense of personal dignity. The latter is incalculably important in stirring man's energy to performance, in the Frostian sense of the word. Yet there is no basic antagonism between science and poetry. They are complementary, like a pair of watch hands. "One of the glories of science," Frost says, "is that it is one part of the humanities." He cites as an example one of his favorite books, Darwin's *The Voyage of the Beagle.* "It ought to be everybody's book;" it "comes into literature on the science side." What he resents is the intrusion of science into things that aren't science. Science appears to have little to do with the *Lebensraum* of the spirit; poetry does. Poetry's role is not only expressing uncommonly what we commonly think and feel; it also gives form and direction to thought and feeling. For when the poem is read imaginatively, a vicarious power is infused, and the poet generates power in the reader by evoking conceptual images.

"I was talking with a college president," says Frost, "and I inquired, 'What is the difference between science and poetry?'" "In the first place," the college president replied, "science is exact." "If that's what you're going to say about it," retorted Frost, "I'll go home." Poetry can be exact in a way that even a college president with a preference for science might recognize. "You might say science and poetry are exact in different ways," Frost explains. "Just what is the exactness of science and poetry? They go together. Poetry comes in haphazard among all the things going on together—science, religion, nature, and history. Unsystematically! The poet has a scrappy mind. If he made a system and then wrote poetry, it would be no poetry at all. They [science and poetry] actually meet because poetry has long been called numbers, and science and poetry both are measure. The poet speaks in measure (which is) the core of them both." Science and poetry have in common not only measure; they also function through "anticipations by imagination"— in Newton's imaginative anticipation of gravitation in the fall of an apple, or Kekulé's anticipation of the benzene ring in the dream of revolving snakes, no less than in Tennyson's anticipation of Messerschmitt versus Spitfire in "nations' airy navies grappling in the central blue," or in Browning's "from life's minute beginnings, up at last/ To man" which, in "Paracelsus," anticipates Darwin by twenty-five years.

As anyone knows who has heard him discuss with brilliance Niels Bohr's atom or uranium and nuclear fission, Frost possesses a general knowledge of theoretical science. His approach to science is empirical. He knows we live in a world in which we can wear glass (or cellulose fibers), hear with a stethoscope an ear of grain on a wheat stalk in its growth, hunt whales with radar, turn wood pulp into sugar, convert coal and oil into edible fats, construct houses of plastics, and counteract the diseases the flesh is heir to by vitamins, antibiotics and sulfa drugs. You would think the cleverness of science would steal the wonders from under poetry's nose. To assume this is to misunderstand poetry, which is still an immemorial wonder. Science, war, poetry, religion, art, politics —what is the point of drive in all of them? What is the will back of them? Frost inquires. He brings together the long forefingers of his two hands, pantomimically, and says again and again—"What is the point of drive? Take science; is it the point, or is it only a bend below the point?" He illustrates manually with the flex of one of his knuckles at the joint. What does science give us? Comfort, safety, security, material pleasures! What is its point of drive? The Alchemist's touchstone? Mechanical slaves? A push-button civilization? Disinterested curiosity? Science is at least "the fine point of daring" in our time.

What is the point of drive in himself? In his poetry? The difference between Frost and many of the formal scholars and most of the scientists is that he can make us realize what they only know. He combines the intuitive apprehension and the curiosity of the exact scientist. The feelers of his mind have eyes in them. His sight is exploratory and sees what is to be discovered, not only what is to be remembered. In some of the poems in *Steeple Bush* the feelers are perpendicular and asymptotic; "Astrometaphysical," for instance, and "The Fear of God." In "Any Size We Please" and "Why Wait for Science" the feelers of his sensibility are horizontal and touch material reality. So it is that he is sometimes little impressed by the implications in brute scientific data. Like Thoreau, he agrees that "a man has not seen a thing who has not felt it."

In "A Wish to Comply" he is mildly caustic about a non-Euclidean universe of mathematical formulae, Millikan motes and abstractions. Anything only one-hundred-thousandth of an inch in diameter isn't very obvious, is it?

> Did I see it go by,
> That Millikan mote?
>
> I rather suspect
> All I saw was the lid
> Going over my eye.
> I honestly think
> All I saw was a wink.

It may be conjectured who is laughing at whom? Whether Frost is laughing at experimental demonstration, or at the gullibility of mankind in wishing to comply with anything beyond immediate sight and retinal verification. "Did I see it go by,/ That Millikan mote?" He didn't and he knows he didn't, for a Millikan mote is the smallest measurable electric charge (which is produced by passing an electric current through a glass tube almost entirely exhausted of air). Millikan motes may be the lowest denominator of the basic stuff in the universe, well and good, but to Frost it is the effect they might have upon him that is important. And this is the point to the poem. "It is not the polypody in my pitcher or herbarium . . . that interests me. . . ." says Thoreau. "The important fact is its effect upon me."

There is one important difference between Frost and Thoreau that throws light on his relationship to science. In Frost's poetry, both levels —the physical and the metaphysical—are conjunctive and co-ordinate, and not paralleled as in Thoreau. The metaphysical grows out of the physical as in evolution the multicellular organism grows out of the unicellular organism. Carried a step further Frost's ideas synthesize the specific and the specific clarifies the idea, as in "A Wish to Comply." Because of this conjunctive association, his poetry is far more than an approximation of the fact. Or, rather, it is an approximation with all that one can pack into what is meant by approximation. By insight, not by exposition, the poet smashes the fact the way the atomic physicist smashes the atom. He renews his words, and releases their vitality until, like match-heads, they explode into light. When he succeeds in getting *all* the dimensions—perception, curiosity, clarity, accuracy, vividness and implication—he extends meaning as well as intensifies consciousness. This is far more than a clarification and an intensification of familiar data. He truly releases the specific to general significance, and, as he does so, gets the dimensions of a fact—its space, time and emotional context. He is, in effect, a vitalizer of the concrete. Like John Donne, Frost might justly say, "Make my dark poem light, and light." He shares with us a world in which the scientist's curiosity is a confirmation of the poet's wonder. The poet is not on the defensive in "Desert Places" or "Why Wait for Science." It is surely a world we make and not just one we find, and as certain as there is evolution, it is certain that one of the makers in our evolving universe is the poet. He is the one who makes us aware.

Thomas Henry Huxley called scientific thinking "organized common sense." Frost's thinking—which we shall call "poetic"—represents the intensification of *un*common sense. He operates in an area of consciousness where science has only tangential relevance—in the perception of beauty and in the awareness of experience at the deep levels of human consciousness. The poet's beauty not only makes luminous the familiar; it also enlightens a world of thought where we know what we feel and

feel what we know. In "Desert Places," Frost projects us a little unexpectedly but nevertheless very forcefully into interstellar space:

> Snow falling and night falling fast, oh, fast
> In a field I looked into going past,
> And the ground almost covered smooth in snow,
> But a few weeds and stubble showing last.

> The woods around it have it—it is theirs.
> All animals are smothered in their lairs.
> I am too absent-spirited to count;
> The loneliness includes me unawares.

> And lonely as it is that loneliness
> Will be more lonely ere it will be less—
> A blanker whiteness of benighted snow
> With no expression, nothing to express.

> They cannot scare me with their empty spaces
> Between stars—on stars where no human race is.
> I have it in me so much nearer home
> To scare myself with my own desert places.

Here he suggests a characteristic difference between poetry and science:
that the former operates in the realm of the imaginable, and the latter
in the realm of the unimaginable. We cannot take in the physical dimensions of the universe, as science reports it, and as the mathematicians and
physicists report it, so overwhelming is its size. Anything measurable
only in terms of millions of times bigger—as some stars are millions of
times bigger than the sun—or the age of the universe measured in terms
of thousands of millions of years is inconceivable. It has no longer personal meaning; only numerical association. So it is with "light years."
Size and time become only comparative symbols, hardly imaginable
conceptions. But a poet knows and respects his orientation in a particular stellar universe, which is, of course, only one of many other
stellar universes drifting in outer space. *"Le silence éternel de ces
espaces infinis m'effraie."* The silence of the infinite spaces terrifies
Pascal; it doesn't Frost.

"Desert Places" is not primarily a poem about cosmic or social
isolation. It is a poem about comparative relationship. Without bravado and with a strong sense of spiritual self-containment, the poet

adjusts our sights so that we see the importance of inner personal matters in comparison with outer impersonal ones. What is implied is the need not only to endure our fatefulness but to understand the bleakness—the absolute zero—of cosmic isolation. The interplanetary void doesn't "scare" the poet, and why should it, in comparison with his own "inward devils" and private "desert places" of startling solitariness? Frost reflects neither the inhumanity of Jeffers's universe, nor the recent edition of the impersonality of a scientific universe; only human relations concern him. This spiritual self-containment is the hard bone of the poet as man.

The mood of "Desert Places" is meditative. The attitude is shrewd and tough-minded. Its special qualities are concreteness, simplicity and directness. In intention it shows us human loneliness can be incredibly intense, and that it is not to be compared with the nonhuman vacuity of interstellar places.

The poem stems from the same root stalk of traditional forms as all of Frost's poems; it unfolds organically and its dynamism comes from its individual elements—image, sound, idea—being actively charged. The orginality is "the turn" which the poet gives the poem in the last stanza. (Here originally the second line of the last stanza read, interestingly enough: "Between stars—on *stars void of* human races." Frost substituted "where no" for "void of" and "race is" for "races.") Frost is not put off by the scientist's description of a finite universe. It is *personal* finiteness that interests him. So in "Skeptic" he uses an image the tightness of which is constricting—he feels the universe "like a caul in which I was born and still am wrapped." But as for the way cosmic things work, he is not greatly disturbed. Not an incurable, but a rugged and sometimes reluctant meliorist, he says:

> The play seems out for an almost infinite run.
> Don't mind a little thing like the actors fighting.
> The only thing I worry about is the sun.
> We'll all be all right if nothing goes wrong with the lighting.

III

In the seventeenth century the Puritans at Massachusetts Bay adapted in a new land a theology with its sanctions prominently embedded in St. Augustine's doctrine of conversion and Calvin's doctrine of predestination. They struck durable roots in the rugged American coastline, and Frost's two Biblicals—*A Masque of Reason* and *A Masque of Mercy*—are twentieth-century cuttings from the original root stalk at Massachusetts Bay Colony. But only cuttings, for to the adherent of Puritan orthodoxy Frost's religious liberalism is light refracted through a skeptic's prism. True to his native cautiousness the sanctions of his belief are not theological, but Renaissance humanistic. His religious temper—intuitive rather than logical in its metaphysical foundations—is blended of the pre-Socratic and the post-Platonic Lucretian. Once, when referring to the days of the great teachers of philosophy at Harvard in the last century—the days of Santayana, James, Munsterberg, Royce and Palmer—he remarked, "The older teachers had large minds that reached right out into the clear." He meant that they had not only intellectual but also spiritual bravery so that they could face the final terror of things. Very active in Frost's religious belief is spiritual daring counterbalanced by humility.

As it is unnecessary to examine his ideas on mass, force, duration, extension, substantiality to know in what his attitude toward science consists, so too it is unnecessary to probe his ideas on immortality, original guilt, redemption, grace, transfiguration, baptism and repentance in order to know his religious belief. Yet there are some questions to be answered seriatim: his conception of and attitude toward God; the nature of his relationship to Christian virtues; what he believes about historical religion; and the reflection of these ideas in his poetry.

Does his conception of God resemble Hegel's metaphysical "Absolute," Spencer's "Unknowable," or Arnold's "Power not ourselves that makes for righteousness"? In a classroom he once discussed *A Masque of Mercy* with a group of graduate students. Someone inquired about his slant toward God. "How do you mean God?" When all the popular notions are freely circulated, then he makes his own selection. "I'm always polite about other people's God," he said dryly. He conceived of God neither as an avenging Jehovah, nor as a Great Mathematician; neither as an enigma, nor as a cunning contriver; neither as a universal anomaly, nor as the inobvious. On the basis of his poetry, to Frost, God is an unseen *reality:* an ultimate divine wisdom beyond penultimate human wisdom. Certainly he does not conceive of a God of dread whose terror is inescapable. Neither is there a "poor intricated soul" upon whom to turn one's brooding eyes and pitying speech. Frost is not disturbed by the dread of God, and he is not obsessed by the writhing of the soul. Nor does he hold God culpable for man's sufferings in a world he never made.

There is also genuine humility in his attitude, which consists in respecting God's purposes and in being worthy of His respect. He does not pretend to understand these purposes as did Aquinas or Volney, the former of whom tells us, like an inside informant, that "all things subject to Divine providence are ruled and measured by the eternal law," and the latter of whom, like one of God's privy councilors, refers to "the regular and constant order of facts by which God rules the universe." Frost keeps well on this side of humility in identifying God's purposes. He is "an Old Testament believer" filled with honest doubt that what he has to offer of himself will be sufficiently acceptable in the sight of God. Any fear of personal insufficiency is not greater than the fear of unacceptability in God's eyes. He could trust himself, but would his poetry measure up? The world of human possibility intrigues Frost's mind as it draws his heart, but a world where one's belief in God is "a relationship you enter into with Him to bring about the future." What can Frost offer more than human wisdom? Will it be enough? This incertitude is what all must live with, and it measures one's piety as it measures trust in God's mercy:

> It is this backward motion toward the source,
> Against the stream, that most we see ourselves in,
> The tribute of the current to the source.
> It is from this in nature we are from.
> It is most us.

What virtues does he commend? Are they Christian virtues like faith, hope and charity, pagan ones like courage, loyalty and honor, or the Roman virtues like *auctoritas* and *pietas?* The virtues he most exalts are love and courage, respect for the human personality (*humanitas*) and respect for tradition (*mores*). What is the source of the virtue? Has personal salvation tormented him? Categorically, no! The Calvinists attempted to justify the ways of God to man through salvation by faith, and Franklin charted the good life on a progress sheet, reconciling a rational morality with the kingdom of God. Frost does not appear to worry about divine grace or Franklin's Art of Virtue. Works are another matter. We might say that works are his grace. Once he said that he always liked "those people who do things well, better than I like those who do people good. I'd rather be judged for doing well than for doing good." By *Complete Poems* you shall know him, and it is a very un-Franklin-like progress sheet.

What does he believe about historical religion? We recall his metaphor of the animated egg beater, which he pantomimed, whirling up the frothy stuff. ("Religion's the froth," he says. "All froth.") In his egg-beater analogy, he is thinking of sectarian theology. Religion, Frost said on another occasion, is when we can say that we aspire to "a full consent." One doesn't aspire to a full consent loaded down with dogma and infected with superstition. Aspiration is the keyword of the effort, as love is the thing itself. Religion is "a straining of the spirit forward to a wisdom beyond wisdom."

One of the most illuminating examples of his God belief is *A Masque of Mercy*. "All I do in this [*A Masque of Mercy*] is reach for something. All the rest is character interest," he once remarked. Like the first *Masque,* this one is a plateau of perspective which overlooks the wide background in his thinking. The *Masque's* drama pivots on what the poet reaches for. Jonah, Keeper, Jesse Bel and Paul —its *dramatis personae*—are all innocent. There isn't a villain among them. The theme, a counter-theme to justice, is mercy, and the point Frost makes is that "mercy is only to the undeserving; only justice is to the deserving." The two twists he gives the Biblical stories are: first, "Jonah couldn't trust God to be unmerciful to a runaway"; and second, "that the Sermon on the Mount was just a frame-up to insure universal failure."

Jesse Bel, Keeper's wife, is a bright, tart-tongued wisecracker, who is temporarily out of love as Jonah is out of faith. Keeper, the bookstore owner, is a moderate revolutionary, a Girondist—not a Jacobin— who would only change the personnel, not the system. A realistic humanitarian, he believes in living up to what can be lived up to. Jonah is a disillusioned prophet who has lost his faith not from anything that God had actually failed to do but from what he thinks God will fail to do at a showdown. He is the "universal fugitive" or "escapist." Paul is the converter who finds his immediate task is to enlighten the God fugitive Jonah on God's mercy-justice paradox. Paul says: "I'm going to make you see/ How relatively little justice matters." Jonah assumes he is under orders to carry out a vengeful Lord's will, by prophesying before an audience that God's threats against "the city evil" will be immediately realized. He runs out on his assumed obligation, but he is not feckless. Jonah's trust in God has been based on the assumption that He would be a stern Old Testament God. Quite on his own Jonah has decided that God won't get tough in a crisis:

> JONAH: I love and fear Him. Yes, but I fear for Him.
> I don't see how it can be to His interest
> This modern tendency I find in Him
> To take the punishment out of all failure
> To be strong, careful, thrifty, diligent,
> Anything we once thought we had to be.

Under the bantering assaults of Paul, the Exegete and Christian idealist, who upholds "the irresistible impossibility" of the Sermon on the Mount, Jonah turns from fugitive to quester, and from runaway to Pilgrim. What Jonah has been shown by Paul and Keeper are the kinds of justice which a man might embrace. First, there is a revolutionary mercy-crossed justice—an intentional justice—which is the aim of pressure groups so that affairs in the state, or the situation in the universe, might be equalized. Next, there is an evil-crossed justice in which a redistribution of everything is sought by violent revolution. Keeper suggests a third kind—the poet's brand. It is a star-crossed justice (which is not explained but which obviously differs from the paternalistic mercy-crossed justice, and from the violent revolutionary evil-crossed justice). It resembles the ideal Frost suggested in his re-action to democracy and the state. Perhaps it is a euphemism for divine justice; the old traditional fateful—it-is-in-our-stars—justice humanized. At least Jonah is aware where his confusion lies:

> I think my trouble's with the crisises
> Where mercy-crossed to me seemed evil-crossed.

To which Keeper replies, "Good for you, Jonah. That's what I've been saying." Paul, after Jonah finds his life through death, makes a significant summary which is the very essence of Frost's own position toward religion, in view of which all the other poems with religious implications are variants. Here the closely reasoned "argument" is sinewed by tough thought ligatures like the following:

PAUL:

We have to stay afraid deep in our souls
Our sacrifice, the best we have to offer,
And not our worst nor second best, our best,
Our very best, our lives laid down like Jonah's,
Our lives laid down in war and peace, may not
Be found acceptable in Heaven's sight.
And that they may be is the only prayer
Worth praying. May my sacrifice
Be found acceptable in Heaven's sight.

KEEPER: Let the lost millions pray it in the dark!
My failure is no different from Jonah's.
We both have lacked the courage in the heart
To overcome the fear within the soul
And go ahead to any accomplishment.
Courage is what it takes and takes the more of
Because the deeper fear is so eternal.

Nothing can make injustice just but mercy.

The ideas in the two New England Biblicals—these altar pieces of a nonsectarian poet—were motivated by the ascendancy of science. They represent the proponent of the humanistic tradition challenging science's right to worldly dominance. If the best that materialistic science can give us is the feeling that we are misbegotten children of an indifferent father, then Frost would shift the responsibility from God to man. In such a crisis of faith the redemption of God is the reality of man, but in the Middle Ages the converse was true and the redemption of man was contingent on the reality of God. Man's presence on earth may not be wholly explicable, but man has reason and he has courage and he has love. These are the explicators that help to justify the ways of man to God. The only fear is not of Hell, or the asylum, or the jail, or the poorhouse; it is the higher, greater fear, the fear of God, and the only medicine for the soul is God's mercy. Immedicable woe *is* then medicable to Frost. Says Keeper:

> I can see that the uncertainty
> In which we act is a severity,
> A cruelty, amounting to injustice
> That nothing but God's mercy can assuage.

Frost advocates God-belief because if man doesn't make his effort acceptable—if he doesn't trouble about the full consent—then he accepts no responsibilities and fulfills no obligations "to bring about the future."

Poetry, then, is intextured with religion and science. Once Frost was discussing contemporary symbols—the cross as symbol of religious salvation and the test tube as symbol of salvation through science. "Here are your two symbols," he suggested. "But where does poetry come in?" he was asked. In a burst of gaiety, he replied, "It's on the loose. Poetry is out having fun." He paused momentarily, and added, "It's interstitial!" This can stand as the poet's unstaunchable confidence in his art. The ultimate word "interstitial" is apposite; poetry *is* within the very tissues of life.

VII

DIMENSION IN TIME AND SPACE

A living art does not produce curiosity to be collected but spiritual necessaries to be diffused.

GEORGE SANTAYANA

1. Image as Signature

Often an image in poem or narrative stands for more than it clarifies in context. Charged with meaning by the intensity of the writer's thought and feeling, it takes on magnitude, like Faulkner's bear, symbol of the primitive American wilderness. "Then he saw the bear. It did not emerge, appear: it was there, immobile, fixed in green and windless noon's hot dappling . . . dimensionless against the dappled obscurity. . . . Then it was gone. It didn't walk into the woods. It faded, sank back into the wilderness without motion. . . ." Sometimes it is a recurrent image with many variations, like Walt Whitman's motile image of the ship. "To leave you O you solid motionless land, and entering a ship,/ To sail and sail and sail!" Sometimes as an image of identity it becomes a personification, like Stephen Crane's army in *The Red Badge of Courage,* that sleeps, thinks, rests, eats, camps, marches, fights. It might be a fixed image like Thoreau's "clear and deep green well" of Walden Pond which the reader looks into as *into* a human countenance, or *at* like Hemingway's bull ring—"high and white and concrete-looking in the sun." It can be intellectual like Emerson's master image of the expanding circle—"the profile of the sphere," which symbolizes "the moral fact of the Unattainable, the flying Perfect"; for around every circle it is possible to draw another *ad infinitum.* And it can be affectional, like the "big still river" which flows right through *Huckleberry Finn,* nourishing the urgent needs of the human spirit with freedom and adventure, activity and companionship.

Many or few, the image is a writer's signature, as eloquent and revealing as the Vincent inscribed on the Van Goghs, the butterflies decorating the Whistlers. The image as signature identifies the writer's work: the tower in Yeats, the moon in Keats, the cave in Shelley, the sun in Blake. Images of smoke and steel are ubiquitous in Sandburg's poetry; hawk and stone dominate Robinson Jeffers's. Sometimes the image is self-conscious as in Walt Whitman's "a kosmos, of Manhattan the son," or provocative like Thoreau's robust cock crowing "if only to wake [his] neighbors up," or playful and ingratiating like Emily Dickinson's self-projected image of a little Amherst tippler leaning against the sun.

But to serve as an identity tag is not the most important function of an image. An image is also a clarifier, appearing when meaning and manner are conjugal. It may have lyrical connotations like Willa Cather's memorable image of a plow glimpsed against the sun setting over the Nebraska prairie—"magnified across the distance by the horizontal light, it stood out . . . heroic in size, a picture writing on the sun." It may be allegoric like the images of Christian's wayfaring in *The Pilgrim's Progress,* legendary as in the Paul Bunyan story, mythic as in *Moby Dick,* mock heroic as in *Don Quixote,* or symbolic like the star in Shakespeare's sonnet "Let me not to the marriage of true minds"—one of Frost's favorite poems. The star is "the ever-fixed mark":

> That looks on tempests, and is never shaken;
> It is the star to every wandering bark
> Whose worth's unknown, although his height be taken.

Often the star image does double duty as in this sonnet; it juxtaposes the physically measurable ("although his height be taken") and the spiritually immeasurable ("whose worth's unknown")—the actual and the ideal, the specific and the abstract. Sometimes it may be found in retrospect to fulfill a third function, integrating the poetry *as a whole.*

The recurring image that enables the reader to identify, clarify and integrate the meaning in *Complete Poems* is the star. The star is one of the chief symbolic images in Frost's poetry, and how important the stars are to him is only too apparent to anyone who has seen him readily identify Altair, Vega and Antares, and other stars as though habitually he travelled by celestial navigation. The transit from earth to star is always within eyeshot as you read him.

When he speaks about "staking out your own sky," he refers to that interesting evening phenomenon of watching the sky break out in stars, and, to drive home the metaphor, he thinks that a writer stakes out the sky with his "bright ideas" as life darkens and as he grows older. As the evening deepens the stars form configurations—the Bull, Orion, the Northern Cross. "I like the constellations as they happen," he says, and we have the sense of his waiting for the individual stars to gather a collective meaning.

"One of the things you must see with me is the freedom of figures," he tells us. "One thing might be a clarification of stars," and to illustrate the freedom and the clarification he will read "The Star-Splitter" and "Come In." The star image releases its own symbolic significance. Individually the star poems are enlightening; together they are constellated and form a pattern in the poet's heavenly carpet. The figure in the carpet is a vision of experience.

Three fields of scientific knowledge—geology, archaeology and astronomy—most particularly the latter—are his special interests. He is a notable stargazer, sharing the distinction with Poe, Whitman and Jeffers in our literature. Less literary as a stargazer than the first, less effusive than the second, and less technically inclined than the third, he has looked at the stars with a scientist's curiosity and a poet's wonder.

"Stars" in *A Boy's Will* evokes the debate between Huxley, agnostic adherent of empirical science, and Bishop Wilberforce, exponent of religious orthodoxy:

> How countlessly they congregate
> O'er our tumultuous snow,
> Which flows in shapes as tall as trees
> When wintry winds do blow!—
>
> As if with keenness for our fate,
> Our faltering few steps on
> To white rest, and a place of rest
> Invisible at dawn,—
>
> And yet with neither love nor hate,
> Those stars like some snow-white
> Minerva's snow-white marble eyes
> Without the gift of sight.

The poet leans toward the empiricist position. Deriving his knowledge directly from reality, he is only faintly moved by the possibility of heavenly concern with human problems. He revises the subjective sentimentalism implicit in his first tentative impression of the stars that shine "as if with keenness for our fate" to the more realistic certainty of the coolly detached, that their light traverses outer space and appears "with neither love nor hate." There are the stars above; there is man below. And never the twain shall unite. This is a way of acquainting us with the nonhuman universe in which, if we do not feel like aliens, at least we are aware of no particular friendliness or greeting by any personal sign from the star-filled sky.

In *New Hampshire* there are three important stellar references: "A Star in a Stone-Boat," "The Star-Splitter," and "I Will Sing You One-O." The first playfully muses on the possibility of a shooting star, or meteorite, falling in a farmer's field, and unwittingly being drawn in a stone-boat and lodged in a stone wall. The poet confesses:

> Some may know what they seek in school and church,
> And why they seek it there; for what I search
> I must go measuring stone walls, perch on perch;

Of the displaced meteorite, he says dryly and with becoming humility:

> Such as it is, it promises the prize
> Of the one world complete in any size
> That I am like to compass, fool or wise.

"The Star-Splitter," a rustic nocturne of the narrative sort, tells how Brad McLaughlin "To satisfy a life-long curiosity/ About our place among the infinities" burned down his house "for the fire insurance/ And spent the proceeds on a telescope." Earning his living as an under-ticket-agent at the Concord (New Hampshire) railroad station, nightly he gazed at the stars through the "velvet black" brass barrel of his telescope. He named the telescope "the Star-Splitter":

> Because it didn't do a thing but split
> A star in two or three the way you split
> A globule of quicksilver in your hand
> With one stroke of your finger in the middle.

Two images reflected in these poems set them off from "Stars." There is Yankee whimsy in the former; humor of situation prevails in the latter. Solid common sense again restrains the poet from overdoing the image in either poem. The closing lines in "The Star-Splitter" intensify Frost's awareness of the separation of man from the universe, a dichotomy which "Stars" underscores. Frost reacts realistically. The chief change in the early poem and the later ones is in tone. Seriousness gives way to playfulness, and certainly to self-mocking interrogation. In "The Star-Splitter" Frost rhetorically asks:

> We've looked and looked, but after all where are we?
> Do we know any better where we are,
> And how it stands between the night tonight
> And a man with a smoky lantern chimney?
> How different from the way it ever stood?

The stellar image in *New Hampshire* which goes deepest is in "I Will Sing You One-O." Hearing in the night a clock in a tower and one in a steeple strike one, the poet thinks of terrestrial and heavenly time. The striking clock ". . . spoke of the sun/ And moon and stars,/ Saturn and Mars/ And Jupiter," and the constellations "spoke for the clock/ With whose vast wheels/ Theirs interlock." Like George Meredith's recognition of "unalterable law" in "Lucifer in Starlight," Frost perceives a human oneness that not only is related to but synchronizes with universal unalterable oneness. "I Will Sing You One-O" differs not only in form but in tone and attitude from the earlier star poems. It is assertive and speculative rather than interrogatory and gently mocking. Moreover, it shows perceptive awareness of unity; it is not haunted by the spectre of separation. The eye of the poet's mind reaches right out beyond the stratosphere into the astronomic universe where changelessness contrasts ironically with the history of man's apparent changelessness. It is as though Frost said, "It is lucky for us that the universe has not altered, and it is not lucky that man has perversely dragged down man and one nation another." The poem is more personal than "Stars." In "Stars" Frost was the spokesman of the *Zeitgeist;* in "I Will Sing You One-O" he is speaking for himself, as he sees things *sub specie aeternitatis.* Metaphysical breadth increasingly characterizes Frost's sidereal slant, and buoyant humor lurks in the texture of the phrase. The stellar image is not always grave; it is now an image humanized by laughter.

In *West-Running Brook* the poet responds with empathy to Sirius and its fellow stars in "Canis Major." His burst of euphoria is exuberant. He identifies the constellation; he describes it in heavenly motion; he asserts his humble (not abject) spirit joyously:

> I'm a poor underdog,
> But tonight I will bark
> With the great Overdog
> That romps through the dark.

In the sonnet "On Looking Up by Chance at the Constellations," he re-emphasizes the attitude of universal calm which prevails beyond the fret and fever of man's rugged activities in historical time and space. The stars in their courses will not greatly disturb our mundane preoccupations, he is saying. The later poems reflect the twentieth-century viewpoint. Frost's heaven is not pictorial like Hieronymus Bosch's, or a projection of the medieval imagination like Milton's version in "Paradise Lost." It is a specific, identifiable astronomic area with place names as on a military contour map. The poet is just as conscious as he ever has been of "empty spaces/ Between stars—on stars where no human race is." He is just as adroit as ever in using the star image, as in "Fireflies in the Garden," to satirize the pretenders of minor intensity. And he is just as perceptive as ever of the beauty of the night sky. But this awareness is no longer separable from scientific implications. Frost now blends the aesthetic with the scientific and the philosophic. All three viewpoints fuse in the following passage from "The Literate Farmer and the Planet Venus" in *A Witness Tree*. After poking fun at the difference between Edison's electric light and the planet Venus, brilliant in the early evening sky, the poet makes a considerable point:

> "Here come more stars to character the skies,
> And they in the estimation of the wise
> Are more divine than any bulb or arc,
> Because their purpose is to flash and spark,
> But not to take away the precious dark.
> We need the interruption of the night
> To ease attention off when overtight,
> To break our logic in too long a flight,
> And ask us if our premises are right."

The distinction between artificial and natural light is amiable and un-ruffled as well as shrewd and practical.

In what he calls a "telescopic" poem, "A Loose Mountain," Frost envisages the star shower called Leonid, like an avalanche off a loose mountain, pelting us with the impalpable drift of its substance. Here he pulls out various stops: bantering tone, philosophic mood and objective viewpoint ("the heartless and enormous Outer Black"), but he never talks big. He keeps well within the eye socket of the tele-scopic lens. Like Lucretius he writes from a comprehensive point of view. Some of the star poems project us into the amplitude of space where the "Watcher of the Void" infects us with sidereal euphoria.

The most direct evidence of Frost's exaltation of the star image is "Choose Something Like a Star," a poem in which adoration joins with the purposive to make the star a symbolic image of an ideal standard and a human steadier. The poet chooses the fairest star in sight—Venus perhaps?—to embody the higher viewpoint by which to keep ourselves becomingly calm and imperturbable, our head clear and cool, our judgment unwarped, "when at times the mob is swayed/ To carry praise or blame too far." In our time the poem seems topical enough; universally topical—as applicable to Rome in the days of the Caesars or Paris in the days of Louis XVI as in the shrill and violent days of fascistic and proletarian dictatorship.

Many of Frost's poems refer to stars; approximately ten percent in *Complete Poems*. It might be said veraciously that he is one acquainted with starlight in the way that Whitman was acquainted with genial sun-light and Poe with the eerie light of the moon. It would be more than he would own to if we found only a symbolic implication in his stellar references. "Aspiratory" is most surely the descriptive word for choosing something like a star, but the true significance of the star as a master image in his poetry consists simply in the latent affection a man has for the phenomena of the natural world. The star, like Emerson's rhodora, is its own excuse for being. He likes "to line the figures in/ Between the dotted stars." He likes to call the constellated stars by their proper names—Leo and Orion and Sirius and the Pleiades. He likes to stay up in the night "to see the star shower known as Leonid." And he likes to read the heavenly signs where a "firedrop" goes "streaking molten down the west." Let the thrush call ever so alluringly in the dark woods at evening, he is otherwise occupied. He is and always has been out for stars.

The star image, which has been here isolated, is as deeply organic in Frost's poetry as the dark woods and the springs, stonewalls and trees, flowers and animals, sun and moon. The significant thing to us is not simply that the star image is more typical than other images, either as a concept or in phrasing, but rather that in its use the poet has not tried to seduce the reader by metaphor or description. Imagery is not argument, and consequently the star image represents exactly what it does, no more, no less. It grows organically out of the experience of the poet and comes to stand naturally for the signature of his spirit.

2. The Poet and Tradition

Stuart P. Sherman once suggested two reasons why writers steep themselves in the forerunners of their craft. Tradition represents "a school of crafts" where the writer with a critical and inventive mind can learn from both the successes and failures of his predecessors, and where he can learn also how to work out his own problems of expression. Tradition is also "a school of manners and moods" where, as Sherman suggested, a writer can discover in the golden periods "a kind of innermost poise and serenity." This poise and serenity, which constitutes an enduring appeal, reigns "only in a mind that, looking, before and after, feels itself the representative of something outlasting time, some national ideal, some religious faith, some permanent human expression, some endless human quest." Sherman believes quite rightly that nothing begets this mood or manner of "enviable tranquillity" like habitual association with those who have it.

Frost has allied himself with tradition in both senses—as a school of crafts and as a school of manners and moods. He has made substantial levies on the great treasure of Latin literature and the Oxford Book of English Verse. And the kind and degree of his attachment to the pre-Socratics and to Lucretius, who have schooled him in a great discipline, have already been discussed. Among his early influential readings, he refers to an elaborate edition of Herrick's poems and Maurice de Guérin's "Centaur." Continuous, cumulative and characteristic, the tradition gives stability, provides a background, and exacts responsibility of the poet, and it also helps to create, unify and express an indigenous culture. *A Masque of Mercy,* for instance, reflects how much Frost has absorbed consciously or unconsciously from many sources, ranging from the Biblical to Milton, and from Bunyan to an anonymous author of one of the ballads of the 1890's. In the Masque are allusions to Blake, Waller, Kipling, Emerson, Browning and Milton, and of these allusions Frost says, "You steal them to new uses."

In 1894, he wrote Susan Hayes Ward that among those he read "in the hope of strengthening his executive faculties" were "The Polish Trilogy" by Henryk Sienkiewicz, that Thomas Hardy had taught him "the good use of a few words," that he drew inspiration from reading Scott and Stevenson, and in poetry, Keats—especially "Hyperion," Shelley's "Prometheus," Tennyson's "Morte d'Arthur," and Browning's "Saul"—"all of them about the giants. Besides these," he added, "I am fond of the whole collection of Palgrave's." He quotes in and out of it, as the phrase goes, as though he owned it. The references and allusions that a poet makes in his poetry are his lien in a great tradition. As a matter of fact, Frost's claim in tradition is by entail; he is one of a determined line of poetic heirs. Like royalty, he ascends as it were by descent.

The interaction of the writer and the great tradition is one of the strange and interesting aspects in literature. Some writers are like the seeds of those flowers which germinated and flowered after a long dormancy in the London craters where the Nazi bombs fell during the Blitz. The Pre-Raphaelites are a little like these flowers—a burgeoning rather than a renewal of tradition. Then there is the little anecdote cited by Walter Pater in *The Renaissance* when he is writing of Pico Della Mirandola. When a shipload of sacred earth from Jerusalem was mingled with the soil of the Campo Santo at Pisa, a new flower sprang up which resembled no flower seen before. It was an anemone with blended colors—a fine flower, "still to be found by those who search long enough for it, in the long grass of the Maremma." This can stand as an analogue for old cultural soil intermingling with new. We do not get John Donnes or Ben Jonsons. If we wait long enough, we get Walt Whitman, Mark Twain, Emily Dickinson, William Faulkner and Robert Frost.

There are at least two ways of being traditional, neither of which is mutually exclusive. Either the writer grows by imitating models, or he seeks and discovers new ways of applying the basic forms which shape style. Frost has taken hints from many sources—from "Lycidas" for this, from Christopher Smart for that. It is what he does with the basic forms in poetry—with the metrical stanza, metaphor, rhyme and rhythm—that indicates his technical renewal of tradition. He communicates the sense of other worlds, other ideas, other poets, and the cross-fertilization of culture. This is a measure of his relationship to tradition. His strength consists partly in the fact that he is related not only to a tradition inherited and conserved, but as well to a tradition renewed and transmitted. Neither a compromiser nor an escapist, he is not an eddy in the main stream; he is confluent and flows into and along in the main stream. Or, even more precise is his own metaphor. He is like a man on an escalator: he goes along with tradition, but under his own power.

In relationship to the tendencies in modern poetry Frost is regarded chiefly as a traditionalist. That he is a traditionalist is true, but what is important is the kind of traditionalist he is. He has a good claim to be considered as a vital, not a formal, traditionalist. It is apparent that he would disagree with William Carlos Williams's contention that a traditional poetic form like the sonnet must be repudiated because it is conditioned by past necessities which are no longer valid, and that a poet must therefore make of his words "a new form." The nub of Frost's demurrer would not be a slavish adherence to the sonnet form per se but a belief that point of view and idiom can adequately vitalize traditional form. By way of illustration, he might point out that more than passage of time or the conditioning factors of past necessities stand between the sight of Proteus rising from the sea or the sound of old Triton's "wreathéd horn" in Wordsworth's "The World Is Too Much With Us" and the sight of "one luminary clock against the sky/ Pro-

claimed the time was neither wrong nor right." The sonnet form is common to both poems, but no one would confuse the varying moods of the poets and the difference in phraseology. Not certainly by ukases and pronunciamentos do we get new forms in art. For William Carlos Williams the object has no continuum and consequently it is perennially destroyed; new necessities impel new objects, and new objects require new forms. For Frost the traditional form should be constantly re-created from within as he shows us in "The Silken Tent."

Frost is related to tradition in a dual way. He takes and he gives. He assimilates and he renews. The source of the intenser vibrations in his poetry is what reverberates from an old and mighty tradition. Yet he is no more strictly conventional by the metrical book than he is conservative by the political party. He not only fashions the forms of English poetry to his purposes; invariably he adapts and enriches them by shaping the common language to his personal idiom. His way to be original is to accept a traditional discipline *without* sacrificing individuality. He draws to his strength, which is a craftsman's love of language, and by effectively transcribing the inflected speech of the human voice, he revitalizes a tradition that is complex, cumulative and continuous. The blank verse in his longer poems has a natural conversational swing to it that makes the English blank verse of other centuries seem literary. This knack of the ear for language is fused with its subject matter in "The Gum-Gatherer," "The Death of the Hired Man," "Mending Wall" and "Birches." With an instinct for communicability he writes for the *listening* audience, and when he is effective, he strikes the heart through the ear.

Frost's linkage with the great tradition of the past is apparent, but how does he stand, let us say, in the context of his time with regard to the *avant-garde?* As a strategist he has made the most of his responsibilities; some of the other American versifiers rode with abandon the lively rocket of the New Movement (1912–1925). When it burst, they faded like sparks in the fire shower. Many of the adherents of modernism have preferred to take their lesson in aesthetics from Pound's "Lesson in Aesthetics" and William Carlos Williams's "To a Solitary Disciple," rather than from Amy Lowell's "Apology"; their lesson in viewpoint from Wallace Stevens's "Thirteen Ways of Looking at a

Blackbird" rather than from Robinson's "The Man Against the Sky"; their lesson in technique from Eliot's "The Love Song of J. Alfred Prufrock" rather than from Frost's "Mending Wall"; and their lesson in the purpose of poetry from Marianne Moore's "Poetry" rather than from Carl Sandburg's "Definitions." In spite of what seems to be conventional traditionalism, Frost is actually not a rear-guard poet in the new movement. If the criterion by which one tests the modernity in twentieth-century poetry is the paralleling of surface meaning with suggestive overtones, then Frost *is* a *modern* poet. This is exactly what Frost is doing in the double-layer poems—in the lyrics, eclogues and sonnets—which have been referred to as parables. Notice, for instance, the number of poems written pre-1912, especially those written around 1905, which in spirit and language anticipate the dicta of T. E. Hulme and F. S. Flint, Ezra Pound and Amy Lowell.

Frost's popular appeal has cost him adherents among the intellectual aesthetes. No doubt about it. Some of these potential adherents have been strangely obtuse in ignoring his technique and ideas. After listening to him correct Robert Bridges's interpretation of verse technique and after listening to his spirited examination of the metrical inadequacies in one of Eliot's "Four Quartets," I should judge that Frost has been insufficiently considered on this side. After all, he is a craftsman in his profession—a *poietes,* a maker—a fact we tried to make clear in Ars Poetica (part II) and in Dimensions in Art (part V).

Frost, unlike T. S. Eliot, had not substantially influenced the course of modern poetry by stamping upon the consciousness of his readers such a dominant image as the waste land. In both form and content Eliot has helped to effect a revolution in poetry. Frost has been successful in turning poetry away from the nineteenth century's rhetorical obsession and toward cadence in natural idiom. He has also renewed the democratic tradition in his poetry by effectively restating human values in imaginative terms. "No choice is left a poet, you might add," he says, "but how to take the curse, tragic or comic." He has taken the curse both ways, leaning a little more to the comic than to the tragic; in method, more observational than speculative; in tone, sanguine rather than disillusioned; and in attitude, intransigent, unsubmissive, impenitent and committed rather than prostrate, abject and indecisive.

3. The Poet's Appeal

Robert Frost's primary problems as a poet have been the problems of all poets in all ages. He had, first, to find out how genuine a talent he possessed. Then he had to find a way to nourish and perfect the talent. And finally, he had to learn how to make his talent an effective part of the movement of his time. No darling of nature, he had to create his own audience, an effort which requires character as well as talent. His trial in consequence has been by existence and by market which "everything must come to." Nor has the "immortal garland" been run for "without dust and heat." It took him over thirty years to come into his own, and at first the praise was measured and temperate, as it should be, but what he has won he seems to have held.

"No doubt," said Santayana, "the spirit of energy of the world is what is acting in us, as the sea is what rises in every little wave; but it passes through us, and cry out as we may, it will move on. Our privilege is to have perceived it as it moves. Our dignity is not in what we do, but in what we understand. The whole world is doing things. We are turning in that vortex; yet within us is silent observation, the speculative eye before which all passes, which bridges the distances and compares the combatants." The vortex of our time has been swirling rapidly, yet Frost has been able to detach himself from it, contain its chaos, order his experience, and make from it "little bits of clarity." This is no mean accomplishment.

What does he reflect of a poet's relationship to society in the twentieth century? A focusing on his personal problems would only go a short way in justification of his effort. He is only one among many poets, and the others must also be considered if any critic is to give an accurate picture of poetry's status in our time. But let us consider a few angles. If depiction of the native scene in American poetry is isolated for special praise, James Whitcomb Riley would stand high. If technical virtuosity is applauded then Thomas Bailey Aldrich would require special attention. If originality in attitude is to be the criterion of excellence, then Stephen Crane's free verse would be acclaimed. Frost combines these qualifications: native materials, individuality in form and a highly personalized viewpoint, yet he is not infertile like Aldrich, never merely folksy like Riley, or predictable in attitude like Crane. None of these factors, either separately or in combination, represents, as we have seen, the relationship in which he stands to tradition. By examining the scope of his cultural appeal we should learn something more about why his response has seemed "original."

The first basis of Frost's popular appeal is his general intelligibility. Once he said, "Some say that we must insist that we write for no audience at all. There must be an audience, an audience invisible, a blend of all the interesting people whom I have dealt with." He is certainly not a professional scholar-poet like T. S. Eliot who addresses either the intellectuals or an élite group of practicing poets. He writes for the lovers of poetry who read for pleasure and enlightenment about up-country New England—the scene off the main drag, the people on the back roads. His appeal is a popular one. We might say that his poetry belongs to the schools as well as to the people. More accurately, we might say that his poetry belongs to the schools as well as to the people in the sense that it belongs to the human heart. An effective poet, he skilfully penetrates the common consciousness at its deeper levels. His poetic sentences cling in the memory. Even when we do not try to riddle his poems' subtle second layer the emotions are still fully engaged. Is it not an important thing to influence one's time directly by making poetry communicable and a utility of the spirit? It is especially so when the poet's acclamation has not come by exploiting his sensibility. Because he has refused to be pressured into poor work, none of Frost's poems has ever appeared in public with only a priming coat.

To be generally effective poetry should have a musical basis, and it should arouse us by evocation and clarity. *Complete Poems* meets each of these requirements. Because it is intelligible, rhythmic and moving, Frost is one of the contemporary poets most widely read by people who approach him as an equal. They are neither mystified by unorthodox forms and eccentric typography nor put off by a cryptic or elliptical use of language. A liking for his poetry is a given, and not, as in some of the *avant-garde* poets, an acquired taste.

In his "talk-songs" he has raised the speaking voice to the level of poetry, not by transcribing common speech but by using words at the pitch of their natural intensity. Whose words? Whose voice? The words and voice-tones heard in the poem's sound track are not those of a New Hampshireman or a Vermonter with inflective tones peculiar to locality. They are simply words and tones common to man. The vocal images are not dialect; they are accent. Anyone can read them, determining the pitch, volume and tempo for himself. What Hopkins says of himself is applicable to Frost. "Take breath and read it with the ears . . . and my verse becomes all right." The world Frost represents is identified by the earmark of the idiom. ("Yankees are what they always were.") It is warmed by sensitive human feeling. ("Weep for what little things could make them glad.") It is informed by a vigilant awareness. ("The strong are saying nothing until they see.") What one man has seen and felt others may see and feel.

Furthermore, his appeal is popular because of a sympathetic understanding of the intimacies of living, which his readers commonly share. No romantic individualist, he has been involved in the normal life of his time, country, section and family, and also deeply involved in conflicts that torment the human heart. Apparently he has learned a great deal from personal tensions, and, by way of compensations, these struggles have honed his insight into problems of human relationship. *Complete Poems* embodies arrestingly some of these intimate tensions. How is it possible to interpret "The Thatch," "The Silken Tent," "The Lost Follower," "The Subverted Flower," and "The Lovely Shall Be Choosers" except in terms of the poet's own life? No writer ever has created what his mind could not imagine. It is a safe bet that if he describes intrafamilial relationships these must have haunted his mind, arising either from personal experience or from experience close to the personal.

Frost has, therefore, been more concerned in discovering values in a naturalistic, than in a divinely ordered, world. He is no vain searcher for esoteric truth like Emerson, whom Hawthorne dubbed "the mystic, stretching his hand out of cloud-land, in vain search for something real." He doesn't want to know what can't be known. ("I don't want to find out what can't be known," says one of the characters in "In the Home Stretch.") When mysticism gets misty, Frost's feelers retreat. He does not make popular, notional and ineffectual guesses about immortality and the hereafter; he tries only to be wise as far as one can see. His vocation is the exercise of the imagination and the recharging of the human spirit with the evidences immediately at hand—in the tree fallen across the road, in the bundles that spill out of the hands, in the door that gets in the way in the dark.

He has also been effective in making people like poetry by personal radiation. There is a rare and irrepressible appeal in his personal magnetism, either *tête-à-tête* or on the platform. A smart showman, he knows how to capitalize on his art without cheapening it. College halls are his favorite pitches where he holds the audience whom he has attracted, not because the poetry is light, but because the showman is able. In the lecture halls, which are his hustings, he meets Cato's stiff requirement of a good speaker: *Vir bonus dicendi peritus* (a man of high character who can make a good speech). Like most men who speak much in public, his words are performers; his hands, prompters; and his talk, experience dramatized—the performance is a play acted with vocal emphasis, facial expression, gesture, pauses and *sotto voce* asides. A fine storyteller in conversation as in poetry, he releases his ideas by artful disclosures, and, by leavening the tall talk with wit, he eliminates all threat of solemnity. It is not surprising that he has established himself as a popular poet—popular in the best sense of the word—in an age when poetry is suspect as a pretentious plaything of academic critics.

A second strong basis in Frost's appeal is intellectual and moral. By dramatizing the familiar essay in poetry (*e.g.,* "From Plane to Plane"), by poeticizing editorials (*e.g.,* "New Hampshire," "Build Soil" and "The Lesson for Today"), and by satirizing topical foibles (*e.g.,* "Departmental" and "To a Thinker") he sets his reader thinking about the nature and destiny of man. What distinguishes his thought is sincerity, in both senses in which Coleridge used the word: first, in impassioned meditation which produces the rhythm and originality of creative expression, and secondly, in rational observation, reflected in the precision and clarity of logical and informed expression. His poems are aimed at the head as well as at the heart. In his reading and in his reactions to the affairs of men, he more nearly resembles a knowledgeable Hellene who borrows, as the Greek did, only to transmute the booty, bee-like, and never to steal, ant-like. Looking freshly at old familiar things is the angle of his particular vision. Experiences worked into him, whereas Whitman, too frequently, gives us the impression that things just stuck to him. "I find," Whitman says in a statement by which we can hoist him on his own exuberance, "I find I incorporate gneiss, coal, long-threaded moss, fruits, grains, esculent roots,/ And am stucco'd with quadrupeds and birds all over." In Frost the ideas grow like plants, like witness trees, with deep roots.

Compared with Emerson, Frost's picture of reality differs in source and expression. The picture of reality in *Complete Poems* comes directly from rational observation re-enforced by meditation. It is a picture that reflects a sense of rangy freedom, and it is stimulating because it is unpredictably various. It comes from an unsystematized attitude. The rigidity of a precisely ordered scheme is a dead end to all innovation and experimentation. The picture of reality projected in Emerson's metaphysic is *a priori* and intuitive. "Idealism sees the world . . . as one vast picture which God paints on the instant eternity for the contemplation of the soul," says Emerson, and so it follows that his optimism is anterior to the empirical aspects of experience. Frost's cautious meliorism, growing out of his experience, has been forged into a subtle weapon. He has not failed to see the outrageous spectacle of human pretension, the fallibility and vulgar errors of man. The very cream of the jest is a human, not a metaphysical, incongruity, which consists in the pretensions of human beings when they try to make natural law adjust to them. These particular people, unlike farmer Brown in "Brown's Descent," haven't learned to bow with becoming grace to natural law like a good Greek.

Frost's effort has been a lively and rugged one, if we are to judge by his passionate belief in poetry as an art. It is more than luck that has enabled him to transmute the common realities into "little bits of clarity." His motivating impulse has been active and aspiratory, not passive and quiescent. The clarity which his poetry reflects is shed on moral experience. Although he is not an overt moralist, his dominant chord is belief in human courage and reason. He knows that man can be sorely beset and that time and eternity dwarf human effort. No sadist, he exults in neither the dilemma nor the suffering. In his poems of experience he acknowledges necessity and respects fate as in "The

Door in the Dark," "Tree at My Window," "Once by the Pacific." But he does not capitulate. In a quiet, unboastful, determined way he rallies the heart with the head. He makes it an imperative condition that intellect and courage be tested by competence and strategy. While the source of the moral inspiration is mystical in Emerson, it is plainly rational in Frost. This may be one reason why the twentieth-century reader feels in *Complete Poems* an immediacy and directness of *rapport* which he does not find in Emerson's writings. The lap of immense intelligence, in which Emerson thought we lay and by which we were informed and energized, seems remote today to man *on his own* in a mysterious, if not implacably alien, universe.

So it is that Frost appeals to our affirmative sense, to man's intelligence and quick-wittedness, and to his energy and courage, all of which are *sui generis* in Frost himself. The vision which gives his poetry its intellectual content is inseparable from the spirit of his country. It does not depend upon nor, of course, does it exclude the people or boundaries of New England. He strikes two national notes: expectancy and affirmation. He gets on top of things and stays there. He appeals to our sense of independence. "Keep off each other and keep each other off." He appeals to our sense of self-belief. "They cannot look out far/ They cannot look in deep,/ But when was that ever a bar/ To any watch they keep?" He appeals to our intellectual resources. "We have ideas yet that we haven't tried." He appeals to our will. "Since he means to come to a door he will come to a door." He appeals to our poise and courage. "They cannot scare me with their empty spaces/ Between stars—on stars where no human race is./ I have it in me so much nearer home/ To scare myself with my own desert places." He appeals to our sense of destiny. "Take nature altogether since time began . . . / And it must be a little more in favor of man." Above all, he appeals everlastingly to our sense of the dignity of the human spirit. "The spinner still was there to spin./ That's where the human still came in."

The third basic appeal of Frost identifies his "original response" —an independent viewpoint, a personal idiom, and a skill in expressive form. The habit of his art is the verbal fun he gets in playing with sound, image and idea. All the originality's in that. Some of his poems have a quality which we find only in the finest lyric in the

Elizabethans, for example, or in the seventeenth-century lyric, or in Shelley's:

> A widow bird sate mourning for her love
> Upon a wintry bough;
> The frozen wind crept on above,
> The freezing stream below.
>
> There was no leaf upon the forest bare,
> No flower upon the ground,
> And little motion in the air
> Except the mill-wheel's sound.

—a quality of deceptive spontaneity. While reading "My November Guest," "Come In," "Stopping by Woods," "Desert Places," "Once by the Pacific," "A Soldier," "Willful Homing," "One Step Backward Taken," "The Silken Tent," "All Revelation," "The Night Light," "The Fear of God," "Leaves Compared with Flowers," and "Spring Pools," we feel there is no imaginable time when poems like these will have only a verbal present.

These lyrics seem to spring full born from an optimum condition. Effortless spontaneity and intactness make them as graceful in form and as felicitous in expression as they are satisfying in content. They penetrate reality. What is seen suggests in its particularity the deeper complexity of experience. The lyric emotion has also a clear, true tone, and a singing element. The words belong to the poet, the voice is his, and a *chant intérieur,* in Brunetière's descriptive phrase, sings through the poem. Like Ulysses, Frost too tries the string of a great bow, which is the bow of poetry, and it sings "sweetly beneath his touch, like a swallow in tone." As a realist he apprehends facts; as a reflective man he comprehends the relationship of these particular facts to the whole; as a poet he releases these facts to significance in "imagery and after-imagery." The synthesis of these three factors has enabled him "to lodge a few poems where they will be hard to get rid of."

Key

Unless otherwise indicated the references to Ripton signify talks with Mr. Frost at the Homer Noble farm in Ripton, Vermont, and the references to Middlebury, Vermont, unless otherwise noted, indicate visits of Mr. Frost at my home. In referring to the English School and the Writers' Conference at Bread Loaf, Vermont, the abbreviation B L E S is used for the former, and B L W C for the latter.

Robert Frost *Complete Poems* (1949)   C P
Personal conversations with Robert Frost   C
Robert Frost's Lecture-Readings   R

Numerals at the left refer to pages in this book. The words of each note indicate the beginning and end of the passage in the text, conversation, or lecture, poem or reference, to which it is related, except for occasional descriptive terms and phrases.

Preface

vii. "a plain citizen."   C   Ripton, Aug. 6, 1949.

I. LOCAL AND PERSONAL DIMENSIONS

1. Epigraph: "He showed . . . with-   C P   p. 288
out."

1. A Foreground Fact

3. "sep-a-ra-tist."   R   Middlebury College, Sept. 27, 1947
4. "There's . . . here."   Ibid.,   p. 634
"So . . . too."   Ibid.,   p. 623
"It's been . . . the world."   Ibid.,   p. 630
5. "They would . . . was true."   Ibid.,   p. 5
"I could . . . have kept."   Ibid.,   p. 447

2. A Sense of Identity

Epigraph: "I come . . . and rustic."	C	Ripton, June 3, 1949
6. "a realmist."	C	Ripton, July 2, 1949
7. "Literature . . . local."	R	Middlebury, May 28, 1936
"strategic retreats."	C P	p. 365
"cannot rest . . . starry."	Ibid.,	p. 199
8. "You know . . . March."	Ibid.,	p. 387
10. "yoke-fellows . . . of old."	Ibid.,	p. 199

3. Traits

Epigraph: "My object . . . other things."	R	Dartmouth College, June 12, 1955
11. "I see what I see."	C	B L E S, June 30, 1950
12. "laziness"; "evasiveness."	C	Boston, Dec. 16, 1938
"I have . . . my ground."	R	Middlebury College, May 27, 1936
14. "catch-as-catch-can."	C	B L E S, June 30, 1950
15. "I give you . . . twenty."	Ibid.	
"I'm an unprincipled . . . matters."	C	B L E S, July 2, 1949
"I'll talk . . . nothing."	C	Middlebury, June 4, 1948
"No, I didn't . . . inexorable."	C	Middlebury, Sept. 25, 1948
16. "I keep . . . insincerity."	C	B L E S, Aug. 4, 1948
"to know something."	C	Middlebury, Sept. 17, 1947
"You know . . . wrong."	Ibid.	
"Let's go slow . . . flowers."	C	B L E S, July 2, 1949
"Sometimes . . . here."	C	Ripton, July 5, 1950
"I like . . . grow."	C	Ripton, July 13, 1948
"I like . . . help."	C	Ripton, Aug. 25, 1949
"the slow . . . decay."	C P	p. 127
"the magic . . . go."	C	B L E S, July 25, 1949
17. "I have . . . book."	R	Middlebury College, May 10, 1950
"a poem . . . universe."	R	B L E S, Summer, 1928
18. "it's antagonisms . . . iridescences."	C	Ripton, June 1, 1948
"I was smart . . . fire."	C	B L E S, June 30, 1950
19. "No, we never . . . real things."	C	Undated
"We never . . . hurt."	C	Middlebury, June 4, 1948
"You'll never . . . year."	Ibid.	
20. "This is mine . . . be mine."	C	Ripton, June 19, 1940

"The gray . . . river."	C P	p. 41
"It's a funny . . . inside."	C	Ripton, June 19, 1940
"scare" . . . "disciplined response."	R	B L E S, Summer, 1928
"I sneaked some . . . given me."	C	Middlebury, Sept. 17, 1945
21. "A furtive worker."	C	South Shaftsbury, Vt., June 2, 1937
"We live . . . the jail."	C	B L E S, July 2, 1949
"No big . . . bothered me."	C	Middlebury, Sept. 25, 1948
"The skill . . . prowess."	R	Cambridge, March 25, 1936
22. "We used . . . disappear."	C	Ripton, June 9, 1949
"I wrote . . . burned them."	R	Middlebury, Sept. 17, 1943
"bulk it."	R	Middlebury College, May 10, 1950
"big and serious."	Ibid.	
23. "Life is more cruel."	C	Middlebury, Aug. 9, 1943
"I can take both."	C	Ripton, July 24, 1943
"I wouldn't . . . my way."	R	Middlebury College, May 10, 1950
"Education is . . . mind."	R	B L E S, Summer, 1928
24. "a work . . . a play."	C	South Shaftsbury, Vt., Sept. 28, 1935
"I'm never . . . fooling."	R	Santa Fé, N.M., Aug. 5, 1935
25. "My life . . . without it."	R	Cambridge, March 25, 1936
"all opinionation."	C	Ripton, June 9, 1949
26. "We'll follow . . . mountain."	C	B L E S, June 30, 1950
"been moved . . . tears."	C	Ripton, June 1, 1948
"Having thoughts . . . freedom."	R	Middlebury College, May 28, 1936
"What is . . . unknown."	R	Ripton, Sept. 27, 1949
"What I . . . newness."	R	B L E S, July 28, 1946
27. "With . . . fingers."	C	Ripton, July 13, 1948
"Damn it . . . flour."	C	Ripton, July 24, 1943 (quoting Jonathan Moses)
"so much velvet."	R	B L E S, July 16, 1925
"semi-rebels, etc."	C	Middlebury, Sept. 22, 1945
"A great . . . peace."	Ibid.	
"Uriel . . . people."	Ibid.	
28. "The people . . . risks."	R	Middlebury College, Sept. 17, 1943
"the greatest . . . great."	C	B L E S, July 28, 1952

"Courtesy keeps . . . Marlborough."	C	Ripton, Aug. 6, 1949
"I'm . . . language."	C	B L E S, July 25, 1949
29. "a reckless reader."	C	Ripton, Aug. 6, 1949
"readatability."	C	Cambridge, Dec. 13, 1946
"We'll be back."	Ibid.	
"The two . . . airforces."	R	B L E S, Aug. 6, 1945
"fresh . . . pages."	C	Middlebury, Sept. 22, 1945
"You're . . . genius."	C	B L E S, July 25, 1949
30. "In the Bay . . . all."	R	B L E S, June 29, 1950
31. "I'd try . . . without one."	Quoted by Mark Van Doren at B L E S lecture, July 21, 1947	
"unexpected connections."	C	Ripton, June 30, 1950
32. "Thorosians."	C	Ripton, Summer, 1946
"When I'm asked . . . Vermont."	Quoted in The Boston Globe, March 24, 1950, p. 16	
"I call myself . . . everything."	Quoted in The New York Times Magazine Section, April 2, 1950	
"I went . . . screaming."	C	B L E S, June 30, 1950
"You're . . . Vermonter."	C	Ripton, July 13, 1948
"I like . . . self-defense."	R	B L W C, Aug. 19, 1953
"At the progressive . . . about."	C	Middlebury, Dec. 25, 1949
"I've digested it."	C	Middlebury, Sept. 25, 1946
33. "Here . . . thirsty."	C	Middlebury, Sept. 25, 1948
"When . . . inhaled."	Quoted in Addison Independent, Middlebury, Vt., June 3, 1949	
"No . . . there."	R	B L W C, Summer, 1949
"scatteration."	C	Ripton, July 2, 1949
"You're . . . thoughts."	C	B L E S, July 2, 1949
"The witticisms . . . yours."	Ibid.	
"You . . . bric-a-brac."	C	Ripton, July 4, 1947
34. "Sometimes . . . amusing."	C	Cambridge, Dec. 13, 1947
"You . . . verbs."	C	B L E S, Aug. 2, 1949
35. "What . . . by."	C P	p. 217
"For . . . forgiving."	Ibid.,	p. 218
"But . . . get."	Ibid.,	p. 421
"And . . . bloody?"	Ibid.	
"The . . . woe."	Ibid.,	p. 471
"Each . . . best."	Ibid.,	p. 523
"And . . . said."	Ibid.,	p. 449

"No, it's insight."   C   South Shaftsbury, Vt., Sept. 28,
                                                  1935
36. "Everyone . . . confusion."   C   Cambridge, Dec. 13, 1947
    "I can . . . process."   C   Middlebury, May 10, 1950
    "If . . . wrong."   C   B L E S, July 22, 1947
    "Everyone . . . age."   C   B L E S, July 21, 1947
    "You . . . background."   C   B L E S, July 1, 1946
    "Democracy . . . itself."   R   Middlebury College, Sept. 17,
                                                  1943
    "Life . . . art."   R   Cambridge, March 25, 1936
    "Observation . . . insight."   C   B L E S, July 15, 1925
    "Life . . . pursuit."   R   B L E S, Summer, 1928
    "There's . . . unities."   C   Cambridge, Dec. 13, 1947
    "Intensity . . . dormancy."   C   Ripton, July 13, 1948
    "All . . . enough."   C   Ripton, Sept. 26, 1953
    "You . . . outsider."   C   Middlebury, Sept. 20, 1955
    "It's . . . vision."   R   B L W C, Aug. 19, 1953
37. "You mean . . . exaggerate?"   C   Ripton, July 24, 1943
38. "When poets . . . no."   C   Ripton, June 1, 1948
    "the four . . . freedoms."   C P   pp. 599, 600
    "of . . . time."   C   Middlebury, Dec. 25, 1949
    "At least . . . somewhere."   Ibid.
39. "And there . . . too."   C   Ripton, July 5, 1950
    "Intelligence . . . important."   Ibid.
    "No, I'm . . . needs."   C   Ripton, June 1, 1948
    "I'm . . . technicalities."   C   Ripton, July 13, 1948

II. ARS POETICA

1. A Theory of Poetry

43. "the separateness . . . parts."   C   B L E S, July 22, 1947

2. Aim as Performance

44. "You see . . . something."   C   South Shaftsbury, Vt., May 13,
                                                  1932
45. "The first . . . self-surprise."   C   Cambridge, March 25, 1936
    "a cool . . . anti-intoxication."   Ibid.

"I suppose . . . ways."   Ibid.
"When . . . network."   Ibid.

3. The Height of Poetry

46. "a straight crookedness."   Preface, *Collected Poems* (1939)
47. "Inconsiderable . . . way."   R   B L E S, July 28, 1952
    "build soil."   C P   p. 421
    "composites."   R   B L W C, Aug. 16, 1952
    "Many . . . soil."   Ibid.
    "the only . . . story."   Ibid.
48. "The best . . . of it."   R   Middlebury College, May 28, 1936
    "I'd hate . . . straight out."   C   Cambridge, March 26, 1936
49. "blazes"; "lights up."   C   Boston, Dec. 16, 1938
50. "free . . . words."   Class talk. B L E S, July 23, 1947
    "The height . . . mischief."   Ibid.
    "Those . . . ear."   R   B L E S, July 28, 1952

4. A Renewal of Words

51. "a performance in words."   C   South Shaftsbury, Vt., May 13, 1932
    "the renewal of words."   C   South Shaftsbury, Vt., May 1931
    "a suggestion of making."   Ibid.
    "That's . . . alive."   R   B L E S, July 17, 1950
52. "I don't advise . . . other way."   C P   p. 56
    "poring over."   C   Ripton, Aug. 6, 1949
    "it . . . words."   R   Middlebury, Sept. 17, 1943
    "a renewer."   Class talk. B L E S, July 17, 1950

5. Composing a Poem

53. "When I . . . non-competitive."   C   Ripton, June 1, 1948
    "work . . . wood."   C   Ripton, July 2, 1949
    "I . . . spot."   C   Ripton, Aug. 25, 1949
    "a . . . command."   C   Middlebury, May 13, 1939
    "a . . . summons."   Ibid.
    "ecstasy . . . mind."   R   B L E S, Summer, 1928
54. "Writing . . . battle."   C   B L E S, July 28, 1952

"presence of mind."	C	B L E S, July 25, 1949
"a resolved perplexity."	C	Middlebury, May 13, 1939
"the pure . . . thing."	Ibid.	
"Rides . . . melting."	Ibid.	
"to touch . . . form."	C	B L E S, July 25, 1949
55. "Regular verse . . . them."		"How Hard It Is to Keep from Being King." (1951)
"How did . . . fulfil it."	C	South Shaftsbury, Vt., Sept. 28, 1935
"Here is . . . dismissed itself."	R	B L E S, Summer, 1928

6. Rhyming

56. "When . . . easy."	R	Cambridge, March 25, 1936
"That's . . . strength."	R	Middlebury College, Nov. 9, 1945
57. "the pervasive idea."	C	Ripton, Sept. 26, 1942
"a series . . . commitments."	R	Middlebury College, Nov. 9, 1945
"I feel . . . rhyme pairs."	Ibid.	
"Suspect the rhymes."	Ibid.	
"If they . . . no good."	R	B L E S, July 6, 1949
"Don't be . . . rhyming pairs."	R	Middlebury College, Nov. 9, 1945
"how valid they are."	R	B L W C, Aug. 20, 1949
"Watch Emerson . . . man."	R	Middlebury College, Nov. 9, 1945
58. "It is . . . scaffolding."	Ibid.	
"Suspect those . . . conventions."	Ibid.	

7. Form

"feminine shrillness."	C	Ripton, June 1, 1948
"We used . . . remake it."	R	B L E S, Summer, 1933
"What is . . . is it?"	C	Ripton, May 25, 1949
"little twists of thinking."	Ibid.	
59. "Neat as a pin!"	C	B L E S, July 2, 1949
"Everyone's . . . head."	R	B L E S, July 17, 1950
"like . . . puzzle-box."	C	Ripton, June 1, 1948
"a thing . . . as spoken."	R	B L E S, July 7, 1921
"the singing . . . the form."	R	B L E S, Summer, 1928

"a-sentencing."   Ibid.
60. "hot . . . cramped."   C   Boston, Dec. 16, 1938
    "creak."   Ibid.
    "squeeze . . . the sentence."   R   B L E S, Summer, 1928
    "to divest . . . ego."   Ibid.
    "You've . . . honesty."   Ibid.
    "All inner . . . two things."   R   Cambridge, March 25, 1936
    "All idea . . . metaphor."   R   B L E S, Summer, 1928
    "a poem . . . association."   C   B L E S, July 6, 1949
    "Cutting . . . mind."   C   Ripton, Aug. 17, 1947
    "by trying . . . the universe."   R   B L E S, Summer, 1928
    "My friends . . . designed."   C P   p. 421
61. "The moon . . . Solomon."   Ibid., p. 550

8. Tones of Voice

    "good sentencing."   R   B L E S, Summer, 1928
62. "Here . . . them."   R   B L E S, July 17, 1950
    "When literature . . . speak."   R   B L E S, July 7, 1921
    "The thing . . . lines."   R   B L E S, Summer, 1928
    "steps right into it."   R   B L E S, July 17, 1950
    "You've . . . dramatic."   Ibid.
    "What we . . . break it."   R   B L E S, July 17, 1950
    "Get . . . writing."   Ibid.
63. "conveys . . . words."   Introduction to *A Way Out* (1929)
    "saying . . . duplicity."   R   B L E S, Summer, 1928
    "Oh!"   C   South Shaftsbury, Vt., Sept. 28,
                                                1935
    "a . . . the."   C   South Shaftsbury, Vt., May 13,
                                                1932
    "I see . . . come back."   Quoted by Professor W. E. Davison,
                                                Middlebury College. ca. 1922
    "tone of voice."   R   Santa Fé, N.M., Aug. 5, 1935
    "a kind . . . the voice."   R   B L E S, July 17, 1921
    "observing ear."   Ibid.
    "the texture . . . a visitation."   Ibid.
64. "But all . . . a thing."   C P   p. 56
    "The metre . . . get variety."   C   South Shaftsbury, Vt., Sept. 28,
                                                1935
    "The sentencing . . . say."   C P   p. 491

"too many . . . delicacy."	C	South Shaftsbury, Vt., Sept. 28, 1935
"There . . . could be."	C P	p. 78
65. "something I . . . my art."	C	Middlebury, May 28, 1936
"Why . . . phrase."	C	South Shaftsbury, Vt., May 13, 1932
"talk-songs."		Quoted in E. S. Sergeant, *Fire Under the Andes* (New York, 1927), p. 295
"on . . . talking."	R	Middlebury College, May 27, 1936
"The tone's . . . isn't it?"	R	B L E S, Aug. 6, 1945
"the reason . . . sound."	R	B L E S, July 6, 1949
"to see . . . different."	R	B L W C, Aug. 18, 1945

9. Motives

66. "the little . . . fulfilled."	C	B L E S, July 2, 1949
"a pretty . . . doing."	C	Ibid.
"the little rounded way."	C	Ibid.
"All I . . . that."	C	Ripton, Aug. 6, 1949
"What we . . . order."	C	Ripton, Sept. 27, 1949
"What is . . . of it?"	C	Ibid.
"making . . . clarity."	C	B L E S, July 21, 1947
67. "I haven't . . . for keeps."	C	B L E S, July 25, 1949
"When I . . . bell."	C	Ripton, Aug. 25, 1949
"the nicest discretion."	C	B L E S, July 2, 1949
"We are . . . to be."	C	Middlebury, May 13, 1939
"that . . . exactly."	R	B L E S, June 29, 1950

III. THE ORGANIC

2. In the Poet

73. "And . . . straight."	C P	p. 273
74. "a synecdochist."		Quoted in L. Untermeyer, *Modern American Poetry* (New York, 1927), p. 181
"gloating."		Quoted in E. S. Sergeant, *Fire Under the Andes* (New York, 1927), p. 295

3. In the Poem

75.	"It was . . . beauty."	C P	p. 517
76.	"When . . . poisoned."	Ibid.,	p. 633
	"A . . . poem."	R	B L E S, July 28, 1952
77.	"There . . . composition."	C	B L E S, Aug. 2, 1954
	"drawing in."	C	Ripton, July 19, 1948
	"the love . . . days."	C P	p. 8
	"with . . . heart."	Ibid.,	p. 6
78.	"Poetry . . . to me."	R	New School for Social Research, Oct. 17, 1935
	"all night . . . this one."	R	B L W C, Aug. 18, 1951
	"I . . . tiredness."	Ibid.	
	"And just . . . abide."	C P	p. 49
78–80.	"I can . . . rhyme."	R	Middlebury College, Nov. 9, 1945
80.	"the purification . . . quality."		Quoted by Professor W. E. Davison, Middlebury College. ca. 1925
81.	"a nice . . . summons."	C	Middlebury, May 13, 1939

4. In the Poetry

82.	"Every poem . . . comes out."	R	B L W C, Aug. 16, 1952
	"It . . . saying."	Ibid.	
83.	"The heart . . . 'Whither?' "	C P	p. 43
	"Don't . . . college."	Ibid.,	p. 421
	"Men . . . or apart."	Ibid.,	p. 31
	"Men . . . far apart."	Ibid.,	p. 391
85.	"A dented spider . . . aright?"		Huntington Library MS. Enclosed in letter to Susan Hayes Ward, Jan. 14, 1912
86.	"amid . . . juniper."	C P	p. 24
	"was . . . wear."	Ibid.,	p. 131
	"tilted . . . air."	Ibid.,	p. 304
	"the power . . . say."	Ibid.,	p. 392
87.	"in the universal crisis."	Ibid.,	p. 519
	"drink . . . confusion."	Ibid.,	p. 520
	"the sweetest . . . knows."	Ibid.,	p. 25
	"One . . . birches."	Ibid.,	p. 152
	"I told . . . life."	Ibid.,	p. 176
	"But these . . . sing."	Ibid.,	p. 277

"still . . . defect."	Ibid.,	p. 303
"a scent . . . wall."	Ibid.,	p. 400
"magnified . . . clear."	Ibid.,	p. 88
"he . . . believe."	Ibid.,	p. 452
"porthole's . . . glass."	Ibid.,	p. 498
"secrete . . . secrete."	R	B L E S, Summer, 1928
88. "so instinctively thorough."	C P	p. 365
"Between . . . me."	Ibid.,	p. 468
"I stopped . . . apart."	Ibid.,	p. 537
"But let . . . frost?"	Ibid.,	p. 180
89. "the heart . . . seek."	Ibid.,	p. 43
"Ah . . . season."	Ibid.	
"to which . . . night."	Ibid.,	p. 151
89–90. "The mind . . . heart."	Ibid.,	p. 240
90. "Life is . . . sinister-grave."	Ibid.,	p. 376
"to use . . . less."	Ibid.,	p. 431
"I have . . . mind."	Ibid.,	p. 482
"collectivistic . . . love."	Ibid.,	p. 481
91. "a sigh . . . death."	Ibid.,	p. 336
"old . . . by-road."	Ibid.,	p. 94
"where . . . elsewhere."	Ibid.,	p. 102
92. "Two . . . streak."	Ibid.,	p. 435
"Far . . . miss."	Ibid.,	p. 436
"too much . . . imagine."	Ibid.,	p. 448

IV. THE PARABLIST

96. Epigraph: "The poet . . . poem."	Quoted in Stallman and West, *The Art of Modern Fiction* (New York, 1949), pp. iv, 449

1. Ulteriority

97. "ulteriority."		Introduction Modern Library edition *Complete Poems* (New York, 1946), p. xvi
"What . . . myself."	C P	p. 25
"The fact . . . knows."	Ibid.	
"grub around . . . worse English."	R	Middlebury College, May 10, 1950

98.	"Everything . . . hinting."	R	B L W C, Aug. 16, 1952
	"Just . . . poetry."	R	Santa Fé, N.M., Aug. 5, 1935
	"Poems . . . meaning."	R	B L E S, Aug. 6, 1945
	"All . . . poems."	R	B L W C, Aug. 18, 1945
	"singly"; "doubly."	R	B L E S, July 2, 1948
	"for . . . people."	C P	p. 227
99.	"I have . . . someone else."	R	Middlebury College, May 27, 1936
	"It is . . . isn't it?"	Ibid.	
	"fresh insights."	C	Middlebury, Oct. 6, 1952
	"It's . . . philosophy."	R	B L W C, Aug. 18, 1951
100.	"Midsummer . . . ten."	C P	p. 150
	"The land . . . lands."	Ibid.,	p. 467
	"And . . . proxy."	Ibid.,	p. 576
	"had eased . . . fan."	Ibid.,	p. 400
	"honest duplicity."	R	B L E S, Summer, 1928

2. Double Vision

102.	"setting . . . supreme."	C P	p. 28
	"the thing . . . form."		Quoted in L. Untermeyer, *Modern American Poetry* (New York, 1950), p. 181
	"Let chaos . . . form."	C P	p. 407
	"the . . . knows."	Ibid.,	p. 25
103.	"extremes . . . at once."	Ibid.,	p. 343
	"a leaping . . . bloom."	Ibid.,	p. 32
	"Men . . . apart."	Ibid.	
	"Leaves . . . mood."	Ibid.,	p. 387

3. Parables

	"sticking . . . heaven still."	Ibid.,	p. 88
105.	"Poetry is . . . eloquence."	C	B L E S, Aug. 9, 1950
	"knock"; "hide."	C P	p. 299
106.	"I was . . . whetter."	Ibid.,	p. 232
	"I found . . . small."	Ibid.,	p. 396
108.	"I have . . . the night."	Ibid.,	p. 324
109.	"Trust . . . bard."	Ibid.,	p. 360
	"Earth's . . . better."	Ibid.,	p. 152
	"This is . . . fond of."	R	B L W C, Aug. 20, 1949

"I lean on that."	R	Middlebury College, Nov. 6, 1945
110. "He learned . . . to be."	C P	p. 152
"The part . . . translated."	R	New School for Social Research, N.Y. City, Oct. 17, 1935
"Yankees . . . were."	C P	p. 173
"I'll own . . . snow."	Ibid.,	p. 180
111. "One . . . conquer."	Ibid.,	p. 152
"Across . . . trees."	Ibid.	
"the sound of sense."		Quoted by W. S. Braithwaite, *Boston Evening Transcript,* May 8, 1915, Part 3, p. 4
112. "not launching . . . carefully."	C P	p. 153

4. Parablist and Symbolist

113. "But . . . behind."	Ibid.,	p. 82
114. "The night . . . to blow."	Ibid.,	p. 364
"The West . . . gold."	Ibid.,	p. 287
115. "In making . . . form."		Quoted in Gorham Munson, *Robert Frost* (New York, 1927), p. 27

V. DIMENSION IN ART

1. Themes

120. "double hints."	R	B L E S, July 2, 1948

2. Relationship to Fellow Man

122. "We're . . . impart."	C P	p. 421
"And . . . once."	Ibid.,	p. 136
123. "Only where . . . future's sakes."	Ibid.,	p. 359
124. "The water . . . a pond."	Ibid.,	p. 358
"The sun . . . chill."	Ibid.,	p. 357
"so pitched . . . bloom."	Ibid.	
125. "It is . . . flake."	Ibid.,	p. 358
126. "You'd . . . heat."	Ibid.	
"But . . . sight."	Ibid.,	p. 359
127. "They . . . stay."	Ibid.,	p. 358
"A wind . . . peak."	Ibid.,	p. 357

"They . . . tool."	Ibid.,	p. 358
"and . . . possum."	Ibid.	
"The . . . beneath."	Ibid.	
"I don't . . . dictionary words."	R	B L E S, July 28, 1952
"all there is . . . to say."	R	B L E S, July 20, 1936

3. A Tragic Sense

129.	"Who wants . . . fool?"	C P	p. 103
	"I'd *rather* . . . you must."	Ibid.,	p. 87
	"they . . . affairs."	Ibid.,	p. 172
130.	"The nearest . . . at all."	Ibid.,	p. 72
131.	"The little . . . of it."	Ibid.,	p. 69
	"Where do . . . I *will.*"	Ibid.,	p. 73
	"Don't . . . don't."	Ibid.,	p. 70
	"Can't . . . lost?"	Ibid.	
	"Tell me . . . chance."	Ibid.,	p. 71
132.	"I shall . . . cursed."	Ibid.,	p. 72
	"It's a paleolithic savage."	R	Cambridge, March 25, 1936
	"The completeness . . . any tricks."	R	B L E S, July 17, 1950
	"Trouble is . . . read him."	R	Cambridge, March 25, 1936
	"You'd . . . satisfied."	C P	p. 71
	"I'll . . . I *will.*"	Ibid.,	p. 73
133.	"My sounds . . . accent."	C	South Shaftsbury, Vt., Sept. 28, 1935
134.	"a-mind to."	C P	p. 71
	" 'twixt."	Ibid.	
135.	"And . . . dull."	Ibid.	
	"She . . . silence."	Ibid.	

4. World of Nature

	"The land is . . . my bones."		Quoted in *The New York Times,* Sunday Book Section, Nov. 27, 1949
136.	"These pools . . . foliage."	C P	p. 303
	"The trees . . . yesterday."	Ibid.	
137.	"sitting alone . . . Michigan."	R	Community Church, Ripton, Aug. 4, 1951

5. A Strategic Retreat

138.	"Back out . . . for us."	C P	p. 520
	"The ledges . . . Pole."	Ibid.	
	"Under . . . saved."	Ibid.,	p. 521
139.	"the great . . . the story."	R	B L W C, Aug. 20, 1949
	"yard-long."	C	Ripton, June 1, 1948
	"cold . . . rage."	C P	p. 521
	"Now . . . dough."	Ibid.	
	"Like . . . more."	C	Cambridge, March 26, 1936
	"glass-blower."	Quoted by Professor W. E. Davison, Middlebury College, ca. 1922	
	"pops like . . . on you."	R	B L E S, July 17, 1950
	"if . . . one way."	R	B L E S, July 23, 1947
140.	"I don't . . . of catchiness."	R	Plattsburg State Teachers College, Plattsburg, N.Y., July 29, 1948
	"If . . . pleased."	R	Middlebury College, May 10, 1950
141.	"We . . . response."	Quoted by Professor Peter Stanlis, Jan. 7, 1943	
	"The . . . rose."	C P	p. 305

6. Fatefulness

142.	"forty . . . World Wars."	R	B L E S, June 29, 1950
	"poems . . . tranquility."	R	B L W C, Aug. 18, 1951
	"fumbled."	R	Middlebury College, May 10, 1950
	"The . . . continent."	C P	p. 314
144.	"We may . . . sane."	Ibid.,	p. 346
	"As if . . . fate."	Ibid.,	p. 12
	"It's . . . brains."	C	Ripton, Sept. 27, 1949
	"how . . . limitless."	Quoted in "Books We Like," Boston (Mass.) Library Association, Inc., 1936. pp. 140–42	
145.	"what will be, be."	C P	p. 313
146.	"But . . . see."	Ibid.,	p. 391

7. Self-Trust

147. "something . . . star."	Ibid.,	p. 575
"It is . . . late."	Ibid.,	p. 456

8. Yankee Comedy

148. "When I . . . stimulates me."	C	Middlebury, June 4, 1950
"A New England Biblical."	*The Atlantic Monthly* CLXXX (Nov. 1947), p. 68	
149. "I don't . . . window."	C	Middlebury, May 21, 1943
"Religion's the froth."	C	B L E S, Aug. 6, 1948
151. "I've . . . wanted."	C P	p. 589
"I'd . . . anywhere."	Ibid.,	p. 590
"The best . . . taken."	Ibid.	
"That is . . . Note Book."	Ibid.,	p. 591
"She wants . . . it is."	Ibid.,	p. 592
"Oh, Lord . . . looking into?"	Ibid.	
152. "All You . . . with anyone."	Ibid.,	pp. 592–93
"God . . . done."	Ibid.,	p. 593
"She's beautiful."	Ibid.	
"We . . . together."	Ibid.,	p. 596
"My forte . . . on."	Ibid.,	p. 595
"Found . . . unreason."	Ibid.,	p. 596
"It . . . answer?"	Ibid.	
153. "Job . . . safeguards."	Ibid.,	p. 601
"It . . . Job."	C	Cambridge, Dec. 13, 1947
"Don't . . . himself."	C P	p. 605
154. "Get . . . surface."	Ibid.,	p. 598
"Disinterestedness . . . virtue."	Ibid.,	p. 601
157. "the conundrum."	C	South Shaftsbury, Vt., Sept. 28, 1935
"There's . . . me."	C	B L E S, Aug. 2, 1947

VI. DIMENSIONS IN NATURE, SOCIETY, SCIENCE AND RELIGION

160. Epigraph: "But . . . matter."	"Education by Poetry: A Meditative Monologue" (Feb. 1931), Amherst Graduates' Quarterly, Vol. 20, No. 2, pp. 75–85

1. Versed in Country Things

161. "The ledges . . . Pole."	C P	p. 520
162. "favor."	R	B L E S, Summer, 1928
"And . . . kept."	C P	p. 447
"prosperous."	C	Ripton, June 1, 1949
"For . . . fulfill."	C P	p. 17
163. "However . . . of ours."	Ibid.,	p. 37
164. "The leaves . . . sleeping."	Ibid.,	p. 43
"The blue's . . . hand."	Ibid.,	p. 78
"with . . . sun."	Ibid.,	p. 117
"the Hyla . . . snow."	Ibid.,	p. 147
"musk . . . springs."	Ibid.,	p. 279
"the petal . . . stung."	Ibid.	
"living . . . drouth."	Ibid.,	p. 311
"though . . . themselves."	Ibid.,	p. 152
"Loud . . . bird."	Ibid.,	p. 150
"each . . . cry."	Ibid.,	p. 20
"that . . . ghost."	Ibid.,	p. 458
"the leafless . . . white."	Ibid.,	p. 391
"Torpedo-like . . . leather."	Ibid.,	p. 349
"Clematis . . . bundle."	Ibid.,	p. 126
165. "The birch . . . noticed."	Ibid.,	p. 517
"There . . . carefully."	C	Ripton, June 3, 1949
"I'd rather . . . such things."	Ibid.	
"Won't . . . revision?"	C P	p. 360
167. "Where did . . . there."	Ibid.,	p. 247
168. "Up where . . . do."	Ibid.,	p. 255
"A little . . . wise."	Ibid.,	p. 341
"We all . . . gold."	Ibid.,	p. 312
"Good . . . neighbors."	Ibid.,	p. 47
"What we . . . die by."	Ibid.,	p. 117
169. "the maples . . . house."	Ibid.,	p. 222
"the sturdy . . . crumbs."	Ibid.,	p. 155
"whispering . . . ground."	Ibid.,	p. 25
"For I . . . desired."	Ibid.,	p. 88
"I may . . . then?"	Ibid.,	p. 290
"stove-length . . . wood."	Ibid.,	p. 171
"The trial . . . come to."	Ibid.,	p. 132
"strategic retreats."	Ibid.,	p. 365

	"You can't . . . winter."	Ibid., p. 180
	"Bring . . . white."	Ibid., p. 16
170.	"Always . . . ground."	Ibid., p. 278
	"Ten million . . . snow."	Ibid., p. 293
	"Far in . . . lament."	Ibid., p. 446
171.	"The hand . . . things."	Ibid., p. 90
	"good blocks of beech."	Ibid., p. 357
	"Except . . . fool."	Ibid., p. 358
	"good hick'ry . . . tough!"	Ibid., p. 228
	"The way . . . mirth."	Ibid., p. 403
174.	"Something . . . God."	Ibid., p. 281

2. Realmist

176.	"to grasp . . . situation."	C P p. 471
	"Freudian . . . by night."	Ibid., p. 557
	"Marxian Muscovite."	Ibid.
	"opinionations."	C Ripton, June 9, 1949
	"realmist."	Ibid.
	"A one-man revolution."	C P p. 429
	"we're . . . other."	Ibid.
	"inside . . . get."	Ibid., p. 425
	"But these . . . human kind."	Ibid., p. 474
	"The opposite . . . is utopia."	R B L W C, Aug. 18, 1951
	"I own . . . reformed."	C P p. 431
	"I never . . . old."	Ibid., p. 407
177.	"brought up . . . Democrat."	Ibid., p. 429
	"it ceases . . . true."	Ibid., p. 74
	"I am . . . against."	C Ripton, Aug. 25, 1949
	"All truth is dialogue."	Quoted in *Time,* Oct. 9, 1950, p. 80
	"I have . . . guise."	C P p. 482
178.	"The world's . . . rolls."	Ibid., p. 427
	"but politics . . . bloody."	Ibid., p. 421
	"But inside . . . I'm personal."	Ibid., p. 425
	"Build soil . . . driven in."	Ibid., pp. 428–29
179.	"Pressed into . . . shape."	Ibid., p. 117
	"He never . . . need."	Ibid., p. 356
	"I have . . . swept."	Ibid., p. 481
	"Socialism is . . . government."	C South Shaftsbury, Vt., Sept. 28, 1935

"For socialism . . . democracy." — C P — p. 423

180. "In socialism . . . stuff." — C — Middlebury, May 9, 1952

"power . . . itself." — C — Middlebury College, Sept. 17, 1943

"It's all . . . changed any." — C — B L E S, July 25, 1949

"an equalitarian" . . . "Cromwell." — C — Cambridge, March 26, 1936

"If you . . . jury." — Ibid.

181. "Live . . . believe." — C P — p. 636

"Seek converse . . . too late." — Ibid., p. 471

"You would . . . my point." — Ibid.

182. "point of drive." — C — Ripton, Sept. 27, 1949

183. "One . . . the humanities." — R — Middlebury College, Sept. 17, 1943

"It ought . . . science side." — Ibid.

184. "I was . . . go home." — On radio, Dec. 11, 1949

"You might . . . them both." — Talk — B L E S, Aug. 5, 1951

"anticipations by imagination." — R — B L E S, Aug. 1, 1951

185. "the fine . . . daring." — C — B L E S, July 3, 1957

"Did I . . . wink." — C P — p. 553

187. "Snow . . . places." — Ibid., p. 386

188. "the turn." — R — B L E S, July 2, 1948

"like . . . wrapped." — C P — p. 549

"The play . . . lighting." — Ibid., p. 555

189. "The older . . . clear." — C — Cambridge, Dec. 13, 1947

"How do . . . people's God." — R — B L E S, July 17, 1948

190. "an Old Testament believer." — C — Middlebury, May 10, 1952

"a relationship . . . future." — "Education by Poetry," *Amherst Quarterly,* Feb. 1931

"It is . . . most us." — C P — p. 329

191. "those people . . . good." — Mr. Frost at Boston Herald Book Fair, Nov. 9, 1937

"Religion's . . . froth." — R — B L E S, July 17, 1948

"a full consent." — C — Ripton, June 1, 1948

"a straining . . . wisdom." — Sermon by Mr. Frost, Rockdale Avenue Temple, Cincinnati, Ohio, Oct. 10, 1946

"All . . . interest." — R — B L E S, July 17, 1948

"Mercy . . . deserving." — R — B L W C, Aug. 18, 1945

"Jonah . . . failure." — C — Cambridge, Dec. 13, 1947

"universal fugitive." — C P — p. 615

192.	"I love . . . to be."	Ibid.,	pp. 623–24
	"I think . . . evil-crossed."	Ibid.,	p. 629
193.	"We have . . . mercy."	Ibid.,	pp. 641–42
194.	"I can . . . assuage."	Ibid.,	p. 641
	"But where . . . interstitial."	C	Middlebury, Dec. 25, 1949

VII. DIMENSION IN TIME AND SPACE

1. Image as Signature

198.	"staking . . . sky."	R	B L W C, Aug. 16, 1952
199.	"I like . . . happen."	Ibid.	
	"One of . . . stars."	Ibid.	
	"How countlessly . . . sight."	C P	p. 12
200.	"Some may . . . perch."	Ibid.,	p. 214
	"Such as . . . wise."	Ibid.,	p. 215
	"To satisfy . . . telescope."	Ibid.,	p. 218
	"Because it . . . middle."	Ibid.,	p. 220
201.	"We've looked . . . stood."	Ibid.,	p. 218
	"spoke of . . . Jupiter."	Ibid.,	p. 265
	"They spoke . . . interlock."	Ibid.	
202.	"I'm . . . dark."	Ibid.,	p. 331
	"empty . . . race is."	Ibid.,	p. 386
	"Here come . . . right."	Ibid.,	p. 509
203.	"telescopic."	Ibid.,	p. 487
	"the heartless . . . Outer Black."	Ibid.	
	"Watcher of the void."	Ibid.,	p. 532
	"when at . . . far."	Ibid.,	p. 575
	"to line . . . stars."	Ibid.,	p. 319
	"to see . . . Leonid."	Ibid.,	p. 487
	"streaking . . . the west."	Ibid.,	p. 523

2. The Poet and Tradition

205.	"You steal . . . uses."	R	B L E S, July 6, 1949
	"in the hope . . . faculties."		Quoted in Huntington Ms. 25338, Huntington Library, San Marino, California
	"the good . . . words."	Ibid.	
	"all . . . giants."	Ibid.	

"Besides these . . . of Palgrave's."   Ibid.
206. "One luminary . . . right."   C P   p. 324
208. "No choice . . . comic."   Ibid.,   p. 472

3. The Poet's Appeal

209. "everything . . . to."   C P   p. 28
  "little . . . clarity."   C   B L E S, July 21, 1947
210. "Some say . . . dealt with."   R   Middlebury College, May 27, 1936
211. "Yankees are . . . were."   C P   p. 173
  "Weep for . . . glad."   Ibid.,   p. 520
  "The strong . . . see."   Ibid.,   p. 391
  "I don't . . . known."   Ibid.,   p. 139
214. "Keep off . . . other off."   Ibid.,   p. 429
  "They cannot . . . keep."   Ibid.,   p. 394
  "We have . . . tried."   Ibid.,   p. 345
  "Since . . . door."   Ibid.,   p. 456
  "They cannot . . . places."   Ibid.,   p. 386
  "Take nature . . . favor of man."   Ibid.,   p. 469
  "The spinner . . . came in."   Ibid.,   p. 355
  "original response."   Ibid.,   p. 451
215. "imagery and after-imagery."   Quoted in E. S. Sergeant, *Fire Under the Andes* (New York, 1927), p. 302
  "to lodge . . . rid of."   Preface, E. A. Robinson's *King Jasper* (New York, 1935), p. x

Index

This index is limited to names of authors quoted, and titles of those poems of Robert Frost that are discussed in detail.

Curriculum Reviewers

Acknowledgments

Every effort has been made to secure permission, but if any omissions have been made, please let us know. We gratefully acknowledge the following permissions:

Susan Bergholz Literary Services: From *The House on Mango Street* by Sandra Cisneros. Copyright © 1984 by Sandra Cisneros. Published by Vintage Books, a division of Random House, Inc., and in hardcover by Alfred A. Knopf, 1994. **Acknowledgments continue on page 495.**

HAMPTON-BROWN
HIGH POINT

SUCCESS IN LANGUAGE · LITERATURE · CONTENT

ALFREDO SCHIFINI
DEBORAH SHORT
JOSEFINA VILLAMIL TINAJERO

HAMPTON-BROWN